Interdisciplinary Inquiry in Teaching and Learning

Marian L. Martinello
University of Texas—San Antonio

Gillian E. Cook
University of Texas—San Antonio

Merrill, an imprint of
Macmillan College Publishing Company
New York

Maxwell Macmillan Canada
Toronto

Maxwell Macmillan International
New York   Oxford   Singapore   Sydney

Cover photo: FPG International, Art Montes de Oca
Editor: Linda James Scharp
Production Editor: Sheryl Glicker Langner
Art Coordinator: Peter Robison, Vince Smith
Text Designer: Patricia Cohan
Cover Designer: Russ Maselli
Production Buyer: Pamela D. Bennett
Artist: Jane Lopez
Electronic Text Management: Marilyn Wilson Phelps, Matthew Williams

This book was set in Souvenir Light and Swiss by Macmillan College Publishing Company and was printed and bound by R.R. Donnelley & Sons Company. The cover was printed by Phoenix Color Corp.

Macmillan College Publishing Company
866 Third Avenue
New York, NY 10022

Macmillan College Publishing Company is part of the
Maxwell Communication Group of Companies.

Maxwell Macmillan Canada, Inc.
1200 Eglinton Avenue East, Suite 200
Don Mills, Ontario M3C 3N1

Library of Congress Cataloging-in-Publication Data
Martinello, Marian L.
    Interdisciplinary inquiry in teaching and learning / Marian L.
Martinello, Gillian E. Cook.
        p.   cm.
    Includes bibliographical references and index.
    ISBN 0-02-376502-X
    1. Interdisciplinary approach in education—United States.
2. Interdisciplinary approach to knowledge. 3. Education—United
States—Curricula. I. Cook, Gillian Elizabeth
II. Title.
LB1570.M3675   1994
375'.00973—dc20   93-29467
                                                        CIP

Printing: 1 2 3 4 5 6 7 8 9   Year: 4 5 6 7

We dedicate this book to our parents, who encouraged us to explore worlds beyond their experience:
Rocco Martinello and Helena Terenzio Martinello
Harold T. Cook and H. Joyce Cook
and
to the teachers and children who will explore worlds beyond those we can imagine.

Preface

Note to the Reader

You are about to experience a different type of text. If you are used to reading text that is explicit and direct in communicating information, you may feel uncomfortable with a more open-ended approach that poses questions for you to consider. We ask that you think of reading this book as an exploration. Initially, you will encounter many questions and few answers. The meanings we want to explore will become clear as you interact with the ideas suggested in each chapter and in the book as a whole. We invite you to approach this book with an openness to different ways of reading and thinking. Like Galileo, Picasso, Faulkner, and other creative thinkers who have changed the direction of thinking in their fields, you should be prepared to break with old models in order to consider different paradigms of teaching and learning.

To the Professor

This text is intended for use as a core text in graduate-level general curriculum and integrated curriculum courses and as a supplementary text in any undergraduate methods course where thematic studies across academic disciplines or a collaborative inquiry approach is presented. The text is designed to model a community of learners as students explore the ideas and exercises provided throughout.

Overview of Chapters

Part 1 provides an introduction to interdisciplinary inquiry. In chapter 1, we present our understanding of inquiry across the fields of study and discuss the habits of mind that are shared by inquirers in the different disciplines. Chapter 2 describes some experiments in integrated curriculum in the United States during the early 20th century and identifies some common questions that emerged.

In part 2, we explain our approach to the development of interdisciplinary theme studies. The selection of themes and the way they differ from narrower topics is the subject of chapter 3. Ways of getting started are illustrated in chapter 4. In chapter 5, we show how interdisciplinary theme studies are related to curriculum standards, and in chapter 6, we suggest how teachers may develop unit studies. Throughout, we relate the habits of mind discussed in chapter 1 to the development of interdisciplinary theme studies. In chapters 7 and 8, we examine the rich variety of resources that can support interdisciplinary inquiry. Each type of resource is described, together with implications for student learning.

Part 3 includes chapter 9, on evaluation of student learning, and chapter 10, on the implementation of interdisciplinary curriculum.

Acknowledgments

Our construct of interdisciplinary teaching and learning has developed over several years of work with elementary and middle-school teachers, the children they teach, and the school administrators who have supported their efforts to develop interdisciplinary theme studies with their students. We gratefully acknowledge the contributions to our thinking made by the extraordinary educators in the San Antonio Independent School District and the Harlandale Independent School District in San Antonio, Texas. We express our special thanks to the faculty and principals of Rogers Middle School and the LINCS Elementary Schools: Charles C. Ball, Beacon Hill, Ferdinand Herff, and P. F. Stewart, and to the summer academy teacher facilitators of San Antonio ISD who helped us to develop and to trial test many ideas. We acknowledge Dr. Edward Tobia, Director of Elementary Curriculum, and Caroyl Green, Director of Secondary Curriculum in San Antonio ISD, and their staffs for their many hours of hard work to develop the interdisciplinary concept in their district's schools. A very special thanks is extended to Dr. Amy Jo Baker for her continuing support of the interdisciplinary concept in the San Antonio district's middle schools and to Juan Jasso and John Maher for similar support in the Harlandale schools.

We gratefully acknowledge Dr. Laurie Pariseau's extensive contributions to chapter 9. Our teacher education students at the University of Texas at San Antonio have helped us to formulate important aspects of this book's treatment of interdisciplinary teaching and learning. We are similarly indebted to the elementary and middle-school students who participated in theme studies conducted by the preservice and in-service teachers we have taught.

The Division of Education at the University of Texas at San Antonio is our academic home, and one of the most supportive places for professional inquiry that we have experienced in our careers.

We greatly appreciate the help that our editor, Linda Scharp, has given us throughout the development of this book, from its conception, through initial manuscript preparation and revisions, and the preparation of the final document. Sheryl Langner, production editor, Ginger Wineinger, copy editor, and Kris Robinson, editorial assistant, have helped us to bring this project to completion.

Our reviewers also deserve recognition for helping us to refine our ideas and to clarify their expression. They are: Theona McQueen, University of Miami—Coral Gables; Robert Eaker, Middle Tennessee State University; Louise M. Berman, University of Maryland; Robert S. Elkins, Humboldt State University; Paul R. Burden, Kansas State University; Jessie A. Roderick, University of Maryland—College Park; Michael A. Lorber, Illinois State University; and Kenneth E. Cypert, Tarleton State University.

Many more people than we have space to acknowledge have influenced our thinking and encouraged us in this work. We gratefully acknowledge their many contributions to our thinking and our learning.

Marian L. Martinello and Gillian E. Cook
San Antonio, Texas

Contents

Chapter Seven

Using Resources for Interdisciplinary Theme Studies   *145*

Chapter Eight

Interacting with Resources for Interdisciplinary Theme Studies   *165*

Introduction

OUR METAPHOR

Interdisciplinary curriculum is distinguished by its ability to invite student inquiry for the discovery of big ideas that link several areas of knowledge. The image that appears on the cover of this book was selected to visually represent that concept of curriculum. The pebble that drops into a pond is like the idea that sparks inquiry. The concentric ripples represent new questions that emerge from the first germ of an idea. The ever-enlarging pattern of ripples refers to the integrated knowledge that is acquired as each question is explored, limited only by the force of the inquirers' enthusiasm for the search. The greater the interest and the more probing the questions, the more encompassing the study, the bigger the ideas that it develops, and the deeper and more meaningful the knowledge the inquirer constructs.

The aim of this book is for children to be creative thinkers. As Piaget (1973) wrote: "To understand is to discover, or reconstruct by rediscovery, and such conditions must be complied with if in the future individuals are to be formed who are capable of production and creativity, not simply repetition" (p. 20).

For too long, teachers have been bounded by the objectives and expectations set by others. Building on the work of Philip Phenix, Schaefer (1967) declared that this "is too monstrous an irony to be tolerated. Teaching," he said, "more than any other vocation . . . ought both to permit and to encourage the pursuit of meaning beyond any current capacity to comprehend" (p. 59). In order to develop inquiring students, the teacher must be a creative inquirer. This book is dedicated to this end.

The social and political experiment that was started in our country more than 200 years ago is still testing the beliefs and principles expressed by the Declaration of Independence and the Constitution and Bill of Rights. The rhetoric of the developing nation's most prominent founders clearly presented the idea that a democratic form of government cannot survive without an educated citizenry. In the early days of the republic, those who held public office were well educated and those who exercised the vote were at least well trained for their occupations. But the waves of immigrants that arrived during the 19th and 20th centuries brought with them cultural diversity, which was perceived by some to threaten the nation's growth. Public schools were established for the "melting-pot" purpose of reducing cultural diversity and training large numbers of immigrant children for productive work in an increasingly industrialized country. It was thought sufficient to develop in those children basic literacy skills, a work ethic, and the ability to successfully apply given ways of doing and thinking to their factory jobs. The school itself was developed from a factory model, and it accomplished its goals.

In the last decade of the 20th century, and looking forward to the changing character of life in the 21st century, Americans are painfully aware of the public school's failure to meet changing social needs. Many students do not complete their basic schooling with sufficient knowledge and skills to be productive members of today's democratic society. The social fabric of the nation has become more complex, with greater diversity of cultural groups and life styles than was the case when the concept of public schools was first implemented on a large scale. Today, the school is challenged to accommodate and to build on the strengths of differences among its students. Industrialization, with its factory jobs, has given way to a new postindustrialism that Wirth (1993, p. 361) characterizes as marked by three major developments: "(1) the electronic computer revolution, (2) the emergence of a competitive global market, and (3) the prospect of serious ecological change." Knowing a model and being able to apply it is no longer sufficient for success in the workplace. Certainly it is inadequate preparation for the exercise of intelligent suffrage or the effective participation in local, state, and national government, and for what Reich (1991) describes as the transnational character of daily work in a global system. Public schooling for the 21st century must accomplish much more than Americans had thought their schools should do. The schools must educate thinking people who have a strong sense of their own locus of control. They must prepare people to use the skills of "symbolic analysis" (Reich, 1991): abstraction, experiential inquiry, and collaboration. They must also prepare people who can enjoy and contribute to a multicultural democracy. The schools must develop people with the abilities and attitudes needed to take responsibility for their own learning throughout their lives—lives in which they are likely to change occupations several times.

The future of this nation is bound more clearly to its schools than ever before. The quality of life for all Americans depends on our ability to adopt a view of curriculum and teaching that reinvents public education for the common good. The ideas we propose in this book are not new. The principles we espouse derive from the work of educational leaders such as Dewey, Piaget, and Bruner. The current resurgence of interest in interdisciplinary approaches to curriculum suggests that this is an appropriate and timely means of educating all young people for the complexities and challenges of life in the 21st century. Some important contributions to this movement may be found in the works of Louise Berman (1968), who describes thinking processes in holistic terms and justifies their development as important curriculum priorities; Heidi Hayes Jacobs (1989), whose explanation of interdisciplinary curriculum clarifies its rationale and its characteristics; Lillian G. Katz and Sylvia C. Chard (1990), who revitalize the significance of the project method in early childhood education; Suzanne Krogh (1990), whose solid discussion of interdisciplinary curriculum development in early childhood education links theory to practice; and Chris Stevenson and Judy Carr (1993), who examine the significance of integrated studies for students in the middle school, with supporting evidence in the form of case studies written by practicing teachers.

Others who describe ways of implementing interdisciplinary curriculum include Ruth Gamberg, Winnefred Kwak, Meredith Hutchings, and Judy Altheim (1988), who explain the development of interdisciplinary theme studies in a particular school; Regie Routman (1991), who discusses integration in the language arts; Susan J. Kovalik and Karen D. Olsen (1991), who explain and detail the interrelationships of integrative studies and the development of scientific thinking in children; and Robin Fogarty (1991), who offers practical suggestions for classroom practice. In addition, the principles of interdisciplinary curriculum have been translated into curriculum by educational agencies such as the California Department of Education (1990), the Colorado Department of Education (1987), and the Oregon School Study Council (Shoemaker, 1989), whose work was developed further by the Eugene School District 4J (1990).

WHAT DO WE MEAN BY INTERDISCIPLINARY CURRICULUM?

We view ourselves as centrists on the continuum that, at one end, defines curriculum as a prescribed course of study (Tanner & Tanner, 1975) and, at the other, as everything that occurs between students and their environments (Hass, 1974). We believe that the formal curriculum is based on the principles and values of the society, with an agreed-upon set of standards, and a scope and sequence that accommodates our best understanding of children's developmental levels. We conceptualize learning as the construction of meaning by the learner. Therefore, we also believe that teachers and learners develop curriculum as they interact with content in various contexts.

Interdisciplinary inquiry allows teachers and learners to explore ideas and to construct meaning within the broad parameters of well-conceived curricular guidelines.

Our concept of interdisciplinary study acknowledges the richness of the separate disciplines, their interrelationships, and their modes of inquiry. In our view, sound learning centers on the deep themes that underlie the content in the subject areas: principles, theories, and major generalizations. We believe that this is best advanced through inquiry that formulates questions from the perspectives of many disciplines of study, organized around universal concepts and generalizations. Interdisciplinary theme studies can exceed conventional standards. They do more than guide student discovery of big ideas; they develop the students' abilities to learn. They prepare students to deal with the unknown. As Reich (1991, pp. 229–230) points out, "For most children in the United States and around the world, formal education entails just the opposite kinds of learning. Rather than construct meanings for themselves, meanings are imposed upon them. . . . Reality has already been simplified; the obedient student has only to commit it to memory." By contrast, Reich adds, in the best schools, "the student learns to examine reality from many angles, in different lights, and thus to visualize new possibilities and choices."

Teachers who develop interdisciplinary curriculum with their students are affirming that they are scholars in their own right, reinventing their practice as they interact with their students and engage them with increasingly complex content within changing instructional settings and situations. There is no one right way to guide student learning; the ways are infinite. Which ones teachers select from the myriad possibilities depends upon their reasoned and intuitive assessment of what is most responsive to the learner's needs. Doing this well takes time, professional know-how, and an unrelenting passion for understanding the multidimensional qualities of human learning.

REFERENCES

Berman, L. M. (1968). *New priorities in the curriculum.* Columbus, OH: Merrill.

California Department of Education. (1990). *Science framework for California public schools.* Sacramento: Author.

Colorado Department of Education. (1987). *Interdisciplinary learning: A resource guide.* Denver: Author.

Eugene School District 4J. (1990). *Education 2000: District 4J integrated curriculum and planning guide, K–5.* Eugene, OR: Author.

Fogarty, R. (1991). *The mindful school: How to integrate the curricula.* Palatine, IL: Skylight.

Gamberg, R., Kwak, W., Hutchings, M., & Altheim, J. (1988). *Living and loving it: Theme studies in the classroom.* Portsmouth, NH: Heinemann.

Hass, G. (1974). *Curriculum planning: A new approach.* Boston: Allyn & Bacon.

Jacobs, H. H. (Ed.). (1989). *Interdisciplinary curriculum: Design and implementation.* Washington, DC: Association for Supervision and Curriculum Development.

Katz, L. G., & Chard, S. C. (1990). *Engaging children's minds: The project approach.* Norwood, NJ: Ablex.

Kovalik, S. J., & Olsen, K. D. (1991). *Kid's eye view of science: A teacher's handbook for implementing an integrated thematic approach for teaching science, K–6.* Village of Oak Creek, AZ: Center for the Future of Education.

Krogh, S. (1990). *The integrated early childhood curriculum.* New York: McGraw-Hill.

Piaget, J. (1973). *To understand is to invent: The future of education.* New York: Grossman.

Shoemaker, B. J. (1989, October). Integrated education: A curriculum for the twenty-first century. *Oregon School Study Council Bulletin, 33(2),* i–46.

Reich, R. B. (1991). *The work of nations: Preparing ourselves for 21st century capitalism.* New York: Knopf.

Routman, R. (1991). *Invitations: Changing as teachers and learners K–12.* Portsmouth, NH: Heinemann.

Schaefer, R. J. (1967). *The school as a center of inquiry.* New York: Harper & Row.

Stevenson, C., & Carr, J. F. (Eds.). (1993). *Integrated studies in the middle grades: "Dancing through walls."* New York: Teachers College Press.

Tanner, D., & Tanner, L. N. (1975). *Curriculum development: Theory into practice.* New York: Macmillan.

Wirth, A. G. (1993, January). Education and work: The choices we face. *Phi Delta Kappan, 74,* 361–366.

Part One

Introduction to Interdisciplinary Inquiry

Chapter One

The Interdisciplinary Qualities of Inquiry

The children were intrigued with the object. It seemed bulky and ungainly, this footwear touted as an aid to walking. Its white upper was a patchwork of leather pieces, double-stitched in place. Here and there, polyethylene moldings formed eyelets, adding strength to those punched in the leather to thread thick cotton laces over a padded tongue. A heavy rubber sole, deeply treaded with zigzags and circles within circles, covered the bottom of the shoe with interesting designs—all different. The trade name, Dunlop, was imprinted in the sole, stamped on the cushioned inner sole, and emblazoned in a lavender-and-green logo on the shoe's side: a spray of laurel leaves surrounding an arrow, with an image of wispy clouds behind. The teacher guided the students to inquire about the shoe: What do you think this means? What is this logo's symbolism? What does the logo represent to people from different cultures?

One by one, the students added their questions to the inquiry: How does culture influence the character of the shoes people wear? How similar are walking shoes in different parts of the world? Where was this shoe made? An inside label read, "Made in Taiwan." Where in Taiwan? By whom? Where did the materials come from? And why those materials? At what cost? Who invented its prototype? And what about the construction of the shoe itself? How was the shoe designed? On what principles? By which formulas? How does the shoe help the walker? Can you walk better and faster with this walking shoe? Why? How was the shoe engineered? This size 71/2 shoe fits a relatively small foot—a woman's foot. Are men's walking shoes engineered differently from women's? Who wore this particular shoe? What were her experiences with walking? What can we tell about her by looking at the pair of shoes? What stories do they tell? What stories are hidden in any pair of shoes?

---

*I*s this inquiry? The questions about the walking shoe seem capable of launching a study that is as clearly focused and question-driven as any conducted by scholars. After all, the question is the cornerstone of all investigation. Each guides the inquirer to diverse sources. Like a jigsaw puzzle, clues can coalesce to reveal previously undetected patterns. Any discovered gaps are sources of new questions that can deepen and widen the inquiry. This exploration of walking shoes became a way to learn about more than "just shoes." It also developed the inquirer's social and cultural, economic, political, technological, and artistic concepts and the ability to discover interrelationships among those concepts that form universal generalizations. Equally important, the process of searching required critical and creative thinking.

Inquiry is the source of new knowledge. Developing the ability to inquire is central to the education of those who devote their lives to explaining nature's mysteries, gaining access to them through the languages and paradigms of the sciences, mathematics, the humanities, or the arts. But inquiry is not solely the province of scholars. Inquiry is also what ordinary people do to learn and to add meaning to their lives. Some seem more adept at it than others. Why?

At a time when the democratic ethic and processes are shaping the political structures and values of many of the nations on our planet, a major responsibility of the public schools is to educate thinking persons. Demographic projections predict that the 21st century will belong to people whose backgrounds are more diverse and less affluent than those of people in earlier times. The United States is an especially interesting case because of its multicultural population and democratic systems. Those systems may not survive without the education of all children through varied ways of thinking and knowing, from their earliest days and throughout their schooling. The greatest contemporary challenge to American public education is to find ways to ensure that this is accomplished.

We tend to look to the separate disciplines of study for direction. Thus, movements in science education have worked for years to develop students' "scientific thinking," and social studies education has fostered "critical thinking and creative problem solving." Central to language arts instruction is the complex use of spoken and written language and interpretive skills in reading. Nurturing students' creative expression is the concern of instruction in the fine and performing arts. Yet American students appear limited in their ability to be self-directed inquirers. What is missing from their education?

To understand inquiry, we need to know how it is done well, and how to recognize its processes in ourselves and others. In this book, we draw from the work of analysts of inquiry, such as Roe (1952) and Kuhn (1970) in the sciences and Hughes (1980) in the arts, and some who explore thinking in several fields, such as Phenix (1964), Gardner (1983), and John-Steiner (1985). The reflections of scientists, mathematicians, computer scientists, writers and poets, and fine and performing artists have given us glimpses into the workings of their minds. Some appear in print, such as James Watson's (1968) reconstruction of the search to discover the structure of DNA and Matisse's *Notebooks of a Painter* (in Flam, 1973). Some are found in video productions of documentaries and analyses of invention and discovery. Other accounts are from personal interviews with scholars at our own university and in our community.

Inquiry may be broadly defined as the search for truth, information, or knowledge (*Webster's,* 1981). In the quest for knowledge, every field is dedicated to clarifying the meanings of "real" and "true." Our interest is in the path toward those goals: *How* is the quest for truth carried on? How are the meanings of "real" and "true" uncovered? How is productive inquiry done in any field—what are its beginnings, its processes, its influences, and its products? And, then, how can we use this knowledge in teaching and learning?

ORIGINS OF INQUIRY

People who work in the *natural sciences* often say that their investigations start with puzzles. Watson and Crick were intrigued by the missing links in the alpha helix that a fellow researcher, Linus Pauling, had proposed toward explaining the structure of DNA. Richard Feynman (1988) found anomalies in the temperature-tolerance data for the O-ring seals that ultimately explained the space-shuttle *Challenger*'s explosion shortly after lift-off in 1986. In a similar way, Stuart Birnbaum (personal communication, 1991) searches for discrepancies in the work of fellow geologists, looking for the gaps in their work, "the things they *don't* explain and the questions they *don't* raise" in their investigations. Scientists are intrigued by the unknown and unexplained. Their curiosity drives their inquiry more often than their human desire for recognition and material reward. Even Watson, who admittedly wanted the Nobel Prize, was helped through the unproductive periods of the search for the DNA double helix by the desire to understand the chemical origin of life.

The studies of *mathematicians,* like those of theoretical physicists, often begin with the test and proof of theories that may have been formulated intuitively. To search for a solution to the "traveling salesman problem," a question that involves finding the shortest tour around a group of cities, Kay Robbins (personal communication, 1992) tried testing the theory of cooperating processes. The theory offers a different perspective on the problem, suggesting a solution strategy that connects independently working computers to share data generated from random searches for the shortest routes. The problem supplies the intrigue; the theory offers a new perspective. Hardy (1940) speaks eloquently about the mathematician's search for proofs. Guillian (1983) adds, "Proof is the idol before which the mathematician tortures himself." Jerome Keating (personal communication, 1991) sees his work as more joyful. He considers his search for evidence to substantiate propositions in non-euclidean geometry as an ongoing and exciting adventure.

Writers inquire into scenarios, characters, and experiences that capture their interest. Eudora Welty (1983) listened for stories in the dialogues of relatives and friends. Short-story writer and poet Nan Cuba (personal communication, 1992) searches her experiences with people for insights into the relationships that infuse her stories and poems. Cuba's story about a brother–sister relationship is drawn from her experience with an adored older brother, but the scenario is imagined. Its "trueness" derives from the integrity of the characters and the setting and the author's deep understanding of each. The same interest is expressed by fiction writer Bill Oliver's (personal communication, 1991) intimate study of his characters. Knowing their favorite scents, tastes, music, and textures, as well as their innermost thoughts, is important to his ability to depict them as authentic characters, even though that specific information may never appear in print. The setting, too, is often imagined in greater multisensory detail than what the writer shares on the printed page.

Inquiry in the *fine arts* derives from a desire to know more about oneself and the universal "self." Printmaker, photographer, and painter Kent Rush (personal communication, 1992) defines his purpose as "to find something beyond what I already know. To get closer to myself so that tangible forms of my work reflect me—the part of me that is more like all of you." It often starts with play, the artist's exploration of ways that images can be used to express perceptions. Matisse (Flam, 1973) talked about forming different perceptions of line, form, color, and light and experimenting with ways to express the designs perceived. In his study of modernism, Hughes (1980) depicts the Cubists as trying to depict *process* by recording all the possible perspectives of their subjects at the same time. Their problem was to capture on canvas ways of seeing that had not yet been expressed in the visual arts.

The *humanities* are similarly driven by questions about human experience. The study of the ancient people of the Lower Pecos River (Ancient Texans: Rock Art and Life Ways Along the Lower Pecos, Witte Museum, San Antonio, TX, 1987) started with the excavation of their rock shelters, their homes. When sites near the Alamo were excavated, I. Waynne Cox and his team of archaeologists at the Center for Archaeological Research, the University of Texas at San Antonio (personal communication, 1991), found artifacts that caused them to wonder about the life styles of people who had lived in the area over the years. The work of historians such as Woodruff Smith (personal communication, 1992) in his studies of China, Gilberto Hinojosa (personal communication, 1992) on the Hispanic experiences in south Texas, and Van Kirk (1980) on women's role in the fur-trade society of western Canada strive to make sense of the past and to explain change. They probe gaps in the historical record about the needs, wants, and life patterns of those who lived at different times in close or distant places and in similar or different cultures. These researchers devote years to their studies because they want to discover the unknown or, by challenging or enlarging existing interpretations, come to better understand human experience.

In all of these fields, the driving force is *passion* to explore and to understand. John-Steiner (1985) refers to passion in the thinking of men and women in every field of study. Inquiry for *educators* is framed by this question: How can children experience that insatiable drive to learn?

MODES AND PROCESSES OF INQUIRY

In *Frames of Mind,* Gardner (1983) presents the concept of *multiple intelligences:* linguistic, musical, logical–mathematical, spatial, bodily–kinesthetic, and personal. Each is a different *form* of thinking that uses particular abilities in varying degrees for special purposes. Gardner's theory describes the diversity of ways in which people perceive and construct meanings. Phenix's (1964) study of *realms of meaning* classifies the areas of knowledge by form and content, the languages of thought, and focus of their inquiry. Propensities for and ways of learning affect how questions are studied and what is learned. John-Steiner's (1985) analyses of thinking in scholars presents the "languages" of thinking as visual, verbal, musical, choreographic, and scientific. She asserts that while many of these modes of thinking are used by thinkers in every field, thinking in some inquiries may be dominated more by one than another.

Modes of Thought

In our search to understand the similarities as well as differences in inquiry across the fields of study, we have found evidence of several modes of thought that seem to fall into three major categories: symbolic, imagic, and affective. The *symbolic* mode includes thinking with words, numbers, or other symbol systems. Inquirers in the literary arts, mathematics, and philosophy may work primarily in this mode. *Imagic* thinking may be visual, spatial, tonal, and kinesthetic–sensate. Visual thinking is often associated with images that form and color the visual artist's experience, the writer's use of static and moving images to construct a scenario, and the kind of spatial imagery perceived by mathematicians, engineers, and architects. Musicians rely heavily on tonal thinking, working through the medium of sound to explore relationships among pitch, tone, rhythms, and harmonic dynamics. Kinesthetic–sensate thinking explores meanings in movements and sensations, a critical aspect of inquiry in dance and in physical sports. *Affective* thinking works with feelings and emotions that can dramatically color, direct, and drive an inquiry. In any of these modes, thinkers use processes of *reasoning* and *intuiting*. Reasoning involves a conscious, step-by-step, logical, analytic approach, while leaps of intuition appear to result from a largely unconscious, holistic process. See Figure 1.1 for a summary of these modes and processes of inquiry.

Figure 1.1
The modes and processes of inquiry

Symbolic: The use of words, numbers, and other symbol systems to perceive, construct, and express meanings, and to form and frame inquiry.

Imagic: The use of images, sounds and tonalities, and kinesthetic–sensory ways to perceive, construct, and express meanings, and to form and frame inquiry.

Affective: The use of feelings and emotions to perceive, construct, and express meanings, and to color, direct, and drive inquiry.

Main Processes
Reasoning
Intuiting

All these modes and processes appear in our readings and discussions about thinking in the arts, the sciences, and the humanities. They refer to both the form in which information is perceived and worked with and the ways it is expressed and communicated. While some fields of study may rely on certain modes or processes more than others, and individual inquirers may be more talented in the use of some over others, all have something to offer *every* inquiry because each provides the inquirer with a different way to perceive the subject, and a different form for framing and conveying ideas. The more diverse the modes of thinking used by an inquirer, the greater the potential for discovery. The power of interdisciplinary inquiry lies in its ability to encourage diversity of thought and, therefore, to increase the explorer's chances of making creative connections and "going beyond the information given" (Bruner, 1973).

The Literary Arts

Writers usually have what Gardner (1983) calls linguistic intelligence, the ability to perform verbal thinking with ease. They delight in the sounds and the symbolisms of words and are particularly adept at perceiving words in different ways and at expressing and communicating ideas through language by using their "inner voice," according to John-Steiner (1985). Most speak of their *love* of words. Eudora Welty (1983) was compelled by the characteristics of words from childhood. She delighted in how they *felt* in her mouth as she formed them, the ways they combined to express images and sensations, and the ways they enabled her to find meanings in people, places, times, and experiences. Cuba (personal communication, 1992) enjoys the detail that words allow her to work with her sensations, feelings, and images, as she did when describing the many dimensions of a fish in one of her stories. It all started for her with questions: "Is it possible to catch a fish with your hands? What kind of fish would be in this location? What would be inside it that would be fascinating?" She saw the fish as a metaphor for life. Everything inside of the fish is representative of life: pleasant and unpleasant, beautiful and ugly. Cuba's study of the fish became a study of the meanings of life.

Oliver (personal communication, 1991) sees the totality of his characters and sometimes the plot of a story in visual metaphors. Most writers are aware of the sensations that help them imagine as they write. There is evidence of visual as well as verbal thinking in their self-reports, and by inference. The reader's ability to form images while reading is testimony to the writer's ability to communicate sensory ideas. The same may be said for the affective mode. Writers use words to speak from and with emotion, and to cause feeling in the reader. Poets, in particular, seem to think simultaneously in imagic, verbal, and affective modes. While words may be their primary vehicle for expression and communication, the way they visualize the placement of each word on the page and the physical appearance and style of the letters influence the thought expressed. Poets may be in the vanguard of those who use language to develop and to express their meanings through imagic, symbolic, and affective modes. The inquiries—the searches literary artists conduct to write in authentic and moving ways—use all of John-Steiner's (1985) "languages" of thought. Only the product is primarily, though not exclusively, dominated by the verbal.

Writers use detective-like reasoning when they develop personas from bits of character traits and when they form a story from puzzle pieces of human experience. Welty (1983) explains how she uses facets of people she has known to create new characters with their own special constellation of qualities that makes them unique, yet reminiscent of others, and therefore believable. Writers also develop insights into their subjects and settings by pulling from deep within themselves new interactions among ideas. "All serious daring," as Welty says, "starts from within." They often express those intuitive understandings through metaphor.

The Fine and Performing Arts

Visual metaphor is often used to think through and express concepts in the visual and performing arts. It usually emerges from intuitive thinking but can also be derived through analysis of a problem. Visual artists' descriptions of their inquiries are alive with metaphor. Rush (personal communication, 1992) speaks of the visual representation of "states of mind." "Drawing," he says, "is perception—a way of knowing." Drawing is also a way to play with visual ideas by encoding them. Gardner (1983) includes the "susceptibility to encoding in a symbol system" as a criterion for the seven intelligences that he identifies (the spatial, bodily–kinesthetic, and musical among them). Visual artists do not claim a symbol system comparable to musical notation or the graphic language used to choreograph the dance or movement strategies in sports, but the physical elements of visual art (line, color, space, shape, and texture) may be building blocks of "symbol" systems for visual thinking. Though linguistic thinking is reported by artists to inhibit their creative work, other types of symbolic thinking may enhance their ability to conduct their inquiries.

Artists have much in common with the theoretical physicist, suggests Stephen Reynolds (personal communication, 1991). They develop imaginative ideas about the world by asking questions on the nature of things and reality. Donald Hodges (personal communication, 1991) uses Charles Ives's 1908 orchestral piece "The Unanswered Question" as an illustration of the composer's use of music to ask and seek answers to philosophical questions about the meaning of life in the universe. He argues that tonal thinking offers new perceptions of the question—new ways of understanding its character.

All the artists we have interviewed underscore the emotional aspects of their work. Rush (personal communication, 1992) speaks of rapport—understanding that is nonverbal—as important to his work. He refers to this thinking as intuitive, holistic, divergent, spatial, and nonverbal. His purpose in inquiry is to intuit meaning from all elements of his life experiences, without contaminating them by his biases or predilections. He refers to Albert Pinkham Ryder's metaphor, which likens inquiry to an inchworm, back legs holding fast to a leaf, its front end leaning forward, feeling outward into space for new experiences and discoveries. Reynolds (personal communication, 1991) characterizes artistic creativity as requiring risk taking, driven by the artist's need to investigate new sources and new processes to enable discovery. Intuitive feelings guide the sense of correctness of perceived shapes and forms, and analytical thinking provides the critical evaluation of one's work. "Art is a snail trail—the track that you leave," Reynolds says. It is a quest for truth that has continuity, pattern, and diversity—a challenge to find as many worlds as we can know.

Mathematics

Central to Gardner's concept of logical–mathematical intelligence is the work with "long chains of reasoning" (Gardner, 1985, p. 139). Phenix understands the essence of mathematics as "a language of complete abstraction" (Phenix, 1964, p. 72). Einstein's (Mantel, 1974) reasoning with images (for instance, his perspectives from a tram moving at the speed of light) and his conceptions of energy and time used imagery to develop a sequence of abstractions that led to the theory of relativity. Visual thinking is critical to Robbins's (personal communication, 1992) computer network to investigate the traveling salesman problem: "Workhorse" computers are linked to a central "blackboard" computer to simultaneously deliver data from their computations to the "blackboard" and, also, to be able to randomly select from that "blackboard" increasingly specialized sets of data. Analogies of teams of workhorses and a centralized blackboard contributed to this solution strategy, and the graphing of quantitative information makes the process possible. Keating (personal communication, 1991) also graphs statistical relationships to see quantitative patterns more clearly. Visual thinking merges with symbolic thinking as symbol systems are used to express discovered relationships between quantitative ideas. Much of this seems deliberate and reasoned, and it is. But equally important is the hunch that may give rise to an inquiry or direct its course: Robbins *senses* that the theory of cooperative functions is rich with potential to yield a solution to the traveling salesman problem. Keating often "sees" solutions to problems, then reasons out the proof. According to Gardner (1983, p. 139), "Many mathematicians report that they sense a solution, or a direction, long before they have worked out each step in detail." Explaining the idea requires the exercise of logic and its symbolic expression.

"No matter how talented you are in your field, no matter how much you know, the work is always difficult when you're at the frontiers of your knowledge. Inquiry is not easy when you're testing the limits of your abilities. But that is what makes it satisfying" (Robbins, personal communication, 1992). The need to understand, to discover relationships, and the desire to invent new perspectives drive mathematical inquiry. And then there is the *joy,* the sheer pleasure of searching.

The Natural and Social Sciences

We have tended to think of the scientific method as a clean and meticulous process of formulating hypotheses, organizing experiments, and collecting data, then analyzing and interpreting the findings in order to test the hypothesis and phrase new ones. Most natural and social scientists depict their inquiries as far less clear-cut and tidy. Watson's (1968) description of the search for the double helix is perhaps the best known testimony to the ins and outs, false starts, and detours of scientific detective work. Every scientist we have interviewed, and the many who contributed to John-Steiner's (1985) analysis, referred in some way to imagic thinking in their work. Most use metaphors and analogies. Many draw. Some, like Watson and Crick, construct models to clarify their thinking through kinesthetic–sensate forms. Sometimes the construction is highly analytical. At other times, it may be associated with flashes of insight. Kekule's discovery of the molecular structure of benzene (which initiated the discipline of organic chemistry) came from a dream of spiraling images that merged in the snake-like shape of a ring (McKim, 1980). Artist Kent Rush (personal communication, 1992) reminds us that dreaming is a form of thinking different from others. Eastern cultures use meditation to enable thinking that breaks the bounds imposed by our restricted sense of self. These are intuitive processes.

But science also involves critical, skeptical analysis of findings. And analysis requires symbolic thinking. Science measures with precision. It explicates hypotheses and builds theories. Scientific thinking challenges the known, searching out what is not understood and what is missing. It seeks to replicate and evaluate. The analytical processes may proceed in imagic modes, but they also need symbolic forms to advance the flow, expression, and communication of thought.

Playing with ideas is as characteristic of scientific inquiry as inquiry in any other field. Watson called it *tinkering.* Bronowski (1973) called it "asking impertinent questions." David Senseman (personal communication, 1991) refers to the pleasure of exploring the fascinating unknown. The affective dimensions of inquiry come through in many scientists' reports of their work. *Playfulness, delight,* and *pleasure* are words scientists use to try to explain the role of those clearly felt but enigmatic sensations that fuel their inquiries. These affective modes of thinking are also integral to the intra- and interpersonal abilities, associated with Gardner's (1983) personal intelligences, that contribute to collaboration, competition, perseverance, and joyfulness in inquiry.

The Humanities

Despite a tendency to think of their fields as primarily analytical, historians, anthropologists, archaeologists, and others who study human experience draw on both analytic and affective modes of thinking. Woodruff Smith (personal communication, 1992) reminds us that history is a cultural activity. The language of history is the language of culture. Studies of human experience seek and search through and for the human voice. They can be inherently interdisciplinary, perhaps more than in any other field of study. Therefore, their inquiry can, and often does, utilize all the ways of knowing associated with the sciences and the arts. Humanities scholars reconstruct the past by interpreting and imagining the patterns suggested by clues in the artifacts of human presence. Understanding the life styles of a people, like those of the Lower Pecos, who dwindled away without trace by the middle of the first century, is an ongoing detective-like hunt (Ancient Texans: Rock Art and Life Ways Along the Lower Pecos, Witte Museum, San Antonio, TX, 1987). Still-unanswered questions about why those ancient Texans painted diverse designs on the small round rocks found in their natural shelters along the Rio Grande haunt researchers. Perhaps more than any other, the subject matter of human experience demands of the inquirer a confluence of modes and processes of thinking.

THE LANGUAGES OF THINKING

Every inquiry is influenced by the language of that particular discipline and its accepted body of knowledge: its laws, principles, and belief systems. Kuhn's (1970) analysis of scientific revolutions explains how accepted paradigms can limit thinking in a field of study. Newtonian physics influenced what and how mathematicians thought about physical relationships until Einstein's theory of relativity challenged the ruling paradigms. The concept of plate tectonics dramatically altered the prevailing views of the earth's geological history. Noneuclidean geometry allowed new geometric concepts to emerge. Modernism in art broke with the long-standing tradition of Renaissance perspective. Each paved the way for new ways of seeing and thinking, sometimes in several fields of study. For example, the concept of relativity affected work in the humanities and the arts as well as in the sciences. Every model, every belief, by its existence enables and limits inquiry. The accepted knowledge of a field both informs and biases our perspectives, as we look at our subject through those lenses.

The language of a field influences how questions are formulated. Linguistic languages have their unique characteristics to describe things, depict action, and to subtly distinguish and discriminate. The descriptive capabilities of English may be challenged by those of the Eskimo languages, and both may be challenged by the superior abilities of Spanish to express nuances in action. Every symbol system carries similar advantages and limitations for inquiry. Mathematical symbols permit some relationships to be expressed better than others. Reflecting on the completeness of bubbles in a wave breaking on shore, Buckminster Fuller said that nature hated pi, because the value is never resolved; 3.1415 . . . goes on forever. By hating pi himself, Fuller looked past it for wholeness and found the geodesic dome, now understood as the molecule formed from charred carbon and referred to affectionately and respectfully as the "Buckey ball" (Perlmutter, 1991). Musical notation enables composers to record orchestrations for large symphony orchestras and very complex tonalities, yet is unable to communicate precisely some rhythmic patterns in jazz.

THE CONTEXTS OF INQUIRY

Equally influential is the context of inquiry: its person, its place, and its time. Individual inquirers bring their personalities, propensities, and backgrounds to bear on what and how they explore. James Watson contributed a generalist's perspective that complemented Crick's specialist orientation. Watson's talents with synthesis as well as his youth and American background brought a special constellation of qualities to the search for the molecular structure of the gene. The inquirer's cultural rearing, including native language, influences ways of perceiving a problem and formulating a question. Growing up male or female in a particular culture will add other layers of influence on any study, some drawn from rearing practices, others from societal biases. August Wilson (Knull, 1988) writes plays about universal human issues, but portrays them from the African-American cultural perspective because he wants to advance understanding of that heritage in a society that seems uncaring as well as ignorant of the black experience. Barbara McClintock's work on jumping genes went unnoticed and unappreciated in her field for decades, largely because of her gender in a male-dominated field. A different example of cultural biases is that for years, research on heart disease has used only male subjects, yet those studies have been the source of treatments for women with coronary illnesses.

The environment in which the inquiry is conducted will also limit or advance its search. Laura Gilpin's photographs, like Ansel Adams's, were unique for their time. Today, with technological changes in photographic processes and the proliferation of images in the society at large, their inquiries would probably be quite different in character. Robbins's study of the traveling salesman problem would not be feasible without high-speed computers. And just as new tools will change the kinds of questions asked, so do contemporary ideas influence how we interpret the past. "The past is a foreign country, they did things differently there" (Hartley L. P., cited in Lowenthal, 1985) expresses in serious terms what Macauley (1979) presents humorously in *Motel of the Mysteries*. Macauley's fictitious archaeologists found it all too easy to find sacred meanings in the mundane objects of everyday life. Interpreters of the past must take care notto allow their contemporary knowledge or preconceived ideas to influence their perceptions.

Every inquiry has the potential to change what and how we understand, but every inquiry is limited by what and how we know. Every inquiry is unique and can break the bounds of tradition, but each is limited by the courage and the imagination of the inquirer.

THE PRODUCTS OF INQUIRY

Every question, if explored with care and thoroughness, guides the searcher to knowledge, newly acquired by the individual or newly discovered in the field of study. Inquiry also raises further questions and directions for study. The findings of one search generate ideas for others and, sometimes, suggest connections that give rise to new theories. Inquiry in any field may produce expanded symbol systems— ways of expressing concepts and interrelationships more clearly and succinctly. The process of inquiry helps the inquirer to grow in content knowledge and in the modes, processes, and skills of the search. People who do not consider themselves scholars in specialized fields of study use inquiry to learn about anything that interests them, to solve problems that affect their lives, to direct their experiences, to find their own truths, and to hone their habits of mind. The ordinary person's inquiry may explore an area of interest, an intriguing question, a mystery, the meanings of an idea, and even the secrets held within an everyday object like a walking shoe. Whatever the problem, subject, or issue, any inquiry that is done with enthusiasm and with care will use some of the same modes and processes of thinking that are used by those who are searching for new knowledge in their field of study.

Habits of Mind

Embedded in the testimonies of the sources we consulted are references to abilities that seem to course through inquiry, supporting the use of the thinking modes and processes we have detailed. Some might term them *skills*. We prefer to call them *habits of mind*. Interestingly, some of the same habits appear important to inquiry in every field. They include the abilities to focus, to simplify, to attend to details, to think fluently and flexibly, to form hunches, to experiment, to search for patterns, to use models and metaphors, and to find elegant solutions, and the affective abilities of risk taking, cooperating/collaborating, competing, and persevering or being capable of self-discipline. Certainly there are others. We start with these, inviting our readers to contribute to the set as we continue this inquiry into interdisciplinary and integrative learning.

Finding and Keeping Focus. "Keep your focus," the coach directs the Olympic athlete before the competition. Good advice. But staying focused is more difficult than it seems. Finding a focus hinges on the way questions are posed. Maintaining the focus depends on which questions are selected. An inquiry can be only as probing as its questions.

Every discipline of study is nurtured by the questions its scholars explore. The idea of questioning as problem definition is usually associated with the scientific method. Natural and social scientists define their experiments through hypotheses, which are really proposed answers to their questions. Although a question may be phrased in different ways, it focuses and delimits the inquiry. The geologist who explores relationships among several variables in the physical world is asking operational questions. An anthropologist studying cultural characteristics of social groups may ask descriptive questions. Both scholars formulate their questions in ways that determine where they will look for answers. The questions of theoretical mathematicians are inherent in their search for proofs; those who apply mathematics, such as statisticians, translate questions from other fields into mathematical language. While writers may not highlight the questions that drive their writing, their poems, stories, and essays are clearly attempts to communicate answers to questions about human experiences, behaviors, and qualities. In effect, they are writing figurative answers to a universal set of questions about the human condition. The works of fine artists, often considered *problems,* are the manifestations of experiments with elements such as light, color, texture, shape, tone, and rhythm. All experiments are framed by questions. The character of the query can determine the success of the experiments. But not all questions are equally clear in guiding investigation. Not all questions can be answered in substantive ways. How well the question is formulated determines the extent to which its answers contribute insights to a study.

Simplifying Questions and Problems. Research is advanced by questions that are simply and clearly phrased. No matter how complex the subject under investigation, most researchers claim to search for the simplest and most direct language to express their query. Scholars in every field maintain a continuing quest for the most succinct, most clarifying "language" to express and communicate what they want to find out. The clearer the question, the greater its ability to isolate significant variables, suggest critical relationships, provide clues to sources of substantive data, and, in effect, to point to the problem's solution. The ability to remove from a problem its complicating, extraneous features is a hallmark of the successful inquirer.

Attentiveness. Eastern philosophy advances attentiveness as the ultimate habit of mind—the means for becoming one with the universe. In Western thought, too, attentiveness is valued. The natural scientist speaks of this as observation and collection of precise data. Some say that it is more important to have impeccably accurate data than a clear interpretation, because interpretations may vary but the data must always be true. Inquirers in the humanities talk about clearly recording measurements of the observable. The mathematician and the theoretical scientist may place less emphasis on observing their environment than on theorizing about it, but they too refer to attending to specific components that complete an idea. Their "thought experiments" examine details in the same way that inventors report seeing all parts of their inventions in their mind's eye. Literary artists refer to knowing every detail of their character's persona, whether or not they ever write them down. Visual artists are equally concerned with details—a drop of color, a shadow, or a spot of light— that contribute to the image, although most casual viewers are oblivious to them. Musicians cannot help but attend to the tone and texture of individual notes. Attentiveness requires discipline and appreciation of how a whole is a collection of individual pieces that each requires perceptual precision to comprehend.

Thinking Fluently and Flexibly.   Based on the work of Guilford (1956), Torrance (1962, 1970) described characteristics of creative thinking associated with the generation of many and varied ideas. He termed these ways of thinking *fluent* and *flexible,* respectively. When asked about their inquiry, natural scientists often cite the ability to look at their problem or their data in new ways. This flexibility in perspective can suggest varied interpretations and, most important, new questions that offer different routes for exploration. The ability to think in maverick ways fuels controversy in every field; it may also overturn accepted ideas and supplant established knowledge. Historians may search for clues to support interpretations of people's lives or events that are different from earlier ones. Journalists look for the new angle on a story. Writers distinguish themselves by finding different ways to speak to universal human experience. Metaphors can give new dimensions to old ideas. Artists combine varied media to create unique visual and auditory images. The ability to generate lots of ideas with facility and to use different perspectives to examine any idea is central to creative production; it is also critical to interdisciplinary thinking.

Forming Hunches.   Analysis and intuition play complementary roles in anticipatory thinking. Some predictions and hypotheses are reasoned out; others, such as conjectures, speculations, and projections, are intuited. Those who work in the "hard" sciences are as likely to talk about the importance of their hunches as those who inquire in the arts and humanities. From the hunches, formal hypotheses may emerge. Natural scientists are concerned with relating variables in hypothetical statements that focus their inquiry. Mathematicians and theoretical scientists work to prove the theorems, principles, and laws that are the hypotheses of their imaginative reasoning. Even when the hypotheses are not couched in formal language, inquirers engage in "if–then" thinking. Historians may search for reasons to justify an interpretation or to project a consequence from historical precedents in the sense that "the past is prologue." Writers also use projection to make their characters behave in response to certain circumstances and to the behaviors of others. This hypothetical thinking may result in the forms sculptors chisel out of an undifferentiated mass of material, in the images painters create, in tonal themes that composers weave into variations, or in the cadenzas and improvisations of performers. Though less formal and sometimes more spontaneous than the hypotheses of research scientists, these creations are nonetheless experiments that test hypothetical ideas often born of hunches.

Designing Tests and Experimenting.   Just as the way in which a question is framed determines what clues will be gathered and which sources will be consulted, the form an anticipation takes delimits the character of its test. Experimentation is generally associated with the sciences. It's what natural scientists are expected to *do.* Social scientists also embrace the experimental method to control and test variables cited in their hypotheses. Mathematicians test mathematical theorems, principles, and laws by searching for proofs and trying out their applications. Humanities scholars also experiment by searching for evidence that supports or refutes their ideas. The process of finding the evidence is an experiment in its own right. Anthropologists experiment by gathering descriptive data on their subjects, sometimes to find patterns that may form a hypothesis and sometimes to test an idea. Writers and performers play out their hunches to see if their audiences can tell whether the actions of characters ring true and the plot is gripping. Attempts to solve problems in the fine arts are evaluated in the studio and rehearsal hall as they are created and recreated; the edited versions are then tested during exhibition and performance.

Searching for Patterns.   No matter how good we are at finding new ways of looking at a problem or topic, no matter how prolific our questions, there can be no synthesis without the organization of ideas. The search for patterns is integral to all learning and, therefore, to the generation of new knowledge. Natural scientists are detective-like in their categorization of the data they collect. This integration of "little" notions into "big" ideas is also a part of the social scientist's investigative method. Literary artists develop their characters from the interaction of human traits and form their stories by articulating the associations among seemingly unrelated happenings in human experience. The search for patterns takes different routes for a painter or sculptor, composer or playwright, performer or actor. But none can solve their special problems without being able to achieve an integrated wholeness.

Using Models and Metaphors.   Models are means that scholars use to shape and communicate their ideas about potential answers to their questions. The scientific method is a model of inquiry that scientists embrace and use as their touchstone. That model has been adopted by many social scientists, who in turn have adapted it to their special problems, language, and types of data. The physical representation of molecular structure is another kind of model that explains abstract ideas. Mathematical rules and principles are also long-standing models of criteria for quantitative inquiries. Even so, as mathematical fields expand to include the applicative methods of computer science and statistics, models for their use are formed and reformed. Humanities scholars use ethnographic models to research their subjects, experimenting with varied approaches to better comprehend the complexity of their subjects. In the fine arts, models for inquiry and expression are formed and reformed by inventive scholars. Inquiry is invention.

Metaphors are a special type of model. They can ascribe concrete and sensual qualities to abstract ideas. They can help make the strange become familiar by calling up images that prompt multidimensional associations. There is often an interplay of rational thinking and feeling through metaphors. Poets and writers use them regularly. The work of fine artists includes visual, textural, and tonal metaphors. Metaphors give ideas a larger form. They help to uncover ways to group related concepts. Scholars in the sciences and humanities use them to advance their search for meaningful patterns. Metaphors and models are vehicles for communicating complex ideas with clarity and succinctness. Knowing how to use and to create models and metaphors is a tool of every inquirer.

Finding Elegant Solutions.   Computers might not have developed to their contemporary power without the application of the binary system. A simple "one–zero, on–off" relationship permits some of the most complex technology and computation in human experience. The binary system's role in the development of the computer is an example of an elegant solution. Physicists claim that energy will not be completely understood until its aesthetic is found. Whatever the problem or question, its inquiry seeks solutions that are transcendent in their richness and simplicity. The search in any field is not for any answer but for answers that are clear and unambiguous and convincingly true—answers that are beautiful. Elegant solutions explain complexities in all fields. Knowing where and how to look for them is a function of any inquiry.

Risk Taking.   The pursuit of elegant solutions to problems sometimes demands breaking with old, established traditions. Inquirers in all fields speak to the ability to do that in calculated ways. Sometimes this means pursuing interests and methods of investigation that are not valued in the field of study. Scientists in any discipline may have to risk loss of acceptance in the field in order to question an established idea or to follow their individual bent. Mathematicians may face professional ostracism if their work challenges accepted beliefs or pursues directions that are not yet accepted. The same is true of the humanities, the social sciences, and the literary and fine arts. Yet change is not possible without the courage to study an inherently interesting topic before its legitimacy is recognized, or to subject the patterns one sees to criticism. Knowing when and how to take risks can determine success in any endeavor.

Cooperating and Collaborating.   Despite the tendency for most disciplines to value individual over group efforts, the ability to cooperate and collaborate with others who are working with related problems can advance an inquiry. This is increasingly true in the natural and social sciences, where team efforts can contribute to interdisciplinary studies. Opportunities to bring different points of view to bear on the same problem can lead to richer solutions. Although mathematicians are usually more solitary experimenters, they too claim to benefit from collaborative work with others who are intrigued by the same problem. Literary artists tend to work alone, as do many composers and visual artists. But writers have editors with whom they share a project and with whom they fine-tune the expression of their ideas. And those who work with sounds or visual images often prefer to be members of colonies of similar-minded and artistically talented people who can serve as respondents and reactors to one another's work. Knowing how to be a productive partner or group member often enhances the search for solutions (Johnson & Johnson, 1990).

Competing. The desire to discover directs inquiry. The drive to excel fuels it. Scientists may strive to be first in cracking a code or finding a pattern that earns a Nobel Prize. They want their findings to appear in the literature before other scholars "steal their thunder." Grantsmanship is a highly competitive enterprise. Mathematicians also work to be first with the proof for a theorem—or with a new theorem. Creative artists may be less concerned with racing others to publish, exhibit, or perform their work, but they too push against the limits of their fields' knowledge and their personal creative talents by competing with their peers or with themselves. Without competition, there would be few revisions and new drafts. The competitive spirit often provides the discipline needed to continue an inquiry even when it is not going smoothly. Knowing how and when to compete most effectively is a habit of mind that must be developed.

Perseverance and Self-Discipline. Every inquiry has its stalemates, its barriers, and its frustrations. No matter how interesting the study may be, there is always a point at which it becomes difficult. At that point, the inquirer may be pushing against the frontiers of personal knowledge or even the knowledge of the field. People persevere in those efforts that have special significance for them. The motivation to continue derives, in part, from the degree of intrigue the search holds. How well individuals can exercise self-discipline also determines how long each is willing to "hang in" when the going gets rough. Learning to exercise self-discipline and to assess the origins of and influences on one's motivations has much to do with productive inquiry. See Figure 1.2 for a summary of these qualities of inquiry.

▼ READER INVOLVEMENT

As you read this book, we suggest that you keep a journal to record your reactions to the readings and your own explorations. Have you used the habits of mind discussed in this chapter? In your journal, tell about the situations and the ways in which you have used these processes in your own inquiries or in your teaching.

IMPLICATIONS FOR TEACHING AND LEARNING

What about children's inquiry? What do the ideas discussed in this chapter mean for students—all students—especially those in elementary and middle schools? We see

Figure 1.2
The qualities of inquiry

Modes of Inquiry

Symbolic: The use of words, numbers, and other symbol systems to perceive, construct, and express meanings, and to form and frame inquiry.

Imagic: The use of images, sounds and tonalities, and kinesthetic–sensory ways to perceive, construct, and express meanings, and to form and frame inquiry.

Affective: The use of feelings and emotions to perceive, construct, and express meanings, and to color, direct, and drive inquiry.

Processes

Reasoning

Intuiting

Some Habits of Mind

Finding and keeping focus

Simplifying questions and problems

Attentiveness

Thinking fluently and flexibly

Forming hunches

Designing tests and experimenting

Searching for patterns

Using models and metaphors

Finding elegant solutions

Risk taking

Cooperating and collaborating

Competing

Perseverance and self-discipline

here important implications for the ways in which curriculum is designed and for the ways teaching and learning develop. Each field of study has special characteristics that demand attention in the planning of educational programs. The modes and processes of thinking and the habits of mind that characterize each, and are common to most, should be exercised through education in the lower schools, before students specialize. Learning in the elementary and middle-school years must prepare students for secondary and postsecondary studies by offering them solid foundations in the major ideas, generalizations, principles, and theories of the natural and social sciences, language and fine arts, and mathematics. They must also learn to use with increasing capability the particular imagic, symbolic, and affective modes of thinking that enhance inquiry in each field of study, through experiences that promote analytical and intuitive processing with varied types of content and in diverse contexts. We believe that the most natural vehicle for accomplishing this is an interdisciplinary concept of thematic curriculum and instruction that is question-driven and investigative in character.

▼ READER INVOLVEMENT

In the course of reading this book, you will be guided to develop an interdisciplinary theme study. In any curriculum development effort, knowledge of the subject matter is mandatory. The design of interdisciplinary theme studies requires knowledge of content from the perspectives of the several disciplines that are relevant to the theme. It also requires intimate knowledge of the modes and processes of inquiry and the habits of mind that should be used by students who explore the theme.

As you develop your theme study, we invite you to investigate a subject as an inquirer. The first step is to select a theme for study. We recommend that, like the teachers whose work is presented in this book, you work with the theme of *patterns of change.*

1. Formulate four or five questions about this theme that you would like to investigate. You may want to find a tangible example of the theme to examine. The illustration of inquiry into a walking shoe that began this chapter might begin a study of causes of change in life styles over time in different cultures. The focus you select will depend, in part, on the availability of appropriate resources.

2. For each question, select resources you can consult, such as books and other print media, places, people, visuals (photographs, drawings, videos, and paintings), and additional sources of information about your theme.

3. Begin your search. In a new section of your journal, record the process of your own inquiry. Make note of

   Your questions;

   The sources you consult;

   The data you collect;

   The dead ends you encounter and how you get around them;

   How you interpret and verify your information;

   The hunches you have; and

   The new questions that occur to you.

Identify the modes of thinking and habits of mind that you find yourself using. Include the pleasures and the frustrations of your search. This journal will be a detective story of your search for clues and the emergence of meaningful patterns that help you to understand your theme.

REFERENCES

Arnheim, R. (1969). *Visual thinking.* Berkeley, CA: University of California Press.

Bronowski, J. (1973). *The ascent of man.* Boston: Little, Brown.

Bruner, J. (1973). *Beyond the information given: Studies in the psychology of knowing.* New York: Norton.

Mantel, H. (Producer & Director). (1974). *Einstein: The education of a genius* [Film]. Princeton, NJ: Films for the Humanities and Sciences.

Feynman, R. P. (1988). *"What do you care what other people think?"* New York: Bantam Books.

Flam, J. D. (1973). *Matisse on art.* London: Phaidon Press.

Gardner, H. (1983). *Frames of mind.* New York: Basic Books.

Guilford, J. P. (1956). The structure of intellect. *Psychological Bulletin, 53,* 267–295.

Guillian, M. (1983). *Bridges to infinity.* Los Angeles: Jeremy P. Tarcher.

Hardy, G. H. (1940). *A mathematician's apology.* Cambridge: Cambridge University Press.

Hughes, R. (1980). *The shock of the new.* New York: Knopf.

John-Steiner, V. (1985). *Notebooks of the mind.* Albuquerque: University of New Mexico Press.

Johnson, D. W., & Johnson, R. T. (1990). *Cooperation and competition: Theory and research.* Edina, MN: Interactions.

Knull, K. R. (Producer & Director). (1988). *A world of ideas with Bill Moyers: August Wilson* [Video]. Alexandria, VA: PBS Video.

Kuhn, T. (1970). *The structure of scientific revolutions.* Chicago: University of Chicago Press.

Lowenthal, D. (1985). *The past is a foreign country.* Cambridge: Cambridge University Press.

Macauley, D. (1979). *Motel of the mysteries.* Boston: Houghton Mifflin.

McKim, R. H. (1980). *Experiences in visual thinking* (2nd ed.). Monterey, CA: Brooks/Cole.

Perlmutter, A. H. (Producer). (1991). *The creative spirit* [Television series, 4 parts]. Public Broadcasting System and IBM. New York: Ambrose Video.

Phenix, P. H. (1964). *Realms of meaning.* New York: McGraw-Hill.

Roe, A. (1952). *The making of a scientist.* Westport, CT: Greenwood Press.

Torrance, E. P. (1962). *Guiding creative talent.* Englewood Cliffs, NJ: Prentice-Hall.

Torrance, E. P. (1970). *Creative learning and teaching.* New York: Dodd Mead.

Van Kirk, S. (1980). *Many tender ties.* Norman: University of Oklahoma Press.

Watson, J. D. (1968). *The double helix.* New York: Mentor Books.

Webster's third international dictionary (1981). Springfield, MA: Merriam-Webster.

Welty, E. (1983). *One writer's beginnings.* New York: Warner Books.

Additional Reading

Boslough, J. (1985). *Stephen Hawking's universe.* New York: Avon Books.

Cheney, M. (1981). *Tesla: Man out of time.* New York: Laurel Books.

Dewey, J. (1933). *How we think.* Lexington, MA: D.C. Heath.

Hoskin, M. (1971). *The mind of the scientist.* New York: Taplinger.

Howard, V. A. (Ed.). (1990). *Varieties of thinking.* New York: Routledge.

Kidder, T. (1981). *The soul of a new machine.* New York: Avon.

Preble, D., & Preble, S. (1985). *Artforms.* New York: Harper & Row.

Ryle, G. (1949). *The concept of mind.* London: Hutchinson.

Shafer, H. J. (1986). *Ancient Texans.* San Antonio: The Witte Museum of the San Antonio Museum Association and Texas Monthly Press.

Shamos, M. H. (Ed.). (1959). *Great experiments in physics.* New York: Dover.

Stern, F. (Ed.). (1956). *The varieties of history.* New York: Vintage.

Tufte, E. R. (1983). *The visual display of quantitative information.* Cheshire, CT: Graphics Press.

Chapter Two

Historical Experiments in Integrated Curriculum

*I*n this chapter, we look at four examples of experiments in integrated curriculum that span 50 years, from the Dewey School, which opened its doors in 1898, to the Bank Street Workshops, which were in operation until 1948.

The stories of these experiments were told by people deeply involved in them: Katherine Camp Mayhew and Anna Camp Edwards at the Dewey School, James S. Tippett and his colleagues at the Lincoln School, E. Oberholzer in the Houston City Schools, and Lucy Sprague Mitchell at the Bank Street College of Education. Oberholzer describes a research study designed to examine the effects of a massive curriculum effort in integrated curriculum in Houston between 1924 and 1930. The other three describe smaller experiments in curriculum that they did not term "integrated," but which incorporated many of the principles and practices that are part of curriculum integration.

In this chapter, we use imaginary scenarios, based upon information given by these authors, to build scenarios of life in these schools. For each site, we have selected a first grade and a fifth grade class to exemplify the activities of the school.

The purpose of this chapter is not only to look at early experiments in integrated curriculum. As in any inquiry, finding information leads to new questions, and the questions that emerge from looking at these examples are critical in any attempt to integrate the curriculum. These questions reemerge at intervals throughout this book.

Looking at ways that the questions have been addressed in the past may help us to approach them with more insight and wisdom as we develop our own integrated curriculum.

THE DEWEY SCHOOL, 1902–1903: THE SCHOOL AS A COOPERATIVE SOCIETY

The Laboratory School of the University of Chicago, later known as the Dewey School, first opened in January 1896 with 16 pupils and two persons in charge. By 1898, after three moves, it was located in an old residence on Ellis Avenue and had a student population of 82. By 1902, the numbers had risen to 140 children, 23 teachers, and 10 graduate assistants.

The main goals of the Dewey School were, first, the development of the school as a cooperative community that would meet the social needs of students and, second, the intellectual development of the child through activity.

Two major assumptions about children were basic to the philosophy of the Dewey School. The first emphasized the differences between children and adults: A child is not a "little adult," and a child's main work is learning. The second assumption was that "the conditions which make for mental and moral progress are the same for the child as for the adult. Therefore the school must meet the unique needs and interests of the child, while providing a situation where the problem-solving processes used by both children and adults can be brought to bear upon those interests and needs" (Mayhew & Edwards, 1936, pp. 250–251).

This learning occurred within a community setting. In *The School and Society* (1900), Dewey speaks of a school as "an embryonic community life" that will "reflect the life of the larger society." This "embryonic community" will in turn produce citizens that can improve the "larger society" by making it "worthy, lively, and harmonious" (Cremin, 1964, pp. 117–118).

In the school, therefore, a major focus was the *social* purpose of education, which can be seen clearly as we look at the interactive work of the 6-year-olds in dramatic play, and of the 10-year-olds in the construction of the Colonial room (see below). Children learned to work together to achieve common goals.

Activities were perceived to arise from the child's own interests and from the need to solve problems that aroused the child's curiosity and that led to creative solutions. In turn, activity itself led to inquiry and to the development of skills (Tanner & Tanner, 1980).

Subject matter was seen as a resource for social and intellectual problem solving. In accord with principles of child development, the selection of subject matter was related to children's experiences and interests, and moved from primarily concrete and physical experiences for the younger children to more abstract and intellectual pursuits for the older groups.

Group 3 (about seventeen 6-year-olds) was located in a big, sunny room that also served as the Biological Laboratory. During the 3 hours of their school day, they spent 1½ to 2 hours in this room; the rest of their day was spent with the 7-year-olds for play and games, or with the younger children for play and music (Mayhew & Edwards, 1936).

The room contained blackboards and a sand table, and had plenty of room for games and activities. A vivarium and an aquarium provided homes for the living things brought in by the children. In this scenario, the teacher shows us around:

Here's the children's first project, the farm. They built the farmhouse and barn from large blocks. This chicken coop is made roughly to scale. The whole class discussed what would be on the farm. We decided to grow corn and wheat, and to have sheep and a dairy. Notice that the pastures have stone walls; the children decided that the animals needed something stronger than these stick fences.

This project involved them in a lot of measuring and number work. They even learned to use a square, triangle, and ruler to help them in the construction. They understood the inch and half-inch, but had some difficulty in using quarter-inches.

Let's go outside. They grew winter wheat on this little 5 by 7-foot plot, which they measured by themselves. They figured out how to plant the wheat, and when they had harvested the grain, they invented a two-piece flail to separate the seeds from the hulls. It worked really well!

Their dramatic play has centered around the farm. We worked out a complicated scenario to get the wheat to the mill and then to the stores, and after they had played it out, the children recorded the process by making diagrams to show what had happened.

The next area of study was the animals on the farm. The children learned about cows and dairy products. At the same time, our cooking lessons focused on the use of milk, butter, and cheese in recipes. We even tried to tan leather in our science lessons, but that didn't work very well.

Next, we studied sheep and wool production. From there, the children wanted to know about other fabrics, so we had an extensive unit on cotton.

Look at the sand table. They are working out how to get water from the mountains to the desert. They've learned a lot about water levels. They even invented a water tower.

Reading and writing is an important part of all their work. The skills grow out of the activities. At the end of the unit on cotton, we put together a play to show how the cotton came from the plantation to the factory and then to the wholesale stores. We also composed a written record of the process that was read at assembly.

I really enjoy this way of learning. The children are so interested in everything, and they constantly absorb new knowledge of materials and processes. Of course, it demands a lot from the teacher, but it is exciting to see the children using their inven-

tive ability to develop these activities. It helps them to understand social relations and organizations, and to be part of them (based on Mayhew & Edwards, 1936, pp. 80–88).

The 10-year-olds (Group 7) were in two groups, under the direction of the head of the textile department and the director of history. They met in one of the dining rooms and at one end of the kitchen laboratory. In this scenario, the head of the history department shows us around the Colonial room that the children built under the supervision of the shop director, Elizabeth Jones.

The children really had to work together closely on this project. The boys chose to work mainly on the furniture, and the girls on the bedding and rugs, but they both worked together on the construction of this fireplace. They had quite a difficult time with this. The first time they built it, the lime was not properly slaked, and the mortar crumbled. They learned that the lime needed to be left in water all night in order to slake adequately. You should have seen their excitement when they first lit a fire and found that the flue drew well! They were very pleased with themselves.

Look at the furnishings of the room. One boy made this little spinning wheel at home. We find that there has been a marked increase in the time children spend on their chosen activities in out-of-school hours. For example, this bedstead was constructed here, but the feather bed and bedding were made by the girls at home.

The children are learning a great deal about early communities and how people depended upon each other, since in projects like these, the children themselves have to act as an interdependent community. This study focuses on the growth of unity among the different Colonies, and the resulting movement toward independence from England. As we go on with the study, we will also examine the social and political development that followed independence. I think that the children understand how the pioneer families had to depend upon themselves at first, and how specialization of labor occurred. As we progress with the study, we will follow the expansion of trade among the Colonies and with Europe. We want to involve the children in concrete experiences at all times. One of the teachers suggested that we have each child become an imaginary sea captain who describes his travels and what goods he carries. This could lead into a study of the Navigation Laws, which are difficult to understand if they are too abstract.

The children have also learned the importance of research. At the beginning of the year, we found that many of the children could not read with ease or proficiency, so for 3 months, we gave much time to collateral reading related to the historical and geographical background to the study. We also gave writing lessons and drill exercises on words and constructions that were troublesome to the children. They did not enjoy this much, but they understood the need to be able to get information from books, and now they are finding the research much easier.

All through the study, the children are acting as independent learners within a community. Our aim is not so much to cover ground but to give the children some knowledge of how social processes were used by the colonists to secure social results, how obstacles were overcome, and the means contrived to attain these results. We want the children to identify intellectually with the problems, just as the younger children identify with situations through dramatic play.

The main study for this group is historical, but it also moves into geography, science, and mathematics as the children construct maps, experiment with materials, and use number concepts to help with scale and proportion. They are also conducting other studies in science, and they really enjoy experimenting with numbers and mastering number processes. They also engage in activities related to the main project in art and music, and cooking, and in their French classes they talk about what they are doing in the activities.

The main value of this approach? I think it is that the children learn to work together and to handle all kinds of social activity, and at the same time they become independent problem solvers. I must say I really enjoy watching the social and intellectual development of the children in this group" (based on Mayhew & Edwards, 1936, pp. 166–171).

The Integrated Curriculum in the Dewey School

Integration of the curriculum emerged both from beliefs about learning and from beliefs about the purposes of schools. Children's interests are not subject specific; they cross the traditional disciplines. The acquisition of skills emerges from activities and inquiry related to a broad central theme, and are explored in the community of the classroom.

Curriculum integration was expected to occur naturally, as subject-area specialists designed activities to explore the problem each group was investigating. However, teachers were not afraid to encourage the children to explore other topics not directly related to the central problem. For example, the group of 6-year-olds, in addition to the counting and measuring they used as they learned about the farm, also used dominoes and blocks to help develop concepts of tens and units, and they read and wrote books unrelated to the farm study. Similarly, some of the 10-year-olds' science studies were focused on Colonial history, but they also studied plants and animals unrelated to the study, and their number work allowed them to explore abstract mathematical principles and processes such as the relationship between multiplication and division.

It must be noted, also, that the central problems studied in each age group tended to have a strong social studies orientation, which makes sense considering the social purposes of the school. Studies in subjects such as science, mathematics, cooking, art, music, and even French were related to the central social, historical, or geographical central theme.

THE LINCOLN SCHOOL, 1926:
THE CHILD-CENTERED SCHOOL

In 1916, Abraham Flexner published his essay "A Modern School" in the *American Review of Reviews,* calling for a school designed "to give children the knowledge they need, and to develop in them the power to handle themselves in our own world" (Cremin, 1964, p. 280). This school would be based upon scientific standards, and would provide a "laboratory from which would issue scientific studies of educational problems."

This "model school" came into existence as the Lincoln School of Teachers College. Situated in Manhattan, the school built a curriculum based upon units of work that took into account children's development, and that used the city of New York itself as a laboratory for exploration and activities.

In 1921–1922, the school moved into a new building in which the children studied units designed to deal in depth with some important aspect of contemporary civilization.

Each classroom was perceived as a real workshop, and children's learning was seen as real work. The goal of the school was "the development of an all-round, harmonious personality." The criteria for units of work developed by the staff of the elementary division (Tippett, Coffin, and the staff of the elementary division of the Lincoln School of Teachers College, Columbia University, 1927) gave a clear indication of the school's philosophy:

1. The unit of work must be selected from real-life situations and must be considered worthwhile by children because they feel that they have helped select it and because they find in it many opportunities to satisfy their needs.

2. The unit of work must afford many opportunities for real purposes and real projects, and it will be something that children can carry into the regular curriculum.

3. The unit of work must stimulate many kinds of activities and so provide for individual differences.

4. The unit of work must make individual growth possible.

5. The succession of units of work must provide for continuous group growth from one level to the next.

6. Each unit of work must furnish leads into other related units of work and must stimulate in children the desire for a continued widening of their interests and understandings.

7. Each unit of work must help meet the demands of society and must help clarify social meanings.

8. Each unit of work must be accompanied by progress in the use of such tool subjects as contribute to that unit.

9. Each unit of work must lead to the development of desirable habits.

Teachers themselves were expected to have a sound background: a thorough knowledge base, an understanding of children and their development, and a lively personality (Tippett et al., 1927). The teacher was expected to use a specific technique that included the following elements (Tippett et al., 1927):

1. To give time for orientation;
2. To set the stage for the initiation and development of educative situations or units of work;
3. To work as a member as well as a guide of the class;
4. To select the educative factors in any unit of work;
5. To do something with the facts and meanings that have been stressed.

Let us look at "real work" in progress in a first grade classroom:

The first grade turned their classroom into a "play village." Houses were constructed out of cartons and cardboard and lovingly painted. Blocks enclosed yards and formed elegant walls and gates. Toy people and animals populated the village; the houses were filled with handmade furniture, drapes, and rugs. Engines, cars, and wagons provided transportation. A theater, a hotel, and stores made the village more than a collection of homes.

In this village the children worked and played. They left it to take real trips throughout New York City: to markets, farms, and factories, to museums and a fire station, and to docks and ferries. From the trips they brought back new knowledge and experience that they used in their dramatic play, language work, science, cooking, and math. They composed their own class stories and learned to read them. They made up plays and composed songs. They used money constantly in their dramatic play: to pay rent, to buy and sell, to go to the theater or the circus, to ride on buses or trains. They used measurement in construction and cooking. Science was an integral part of the exploration: The children conducted an experiment with the power of steam. Artwork centered around the trips and the project itself, from painting pictures to designing booklets to printing fabric for curtains for the houses.

The fifth grade unit on water transportation grew out of a third grade boat unit, and out of the children's own interest in boats and their uses. In the fifth grade, students were able to explore the subject in more depth and detail than was possible at the third grade level.

During the first 3 weeks of the year, the class studied the topic in a general way and developed an extensive list of questions to be explored:

Do we really know when boats began?

Why did people need larger boats?

Why did the Roman galleys have several banks of oars?

Why did sailboats change to steam?

In order to prepare for individual study, the whole class worked together on two topics, "Primitive Boats and How They Began" and "Early Sails and How They Began." Students then selected different topics and worked on them individually or in very small groups. Each student set a date for the completion of the report. The report was read to the whole class, criticized, and either accepted as complete or returned for revision. Completed reports were contributed to a class "boat book."

From the beginning, the unit took a historical approach to the topic, and this led to two major class projects: a book of linoleum-block prints of ships, and a painted burlap frieze depicting the history of water transportation from the earliest history to the modern day. These projects were organized and developed through extensive committee work by the students.

Field trips related to the study included a ferryboat ride from Manhattan to Staten Island to see harbor boats, and visits to a square-rigger that had been turned into a museum and to the Brooklyn Navy Yard.

Work on the unit incorporated extensive reading and writing, research, vocabulary work, accurate measuring and elementary geometry, scientific study of navigation and flotation, geographic study of maps, artwork, music, dancing, and industrial arts, all related to the topic.

The year's work culminated in a special school assembly, where the students gave a variety of reports, songs, and dances (based on Tippett et al., 1927, pp. 74–88, 184).

The Integrated Curriculum in the Lincoln School

The curriculum in the Lincoln School was deliberately organized around broad, cross-curricular units of work designed to provide children as nearly as possible with "real-life situations" (Tippett et al., 1927, p. 29). These units of work might incorporate virtually all the traditional subjects or be closely focused on one subject area such as social studies, science, or music. In their reports for the year, teachers were required to indicate the subject areas that had been incorporated in the units of study (Tippett et al., 1927).

More than one unit of study was frequently in progress at one time. Sometimes a smaller unit was related to the major unit. For example, in the second grade class, a map-making unit might be going on concurrently with a study of how foods reach the city from the farm. At other times, unrelated units might be going on simultaneously. In a fifth grade class, a study of marimbas and marimba making instigated in the creative music class might be concurrent with a larger unit on Colonial history.

Skills subjects such as math and reading were frequently linked to a unit, but, if necessary, were taught separately. For example, if a unit did not include any opportunities for arithmetic, separate lessons would be taught, or if specific skill or knowledge was needed, special lessons would be given. Sometimes, as in a second grade classroom, daily reading or other skill lessons were built into the schedule (Tanner & Tanner, 1980).

Flexibility in meeting the goals of the school was a hallmark of the Lincoln School—and these goals were clearly child-centered. Children were involved in the selection of units, and the units were designed to be broad enough to allow for individual interests. The teacher was guided by two considerations: "The unit must be kept near to present needs, and it must be thought worthwhile by the child" (Tippett et al., 1927, p. 31).

THE HOUSTON CITY SCHOOLS, 1924–1930: INTEGRATING CURRICULUM IN A LARGE CITY SCHOOL DISTRICT

Curriculum change in a large urban school district is a ponderous business. At the time of the study conducted by Oberholzer (1937), 1929–1930, the Houston school district had a population of 325,000, a student body of 60,000, and 1,800 teachers. The Houston City Schools spent 8 years in research and study, and produced more than 300 bulletins (over 10,000 pages!) before beginning to implement the integrated curriculum (Oberholzer, 1937).

This "scientific" development of the curriculum followed the guidelines described by Bonser (1926) in part 1 of the *Twenty-Sixth Yearbook of the National Society for the Study of Education,* which were as follows:

1. The development or choice of acceptable criteria or standards for selecting materials;

2. The organization and presentation of selected materials for children under conditions as exactly comparable as possible to those of other children using different materials; and

3. Testing results to find the outcomes of teaching the selected materials and comparing these with the outcomes from the materials used by the control groups.

When implementation did occur, it was carefully controlled and "scientifically" monitored. The curriculum was introduced gradually, and an experimental study was conducted with selected fourth and fifth grade teachers to examine the effects of the integrated curriculum.

A first-grade teacher speaks:

I teach first grade in the Houston City Schools. I have taught here for 12 years. We have had many changes in our district in the past few years. First, they changed the organization of the schools. We used to have Grades 1–7 in the elementary schools. Now we have K–5 in the elementary school, and Grades 6, 7, and 8 are placed in junior high schools. Kindergarten is optional.

At the same time, the district decided to try a new type of curriculum called "the integrated curriculum." It was really hard work to get it in place! Committees were working on it for years. We kept hearing about it, but we weren't sure what it meant. I was selected 2 years ago to try out a unit on family life. It is now an 18-week unit, but I just tried part of it for 6 weeks. The children enjoyed thinking about things they know and understand.

Last year, we started this new program by introducing what they called a "fusion course" in social studies; we taught a general social studies course instead of separate classes in history and geography. It worked really well with my little ones. We were encouraged to work on topics drawn from the children's interests instead of learning dates and places. We learned about homes, the responsibilities of family members, and our own neighborhood.

This year, we are using the district Handbook for Teachers to help us plan integrated units on family life and community life. The controlling theme is interdependence. That theme is used in all the grades, but in different ways. In a faculty meeting, one of the district supervisors talked to us about the philosophy of the new curriculum. Basically, it is a problem-solving approach. Education must teach pupils to grapple with the economic, social, and political problems of life. The new curriculum uses an activity approach. Pupils learn to think intelligently about problems at their own level, and to use material from any subject area to help solve the problem.

The Handbook has lots of ideas for us to use. My principal says we can try out the ideas, but he is a bit worried about reading and math. He says we should make sure the pupils learn all the skills they used to. That will be hard, but I think I can do it. I am looking for children's books I can use in place of the history and geography texts. He wants us to send the children to special teachers for art and music. I work well with Miss Black, the art teacher, and Miss Newman, the music teacher, so I hope we can plan some activities together. I am excited about the new curriculum and I am looking forward to trying it in my classroom (based on Oberholzer, 1937, chaps. 2, 3, and 8; appendix 4).

In the research study, fourth and fifth grade teachers participated voluntarily in a carefully controlled experimental research study to examine the effects of the new curriculum. Three groups of teachers were identified, two experimental groups and one control group. The first experimental group, type A, was selected to use the integrated curriculum without restrictions as to time distribution, choice of materials, or specified expected outcomes. The second experimental group, type B, used the integrated curriculum but with specific objectives and desired outcomes, and with specified time distribution. The control group, type C, was divided into two halves. One half used the old curriculum taught in traditional ways, but incorporated the fusion course in social studies; the other used the new units in the integrated curriculum, but taught them in traditional ways using the old time distribution for different subject areas.

In this imaginary scenario, a fifth grade teacher describes her experiences:

I was very excited when I was selected to be in a study of the new integrated curriculum. My principal recommended me, and I filled out a questionnaire. I was to be a type A teacher. That meant that I had lots of freedom to use the new curriculum. I had to cover all the fifth grade topics, but I could do it at my own rate. I had the pupils all day, and I was not allowed to divide the day into subjects; the pupils did not even go to art or music! I used the district Handbook for Teachers to help me plan the units, but I used other materials as well.

The theme I found most interesting was the one on "Life on the American Frontier." It was related to the controlling theme of adaptation. Some of the problems we explored in this unit were:

How are houses built to adapt to the environment?

How did settlers change their eating habits?

What clothes did people wear, and why?

What kind of education did the children have?

What kind of inventions and tools helped the people adapt? (Later this question was explored again in the unit on cotton.)

How was the land divided up for the settlers? How did they know where to settle?

The pupils studied how different settlers in Texas adapted to life here: Indians, Mexicans, Anglos, Germans, and others. Some of the pupils brought family keepsakes to make an exhibit of different cultures. The pupils were also very interested in the historical characters, and some of them wrote biographies of important leaders in Texas history. These questions involved the pupils in history, geography, science, math, music, art, and even cooking, and they did a great deal of reading and writing all through the unit. I think their reading and writing improved. One child said, "I have read more books than I have ever read before because I wanted to find out new things for myself."

The parents were very supportive. One parent wrote, "My son has done better this term than he ever did. I think one reason is that the increased freedom in the room keeps him from getting so nervous. He feels more at ease."

We also covered units on the cotton industry (related to the theme of interdependence) and two other historical units, "From the Old World to the New" and "The Making of Americans." All the units were related to life in Texas and in Houston.

For the study, we had to keep records and answer questionnaires. I really liked this approach. As I said in the questionnaire at the end of the year, "Each school day has been a day of real living both for the teacher and the children" (based on Oberholzer, 1937, chaps. 2, 3, 8; appendices 4, 25).

The Integrated Curriculum in the Houston City Schools

The integrated curriculum was based upon the work of Dewey and Kilpatrick. The school was seen as "an effective social agency" in which two prime considerations were "the nature of the child" and "the social function of the school" (Oberholzer, 1937, p. 8). The curriculum was designed to promote the development of the child both as an individual and as "a member of the social group who participates in promoting social progress" (Oberholzer, 1937, p. 9). Dewey's twin themes of the "embryonic community" and the school as an agent for social progress are apparent here.

This curriculum, unlike that of the Dewey School and the Lincoln School, which was expected to emerge from the interests of the children, was carefully developed around "big themes." *Interdependence* was addressed at all grade levels except Grade 4, *control over nature* in Grades 2 through 7, *adaptation* in Grades 3 through 7, and *cooperation* in Grades 6 and 7. There seems therefore to be a pattern of development from more concrete themes to those that are more abstract.

The topics addressed within each theme were all clearly in the area of social studies, and followed three organizational patterns that may reflect the old course of study and the state-adopted texts. There was a chronological study of history, from "Primitive Life" in Grade 2 to "The Industrial Revolution" in Grade 7, and a mixture of the "expanding environments" organization and topical study in geography. It is not clear just how the other subject areas were incorporated into the curriculum, but the teachers were encouraged to use the *Handbook for Teachers* for ideas, and to teach skills as the need arose.

The Houston curriculum manifests some of the limitations and frustrations of large-scale curriculum development in the public schools. The committees struggled with the existing situation: a curriculum already defined by a subject-oriented course of study and by state-adopted texts, a mixture of well-trained and less adequately trained teachers, a perennial shortage of resources in a growing city, and the lack of means for educating the general public. In spite of all this, the curriculum incorporated the flexibility necessary for a child-centered approach, with provisions for varied activities in large and small groups.

As in most integrated-curriculum work, the teacher had a high degree of flexibility and responsibility in organizing the classroom, selecting resources, deciding when to emphasize concepts and when to focus on skills, and planning activities that "serve best as a means to an end."

The results of the experimental study demonstrated success in skills achievement, more time for "enriched education," problem-solving activities, and creative work, higher levels of achievement, and more learning among the experimental groups than in the control groups. In addition, comments from principals, teachers, children, and parents indicated gains in the development of "pupil initiative and self-reliance, . . . pupil attitudes and appreciations, . . . motivation of study habits and skills, . . . organization and procedure, . . . [and] teacher improvement" (Oberholzer, 1937, appendix 25).

It seems that in Houston, the integrated curriculum was carefully planned, conceptually based, and thoughtfully implemented.

THE BANK STREET WORKSHOPS, 1943–1948: TEACHER EDUCATION FOR CURRICULUM DEVELOPMENT

The Bank Street Workshops were designed to take the principles and practices of curriculum from the Bank Street College of Education into the public schools. The Bank Street College of Education developed out of the Bureau of Educational Experiments, founded in 1916 by Lucy Sprague Mitchell to try to bring together the movement toward building experimental schools with the movement toward developing a science of education (Cremin, 1964).

The purpose of the first workshop, in 1943, was "to work with [New York] teachers in *their* school, with *their* children, in *their* physical and social neighborhood, and in that concrete situation to work with them realistically to build a curriculum suited to children in modern-day United States" (Mitchell, 1950, p. 81). For the first 3 years, three of the Bank Street staff worked intensively with about half the teachers and three of the administrators in a large urban elementary school of some 1,700 students. The curriculum was revised twice during the Workshop experience, with increasing involvement and ownership among the teachers. In 1946, the program was expanded to two additional schools, and three teachers from the original school were assigned to work full-time with the Bank Street team in the new Workshops.

In the following imaginary scenarios, two teachers describe the program.

I am a first grade teacher, and I have been in the Workshop for 1½ years. I was one of the first 26 teachers in the Workshop program at our school. When the Bank Street leaders told us about it, I was excited, but also worried. It all seemed so strange! I liked the idea of using and widening children's interest, but I didn't know how. All I wanted at the beginning were concrete suggestions that I could use in my classroom. Now, at the end of a year and a half, I understand how naive I was! The Bank Street staff were wonderful. They helped us to develop our own ideas, but they showed us how to do it. For example, Miss P., the Bank Street leader who worked with the kindergarten, first, and second grades, helped me to develop a neighborhood study for my first grade children. She suggested trips around the school and in the neighborhood that would help children to explore topics like "Workers in the School and the Neighborhood," "Transportation," and "Food."

The children loved the trips, and so did I. They were so interested in everything they saw. We explored the school and the local neighborhood, visited the Hudson River and the Harlem River, and the pushcart market on Eighth Avenue, and looked at all kinds of transportation. When they built a new curb along our street, the children were fascinated, and asked the men all kinds of questions.

I now understand that this approach means thinking about the curriculum in a completely new way. I was amazed to see how many of the old subject areas were included in the home–school–neighborhood unit: health education, reading, language, literature, art, science, penmanship, and number. I have seen the children growing as thinkers, as artists, as scientists, and as social beings. And I thought that this was just a social studies unit! (based on Mitchell, 1950, pp. 472–476)

I think one of the most important things about this approach is that children begin to see relationships, and as Miss P. pointed out, seeing relationships is thinking. The children are beginning to identify with an ever-broadening group of people, and I think this will help them in later grades to identify with people they can't know personally.

I've changed in the ways I think about learning. At the beginning, I thought that the trips, the related play, and the art activities were just to get children motivated for real learning. Now I understand that these activities are real learning experiences in themselves.

Now I want to know more for myself. I want to learn more about my own city of New York. I have learned to ask questions! This approach is very hard work, but is gives me a lot of satisfaction because I am learning and I see the children's development, too.

I am looking forward to the next stage in the Workshop. We are already thinking about the curriculum for the whole school. I used to think that curriculum was the curriculum guide we had to follow. Now I see that it is based on our philosophy and beliefs, on our understanding of children and their development, and the physical and social setting in which the children live. Our first grade curriculum will still focus on home and school in relationship to our neighborhood, but this time around, I think we will understand more clearly how the parts fit together, and what we are trying to do. I am so glad to be involved (based on Mitchell, 1950, pp. 93-95, 129-141, 198-213, 472-476).

At the same time, a fifth grade teacher describes the program from her point of view.

I sometimes think that the Workshop approach is easier for the younger grades than it is for us. We have so much content to cover! In Grades 5 and 6 we have to address the general theme "Living Together in the United States and in the World." That means we have to cover the history of the United States from the explorers to the present, the geography of the United States, the rest of the Western Hemisphere, and Europe, and now a new addition called "Living and Working Together in the World."

The fifth and sixth grade teachers are working on this challenge in the Workshop. Last year we put all the U.S. history into Grade 5, and the relations with the rest of the world into Grade 6. It really didn't work. We had too much content, and the sixth grade curriculum was too abstract and mature for the students.

In our planning discussions, the committee did agree on some approaches. It was agreed that the way people lived and worked together was always to be linked to the physical environment: landforms, waterways, climate, native vegetation and animals, and natural resources. The opening topic in each grade would be focused on the present, and a study of present life and work in New York City was to continue all year. We decided to look at history in terms of significant movements and events rather than dates, wars, and political history. And we wanted to include an increasing focus on social values and relationships among people.

These discussions led to practical questions of what to put in each grade, and how to integrate history with geography. We decided to base our curriculum on what we know about 10- and 11-year-old children—their intellectual curiosity, their desire for adventure, and their growing sense of values. We looked at two big themes: the relationships of people to their environments and to one another. Within these two big themes, we wanted the children to use direct experiences that would help them to see the world as a laboratory, a place to find out things that interest them. Science is a big part of our curriculum. And of course we want children to think! We finally put together a curriculum we can work with.

It hasn't been easy, though, even with the new curriculum outline. At the beginning, I didn't see the point of beginning with the present. It seemed more sensible to put it at the end, after we had studied the past. Miss B., one of the Bank Street workers, helped me to find a theme, "How We Became What We Are." I must admit that this has helped the children—and me!

We began work on a mural. At first, it didn't work too well. All the children had different ideas, and anyway they don't draw too well. Miss B. suggested that we use their ideas anyway, and then try to find a theme. We took a trip to the Museum of the City of New York so that the children could compare transportation of long ago with that of today. We never really did find a narrow theme, but the mural showed the flow of history. We also put on a play with scenes about ideas like "Trade" and "Traveling." It worked pretty well, and one girl even said that it made history come alive.

Miss B. thinks that we could use the play and the mural to help children develop more questions to explore about the people in our history. Where did people come from? What were they like? Where do their descendants live? I think this is a good idea. The children are beginning to be able to do their own research in the library now.

I have learned a lot from the Workshop. At first, I did not see how you could put history and geography together. Now I see that history and geography and science are all parts of the same discovery method.

The Bank Street workers have been very helpful. They come in sometimes and work with my class. Then I can understand what they mean. They listen to us in the discussion sessions, and help us to clarify our ideas. This new curriculum comes from the Workshop, not from Bank Street. We meet every week to talk about what we are doing. Sometimes we have guest speakers, like the high school science teacher. Last year we made maps. I learned a lot about map projections, and why my unit wasn't working. They even took us on a field trip around the neighborhood so that we could learn how to help children look more carefully and raise good questions.

Perhaps the most important thing I have learned is to look at children's development and their environment, and then to work out the social ideas that we will bring out in discussion and activities whenever we have an opportunity. These big social ideas have made my teaching make more sense. I have always liked history; now I'm beginning to understand why I like it, and how to help the children like it, too (based on Mitchell, 1936, pp. 97–98, 142–183, 246–272).

The Integrated Curriculum in the Bank Street Workshops

In the early days of the Workshops, teachers did not understand the integration of the curriculum. They liked the idea of units as experiences in which content from various areas of the curriculum might be used, but they perceived the units as something to be added onto the regular course of study.

Social studies was deliberately selected as a starting point in the curriculum, since this subject area lent itself most readily to student involvement and social interaction. History, geography, and civics were obviously part of the new social studies, and science was also added. Major themes were identified for different grade levels: "Living and Working in the Home, School, and the Neighborhood" for kindergarten, first, and second grades; "Living and Working in New York City and in Different Kinds of Communities" for Grades 3 and 4; and "Living and Working Together in the United States of America and the World" in Grades 5 and 6, an organization that exemplifies the "expanding environments" pattern still common in elementary social studies curriculum.

As the Workshop meetings continued, teachers explored with Bank Street staff ways in which activities in dramatic play, art, language, music, and other subjects grew out of the core experiences. However, in the Workshop program, there was never any effort to build a completely integrated curriculum. Indeed, in the second phase of the Workshops, the emphasis was upon building a sound vertical social studies curriculum rather than broadening the curriculum across other subject areas. Integration continued to be informal rather than structured.

At the beginning of the Workshops, the teachers were interested in *how* to implement the new ideas, not in the underlying philosophy or assumptions about children and learning. In the second phase, there was an important shift in the teachers' approach to curriculum building. After 3 years in the Workshop, they began to see how knowledge of children's development, of the environment, and of a basic philosophy of education were essential bases for curriculum development.

The story of the Bank Street Workshops is a fascinating story of intensive staff development and curriculum building. Some of the findings from the Workshop experience are significant in any curriculum development in which teachers are involved.

The teachers went through the following stages of professional growth:

▼ An early lack of self-confidence that led them to seek for specific directions and prescriptions;

▼ A desire to acquire more background knowledge and content;

▼ Growth in understanding the concept of curriculum building; and finally

▼ Relating their job to the world outside the school (Mitchell, 1950).

It is interesting to note that these findings closely parallel the "stages of concern" identified by Gene Hall and his colleagues as they studied teacher development some 30 years later (Hall & Loucks, 1978).

As the teachers developed more self-confidence in their own ideas and their ability to work creatively with children, their professional attitude changed. They became enthusiastic, inventive, and willing to experiment. They worked hard, but they obtained deep satisfaction from their creative endeavors (Mitchell, 1950). While they became increasingly impatient with the strictures and limitations of public school teaching, they were also better equipped to deal with these problems and to develop true learning environments for their students.

▼ READER INVOLVEMENT

What did you learn from these attempts to implement interdisciplinary curriculum? What implications do these stories have for your own situation? What new questions do you have about interdisciplinary curriculum?

QUESTIONS THAT EMERGED FROM THESE EXPERIMENTS IN CURRICULUM

In each of these settings, from the Dewey School to the Bank Street Workshops, common questions emerge that are of great significance to anyone engaging in the development of integrated curriculum. The questions have no easy answers, but they must be explored for every new endeavor. How was each issue handled by these experimental schools?

How Is a Philosophy Developed and Implemented?

The Dewey School was designed as a laboratory to test Dewey's ideas about methods, curriculum, and organization. These ideas emerged from 20 years of study of philosophy, teaching, writing, and social service. The basis for his philosophy has been traced to sources such as Kant, Hegel, Rousseau, William James, and Jane Addams (Brickman, 1962; Cremin, 1964; Tanner & Tanner, 1980).

This philosophy was clearly articulated in Dewey's own writings, and was put into practice by a small group of dedicated teachers under Dewey's own leadership.

The Lincoln School, too, was founded largely upon the work of one man, Abraham Flexner, who in turn was strongly influenced by Dewey. In the early years of the 20th century, new experimental schools were developing rapidly in many places across the United States. Flexner, who had undertaken a survey of the Gary (Indiana) schools in 1917 (Cremin, 1964), took a strong stance against the remnants of the traditional curriculum that he saw even in some of the so-called progressive schools. He argued that "if a subject serves a purpose, it is eligible to the curriculum; otherwise not" (Flexner, 1923, p. 99), and insisted that the "scientific spirit" was to infuse the Model School, and to make it a place in which to test educational beliefs (Cremin, 1964).

The Lincoln School was created as an educational laboratory in which to try out Flexner's ideas. The teachers were committed to the principles upon which it was founded, and the story of the Lincoln School, *Curriculum Making in an Elementary School,* written by the staff of the school in 1927, shows clearly their commitment and involvement (Tippett et al., 1927).

In Houston, the philosophy that supported the integrated curriculum was based strongly upon the work of Dewey and Kilpatrick. The ideas for implementation of the new curriculum seem to have come from the administration in the district, but there was a commitment to teacher involvement in its development. The committees that met for 8 years before the curriculum was implemented included teachers as well as administrators. Implementation was not imposed, but teachers were encouraged to use the new curriculum to the extent that they felt able. Indeed, the experimental study identified three groups of teachers: One group who implemented the new ideas fully, one group who implemented the new curriculum within the old framework, and a control group who continued to teach in the traditional way.

The Bank Street Workshops also involved teachers. Indeed, the purpose of the Workshop was to enable teachers to develop the new curriculum at their own speed and in their own way. The first Workshop initially involved only about half the teachers in the school. It was 3 years before the principal decided to make the Workshop curriculum the official social studies curriculum for the school. The philosophy supporting this curriculum was clearly Deweyan. It was, however, introduced by the Bank Street staff in a way that supported their beliefs that the school was a place where experiments and scientific problem solving were carried out at all levels, including the level of curriculum development.

It is apparent from these examples that the development of integrated curriculum should be based upon certain principles and practices:

▼ A sound vision of the larger purposes of schooling;

▼ A long-term commitment to change, understanding that real change takes time;

▼ The involvement of teachers as experimenters in an experimental setting where children too are experimenters;

▼ A willingness to allow teachers to make choices about the amount and types of involvement they wish to have; and perhaps above all,

▼ The importance of putting principles into practice at all levels of the school community: in administration, teaching, and learning.

In this book, we support the same principles. Our own philosophy is presented in chapter 1 and serves as the foundation for the entire book.

Should the Integrated Curriculum Be Implemented Intensively or Extensively?

The Dewey School, the Lincoln School, and the Bank Street Workshops are examples of intensive, small-scale curriculum implementation. Houston provides an example of an extensive, large-scale implementation. There are advantages and disadvantages to each approach, detailed in Figures 2.1 and 2.2. These should be borne in mind when planning to implement an integrated curriculum in a specific school or district.

Who Determines the Content of the Curriculum?

In any curriculum that is built around children's interests, there is a tension between meeting the needs of the child (as perceived by adults) and satisfying the desires of children (as perceived by the children themselves). This tension is an underlying factor implicit in the accounts of the Dewey School, the Lincoln School, the Houston schools, and the Bank Street Workshops.

Figure 2.1
Small-scale implementation

Advantages	Disadvantages
It encourages on-the-job experimentation.	It affects only a limited number of children.
It is likely to be supported by all involved.	The population may not be representative, so the ideas may not be transferable.
Children can benefit from the new approach immediately.	It may be difficult to implement within the constraints of a school system.
It is likely to provide a clear and successful model for others to emulate.	

Figure 2.2
Large-scale implementation

Advantages	Disadvantages
A large number of children are served.	Much time must be devoted to prior planning.
There is support from the central administration.	Not all teachers are willing or able to implement the new curriculum.
It facilitates the provision of appropriate books and resources.	Teachers may not understand the philosophy, and so may carry out the principles inappropriately.

At the Dewey School, the children had limited choices. Dewey stated that the Dewey School would offer "a much larger degree of opportunity for initiative, discovery, and independent communication of individual freedom than was characteristic of the traditional school" (Mayhew & Edwards, 1936, pp. 6–7). However, it was clearly the task of the teacher to determine both the broad curriculum, albeit related to children's interests and developmental stages, and also the daily business of the classroom. The teacher provided the major ideas and framework for the curriculum; within that framework, each child was encouraged "to contribute, either out of his past experience or his imagination, ways and means of meeting the problem of needs that might arise under new circumstances" (Mayhew & Edwards, 1936, p. 81).

At the Lincoln School, the tension is more evident. Flexner, writing in 1917, suggested a curriculum "built out of actual activities in four main fields which I shall designate as science, industry, aesthetics, civics." Children "would be interested in problems and the theoretical basis on which their solution depends" (Flexner, 1923, p. 103). This sounds like a fairly teacher-centered approach. However, the guidelines for the selection of units described by Tippett and his colleagues in 1927 reflect a more child-centered approach. The unit was to be selected from "real-life situations" that the child should consider worthwhile "because he feels he has helped select it." The unit was required to give "opportunities for real purposing and real projects," to "provide for individual differences," and to "stimulate in the child the desire for a continual widening to his interests and understandings" (Tippett et al., 1927, pp. 31–37). The children's questions and interests were an integral part of each unit, but the teacher had the responsibility for developing the units, planning learning activities, and maintaining high standards of growth and development for every child (Tippett et al., 1927).

The Houston curriculum was designed by committees of teachers. The individual classroom teacher was given considerable flexibility in its implementation, so that students could "be recognized as individuals and permitted to progress in accordance with their learning ability" (Oberholzer, 1937, p. 10). As teachers became more confident in implementing the integrated curriculum, "pupils were assisted in setting up their own objectives and in helping to organize activities" (Oberholzer, 1937, p. 17).

The Bank Street Workshops were clearly designed to enable teachers to develop curriculum to meet the needs of their own students within their own unique situations. Learning about child psychology became an integral part of the teacher's training, and by the second stage of the Workshops, 3 years into the project, teachers wanted to experiment within the framework of the curriculum to "interpret the prescribed curriculum content in ways that were best for children's growth." They learned to give the children freedom to explore their own interests within the broad units, and were excited to discover that this resulted in "new interests, new zest for observing and finding out, new habits of tackling a problem by thinking out relationships, [and] new ways of expressing their thinking and feelings" (Mitchell, 1950, p. 337).

From these examples, some principles emerge as we consider the question of who determines the content of the integrated curriculum:

▼ Teachers have the responsibility for designing the broad framework of the curriculum;

▼ The curriculum is built around known developmental stages and interests of students;

▼ When the integrated curriculum is first introduced, teachers take responsibility for selecting specific topics and learning activities;

▼ As teachers become more confident and comfortable with the new curriculum, they are more willing and able to give children more responsibility in selecting learning activities;

▼ As children work in a free, problem-solving atmosphere, they are able to make better curriculum choices for themselves.

As we think about developing our own integrated curriculum throughout this book, we need to think about the current situation—the levels of understanding, commitment, and experience concerning the integrated curriculum among the teachers. The developmental level of the children and the amount of prior experience they have had in making curriculum choices are even more important considerations.

To What Degree Does an Integrated Curriculum Incorporate All Subject Areas?

This question has been addressed for each of our examples earlier in this chapter. A brief review may help to give additional focus.

In the Dewey School, social studies was the major area of study, which is in accord with Dewey's ideas of the school as an embryonic community. Other subject areas were included as they occurred naturally in the major "activities," but skills areas were also addressed as separate subjects.

The Lincoln School curriculum was deliberately organized around "units of work," which were based upon a variety of subject areas: social studies, science, music, arts and crafts, or a combination of two or more of these. Each unit was expected to incorporate a variety of subjects, but skills were also taught separately, either as a regular part of the school day or as the need arose.

The Houston curriculum was consciously designed as an integrated curriculum. However, it had a strong social studies bias; indeed, the names of the units seem to have been drawn directly from the old history and geography syllabi.

The Bank Street Workshops were centered clearly and deliberately upon social studies, with science integrated as closely as possible. Here the integrated nature of the curriculum emerged slowly and naturally over time, and the degree of integration seems to have varied from fairly limited, as in a sixth grade unit on "Earth Forces in China" to a broad interdisciplinary unit on "Our Neighborhood" in first grade.

How much integration does an integrated curriculum involve? It depends primarily upon the type of topic or theme. Generally speaking, the more abstract the theme, the greater the degree of integration. Specific topics tend to limit the amount of integration. For example, "Transportation" can apply directly to nearly all the major subject areas, while "The Civil War" is more likely to be limited mainly to history and perhaps some geography. (See chapter 3 for a broader discussion on the selection of themes.)

There is, however, no magic formula. It is more important that the curriculum be relevant and significant to the learner, and that activities and ideas naturally involve interdisciplinary and cross-disciplinary thinking and questioning, than that every subject area be forced into the "integrated curriculum."

How May Skills in Reading and Math Be Taught?

This question is, of course, related to the previous one, but because it is a perennial question that faces us as we engage in integrating the curriculum, it deserves special attention.

In all the examples, it is clear that while reading and mathematics are part of the units and activities, the theme studies did not provide complete coverage of the skills needed in these areas. There was therefore provision for specific skills instruction.

In the Dewey School, for example, the children engaged in "number work" that explored mathematical principles through games and inquiry unrelated to the major areas of interest. In the Lincoln School, arithmetic and reading were taught separately if the unit of work did not make adequate provision for skills instruction, or specific skills were taught as needed.

The Houston curriculum did not really address this problem. The study of fourth and fifth grade teachers incorporated three different approaches, from totally integrated to totally subject-oriented. In the totally integrated group, skills were taught "when a teacher saw a need, and to whatever extent the teacher decided," while in the control group, skills were "taught in regular subject periods as set up in the daily schedule" (Oberholzer, 1937, p. 25). It is interesting to note that the results of the study indicated that a comparison of the experimental and control groups showed similar achievement in reading, spelling, and arithmetic. As Oberholzer pointed out, "The pupils . . . using the integrated units did not suffer in their achievement in the subjects commonly known as the 'three R's'" (Oberholzer, 1937, p. 131).

The Bank Street staff worked hard to help the teachers see how the activities in one subject area led to activities in reading and mathematics, and teachers began to understand how children learn "to read and write by being 'taught backwards'—that is, by getting interested in something they could really do" (Mitchell, 1950, pp. 345–346). It appears, however, that formal skills instruction, particularly in math, was continued along with the activity curriculum.

The extent of additional skills instruction needed depends upon the selected theme and the children's needs. The main question here is not so much how to incorporate reading and math *into* the curriculum but rather to see how activities emerging naturally from children's inquiry and problem solving help them in the development of verbal and numerical literacy.

How Is Success Evaluated in the Integrated Curriculum?

Apart from the study conducted by Oberholzer in Houston, our examples show little evidence of formal evaluation, and we think that this relates directly to the goals and purposes of the schools and programs. If you look at their stated purposes, then the story of each example is itself the evaluation.

The Dewey School was set up as a social experiment. The descriptions of the groups in action describe that social experiment where children did work together on projects that both mirrored the larger world and helped them develop skills to live productively in that larger world.

The story of the child-centered Lincoln School is a series of accounts of child-centered units of work in which the children explored their neighborhood and through those experiences learned to make sense of the larger human community.

The Bank Street workers modeled, demonstrated, and, true to the philosophy they were teaching, enabled teachers to build curriculum based upon beliefs about learning, understanding of children, and knowledge of the environment. Their book chronicles that process, and again the story is the evaluation.

Meanwhile, in Houston, Oberholzer posed questions and collected data from experiments designed to answer those questions. The success of the experiment is measured by the degree to which the responses satisfied the questions.

It is tempting to think of evaluation only in terms of cold, hard data, scientifically collected and collated, and indeed this type of evaluation has its place. But the integrated curriculum is dynamic, interactive, situational, and creative. There is no single model; thus there cannot be a single model for evaluating success.

This does not let us off the hook, however. If we choose broad and far-reaching goals, we must find broad and far-reaching means of evaluation. In chapter 9, we explore some of these approaches. Mayhew and Edwards, Tippett, Oberholzer, and Mitchell tell us stories that themselves reflect the beliefs of the storyteller. Because these authors were deeply involved in the project they describe, their evaluation *is* subjective, and it rings true through the richness of the story.

How then is success evaluated? In ways as rich and deep as the project itself deserves.

How Is the Larger Community Related to Schooling and the Curriculum?

This final question goes far beyond the details of teaching and learning, yet is probably the most important of all. It comes full circle to the vision and the philosophy of each of the experimenters in our four examples.

For Dewey, the answer to this question was clear. He wrote that "education could prepare the young for the future social life only when the school was itself a cooperative society on a small scale" (Mayhew & Edwards, 1936, p. 5). At the same time, the school has a responsibility to the larger society. In 1901, Dewey wrote of the social purpose of curriculum "in maintaining the intellectual continuity of civilization" (Dewey, 1901, pp. 193–194; Cremin, 1964).

The Lincoln School put into practice Flexner's vision of a Model School, a school with two major purposes: the intellectual and aesthetic development of the child that would in turn serve a society in which "abstract thinking has probably never before played so important a part" (Flexner, 1923, pp. 100–101).

In Houston, Oberholzer pointed out that "the wealth of the nation is bound up in the welfare of its youth," and that "the child with an inquisitive mind and a creative desire . . . is now generally recognized as the center of interest around which all forward-looking changes in American public education should be made" (Oberholzer, 1937, p. 4).

In all these examples, we see a common purpose: the development of the individual, leading to the development of society.

This purpose is reflected at another level in the Bank Street Workshops. Mitchell describes graphically the professional development of the teachers as curriculum thinkers and as continuing learners, and then indicates that as the teachers became more creative in their own jobs, they also related their jobs increasingly to the world outside the school, both in the profession and in the larger community.

Schools inevitably reflect the current values of society, and, in fact, are intended to conserve dominant values. This may help to explain why the apparently successful ventures in integrated curriculum described in this chapter did not survive, and why this approach appears to require reinvention. Schools tend to be reactive to societal demands rather than proactive in preparing children, as adults, to shape society. However, in places where primary attention is given to examining the ways that children learn and what they will need for the world of the future, child-centered, inquiry-based movements in curriculum continue. Cases in point are found in the current concerns for developmentally appropriate practice, whole-language instruction, emphasis on science process, and approaches to developing mathematical literacy. But these are partial attempts. Curriculum for integrative learning applies these concepts in all subject areas. Although the four experiments described in this chapter did not survive, there are schools where successful interdisciplinary programs have been in progress for years. Among these are the Town and Country Schools, and lab schools at places such as the Bank Street College of Education in New York City and Nova Scotia's Dalhousie University. Experiments in secondary education such as Foxfire and the Dalton School are additional examples.

Our four examples give us a view of the integrated curriculum in action. How may we understand their stories, adapt their ideas, and answer their questions in our own world, with our own students, in our own time? These questions frame the inquiry of this book.

▼ READER INVOLVEMENT

Continue to develop your own theme study. Under each of the four or five main questions you have identified, list the major resources you could consult to explore those questions. Select one or more, and collect data that will help you answer the question. What new questions emerge as you collect the data? Record these ideas in the inquiry section of your journal.

REFERENCES

Bonser, F. G. (1926). Curriculum making in laboratory schools of experimental schools. *Twenty-sixth yearbook of the National Society for the Study of Education* (Pt. 1). Bloomington, IL: Public School Publishing.

Brickman, W. W. (1962). Introduction. In J. Dewey & E. Dewey (Eds.), *Schools of tomorrow* (pp. ix–xxviii). New York: Dutton.

Cremin, L. A. (1964). *The transformation of the school.* New York: Vintage. (Original work published 1961)

Dewey, J. (1900). *The school and society.* Chicago: University of Chicago Press.

Dewey, J. (1901). The place of manual training in the elementary course of study. *Manual Training Magazine, 2,* 193–194.

Flexner, A. (1916) A modern school. *American Review of Reviews, 53,* 465–474.

Flexner, A. (1923) *A modern college and a modern school.* Garden City, NY: Doubleday.

Hall, G., & Loucks, S. F. (1978). Teacher concerns as a basis for facilitating and personalizing staff development. *Teachers College Record, 80,* 36–53.

Mayhew, K. C., & Edwards, A. C. (1936). *The Dewey school.* New York: Appleton-Century.

Mitchell, L. S. (1950). *Our children and our schools.* New York: Simon & Schuster.

Oberholzer, E. (1937). *An integrated curriculum in practice.* New York: Teachers College Press.

Tanner, D., & Tanner, L. N. (1980). *Curriculum development: Theory into practice* (2nd ed.). New York: Macmillan.

Tippett, J. S., Coffin, R. J., & the staff of the elementary division of the Lincoln School of Teachers College, Columbia University (1927). *Curriculum making in an elementary school.* Lexington, MA: Ginn.

Additional Reading

Dewey, J. (1956). *The child and the curriculum and The school and society.* Chicago: University of Chicago Press. (Original work published in 1900, 1902)

Dewey, J., & Dewey, E. (1962). *Schools of tomorrow.* New York: Dutton. (Original work published 1915)

Kilpatrick, W. H. (1918). The project method. *Teachers College Record, 19,* 319–335.

Kilpatrick, W. H. (1931). A reconstructed theory of the educative process. *Teachers College Record, 32,* 530–558.

Part Two

Development of Interdisciplinary Theme Studies

Chapter Three

Developing Themes

GUIDELINES FOR DESIGNING THEME STUDIES

The design of theme studies is a creative enterprise. Varied approaches to developing interdisciplinary curriculum have been reported in the literature. Taba's (1962) classic linear model for curriculum development incorporates seven steps:

1. Diagnosis of needs;
2. Formulation of objectives;
3. Selection of content;
4. Organization of content;
5. Selection of learning experiences;
6. Organization of learning experiences; and
7. Determination of what to evaluate and of the ways and means of doing it.

Taba also viewed learning as interrelational, defining three major elements: (1) the learning materials (everything the learner interacts with); (2) the nature, abilities, and interests of the learner; and (3) the structure, form, and sequence of the learning process. However, Taba points out that curriculum development is a complex process, and that efforts toward curriculum integration should begin at the grass-roots level: " . . .The major criteria of a good curriculum and ideas about organizing the curriculum acquire meaning only as they are applied to some tangible content. What integration of learning actually is and which elements of curriculum can be brought into an integrated relationship cannot be determined in the abstract, but only by testing on some concrete subject—or on such sampling of subjects as the variations in their basic structures dictate. . . .The possibilities of active discovery methods of learning and their limits can be worked out only by experimenting with a variety of ways of stimulating them" (Taba, 1962, p. 345).

Hartoonian and Laughlin (1989) recommend designing theme studies by identifying major ideas about human experience that cross grade levels at increasing levels of sophistication. They propose that students experience the components of social inquiry: seeking comprehension and conceptualization of the topic, explaining causality, investigating the truth or validity of explanations, and creating extensions for inquiry into new issues. Jacobs and Borland (1986) offer a four-step plan including: (1) selecting a theme, (2) brainstorming associations, (3) formulating guiding questions for inquiry, and (4) designing and implementing activities. In our experience, a broad sequence has emerged that appears to offer useful guidelines for teachers and students to follow during their initial efforts in designing theme studies (see Figure 3.1). These steps serve as benchmarks in our exploration of how theme studies may develop at different grade levels by teachers with varied interests and perspectives. The first, selecting a theme, is explored in this chapter. Taken in sequence, the remaining steps are examined in subsequent chapters.

Figure 3.1
Guidelines for designing theme studies

1. Select a theme.
2. Develop a web or use other ways to build a wealth of ideas.
3. Identify questions through the lenses of different disciplines.
4. Identify concepts; formulate generalizations within the theme.
5. Meet local curriculum requirements and frameworks, e.g., school, district, and state guidelines.
6. Map the general sequence.
7. Formulate questions for student inquiry.
8. Develop ideas for learning-activity clusters.
9. Identify content and process objectives.
10. Design learning activities.
11. Choose culminating projects.
12. Use resources to explore questions.
13. Decide on record keeping, reporting, and ongoing assessment.

ALTERNATE WAYS OF DEVELOPING THEMES

In the pages that follow, we present several methods, considerations, and criteria for designing theme studies. In working through this process with several groups of classroom teachers, we have discovered that different teachers use varied approaches to the development of equally successful theme studies. There appears to be a continuum that presents the teacher's role as:

Teachers who are new to theme studies or whose primary teaching style is like that of a director or a conductor often prefer to monitor the development of the curriculum by thinking through the process in considerable detail before beginning a theme study with their students. Others, on the continuum between director and guide, may like to begin with their own ideas, then ask their students for input, and synthesize the two sets of data as they plan theme studies. Throughout their planning, these teachers will structure the theme study so that it is well integrated with the regular curriculum guidelines. These may be influenced by national and professional organizations, adopted texts, district curriculum guides, and district and state standards.

Teachers who are very comfortable serving as instructional guides will often introduce a thematic idea to their students and solicit student-generated ideas for its exploration in the earliest planning stages. Using the students' ideas as the primary focus of the study, these teachers plan the interdisciplinary thematic curriculum with reference to district and state standards. Their curriculum plans become "maps" to guide the students' exploration of their own interests within the boundaries of teacher-framed options.

The mentor role is taken by teachers who are experienced with interdisciplinary thematic teaching, and who feel comfortable working with their students in open-ended ways, while staying true to established curriculum standards. In this role, the teacher becomes a member of the research team, collaborating with students in identifying themes for study, reacting to their ideas for exploration, suggesting ways to proceed, and even participating in some of the searches.

In this text, we start with the most teacher-directed approach to designing interdisciplinary theme studies because we believe that it is easier to open up a structured process than it is to superimpose structure on a very open one. We also think that teachers who are designing interdisciplinary theme studies for the first time, and those who have limited experience with the concept, may find that a directive role is the most comfortable and is most likely to ensure success in promoting student learning. We want to make it clear from the outset, however, that we believe student ownership of the curriculum must be integral to interdisciplinary thematic studies. The more involved students are in directing the course of their learning, the greater the likelihood that they will become self-directed learners. Therefore, we encourage teachers to move from directive planning to increasingly more cooperative planning of theme studies with their students, as their pedagogical preferences, situations, and opportunities permit.

One of the dangers inherent in allowing students great latitude in directing their own learning is that they may not challenge their assumptions or may, indeed, formulate inaccurate concepts or principles. The literature in science and museum education shows that children, and also adults, may cling to misconceptions even when presented with evidence to the contrary (Osborne & Freyberg, 1985; Philips, 1991). Such misconceptions bias perceptions and, thus, interfere with accurate learning. However, teachers who work as mentors and co-researchers can monitor the accuracy of student learning as the theme study progresses.

TOPICS AND THEMES

In *To Build a House*, Barber, Bergman, and Sneider (1991) present the philosophy undergirding the Lawrence Hall of Science Great Explorations in Math and Science (GEMS) thematic approach to teaching science. Using the *house-building* metaphor, the GEMS staff places thinking processes at the foundation of thematic curriculum. Themes of study make up the framework of the curriculum. Content knowledge provides building blocks to fill that framework, which are mortared and nailed together by student enjoyment and curiosity.

A pile of rocks in a pasture or a stack of bricks on a city street cannot amount to much until they are given form. They are like inert knowledge: present and potentially useful, but having no power to move itself. Content knowledge offers us building blocks to construct our learning. But those stones or bricks need form—a framework or scaffolding to help us connect them with other ideas and develop dynamic knowledge that can be transferred to other formats and applied in different contexts. Topics of study can provide great quantities of isolated information. But themes give them form because themes give rise to big ideas, which serve to integrate discrete bits of knowledge and develop frameworks that enable meaningful and purposeful learning.

Themes are large ideas that integrate the concepts of different disciplines. Themes can be concepts such as adaptation, survival, or environment. They can be linked concepts that become generalizations, such as "Living things develop adaptations to their environments that enhance their ability to survive in those environments." Themes may also be issues (Golden, 1986). Environmental issues are clearly interdisciplinary, e.g., "How can people's actions change our planet?"

The study of a topic can be interesting to an individual and offer opportunities for in-depth study and productive inquiry, but topics are limited in scope and usefulness. To return to the house-building metaphor, some topics may have little to contribute to the students' development of scaffolding. They are like loose bricks that need form before they can become dynamic knowledge. By contrast, big ideas or themes provide the scaffolding for understanding. They provide emphases in the curriculum that are worthy of students' learning time and involvement.

DETERMINING THE VALUE OF BIG IDEAS

There are several criteria that help determine whether a theme is important enough to warrant children's study. A meaningful theme should pass the test of each and all of the questions listed in Figure 3.2 with an unqualified *yes*.

DEVELOPING THEMES FROM TOPICS

Most worthwhile themes for interdisciplinary curriculum are not found in textbooks. Some may be found in the professional literature (e.g., Hartoonian & Laughlin, 1989; Rutherford & Ahlgren, 1989; Shoemaker, 1989). The best interdisciplinary theme studies are selected and developed by teachers and students to meet their varied needs in different environments. Teachers can exercise their professional judgment best when they select theme studies with particular developmental levels, curriculum standards and goals, student inquiry, and available resources in mind. We believe that the meaningfulness of theme studies comes in part from the diversity of their sources. These include:

1. Children's common interests
2. Children's and adolescent literature and trade books
3. Textbook topics
4. Current events
5. Local sites and community resources
6. Cultural heritage
7. Children's special and temporal interests
8. Teachers' interests or expertise
9. Objects and artifacts
10. Abstract concepts

Figure 3.2
Criteria for significance

1. Is the big idea true over space and time?
2. Does it broaden students' understanding of the world or what it means to be human?
3. Is the big idea interdisciplinary?
4. Does it relate to students' genuine interests?
5. Does it lead to student inquiry?

These sources for interdisciplinary curriculum design are easy to find. They are discussed in detail later in this chapter. More difficult is developing meaningful themes from interesting but inherently limiting topics. There are several ways to accomplish this. We explore here (1) the *question-driven approach,* (2) the *significance approach,* and (3) the *literature-based curriculum approach.* To illustrate their use in a second grade class, we have chosen a common topic of study in the primary grades: dinosaurs. We anticipate that our readers may apply one or more of these ways to their own interdisciplinary curriculum design and, perhaps, may develop their own approaches.

The Question-Driven Approach

The question-driven method of developing a theme from a common topic examines the topic as a subject of inquiry. Teachers may begin by forming their own questions or, better, by asking students to create a list of questions about the topic that they would like to explore. Some teachers prefer to build on students' lists. Others like to offer students a starter set of questions to build upon. In all cases, questions are formulated from the perspectives of different disciplines of study. See Figure 3.3 for an illustrative sampling of questions (in adult language) for the topic *dinosaurs and fossils.*

These questions suggest the kinds of big ideas that a study of dinosaurs can support. Looking across those generated from different perspectives, we can find several concepts: life cycles (life, growth, death, reproduction), adaptations, geologic time, location, locomotion, migration, transformation, language, legend, habitat, extinction, and tales, among others. Many possible generalizations are also evident. Second grade children may have demonstrated interests that lead to generalizations such as:

▼ Animals are adapted to their habitats in the ways they feed, move, reproduce, protect themselves, and care for their young.

▼ Changes in environment cause adaptations to occur and survival depends on successful adaptation.

▼ Animals, plants, and humans continue to be interdependent throughout time.

Each of the themes can be tested against the criteria introduced above:

1. Is the big idea true over space and time?
2. Does it broaden students' understanding of the world or what it means to be human?
3. Is the big idea interdisciplinary?
4. Can it lead to student inquiry?

Figure 3.3
Questions about dinosaurs asked from the perspectives of different disciplines of study

Discipline	Questions
Paleontologist:	What clues do fossil remains hold about the physical characteristics of different dinosaurs? Which were meat eaters? Plant eaters? How were they adapted to their habitat? What kinds of social groupings did they have? Why did they become extinct? What different kinds of fossil evidence did they leave (bones, tracks, mold impressions)?
Geologist:	What does the placement of dinosaur bones in the rock strata tell us about the geologic time when dinosaurs lived? How long ago did they live? What were the physical characteristics of the earth at the time?
Biologist:	What plants and animals lived during the time of the dinosaurs? What happened to them? What was their food web? Which of those plants and animals became extinct? Why? Which continue to this day? Are birds or lizards the living descendants of dinosaurs? How can you tell a dinosaur from other prehistoric animals? Where did baby dinosaurs come from? How did they reproduce? Were dinosaurs warm-blooded or cold-blooded?
Anthropologist:	Why are people intrigued by these prehistoric creatures? Which culture groups are most interested in them? Why?
Geographer:	Where on earth were the dinosaurs located? What landforms and bodies of water were around when dinosaurs roamed the earth?
Fine Artist:	What were the textures of dinosaur coverings? What did they look like? What colors were they? What did their habitats look like? Feel like? Sound like? How do we depict dinosaurs in paintings, sculptures, and films?
Musician:	What sounds did dinosaurs make? What patterns of sound did they use to communicate with one another?
Mathematician:	How far did dinosaurs roam or migrate? How fast did they move? What was the carrying capacity of the areas in which they lived, i.e., how much area and what food supplies did they need to support their populations? How can we measure time? Distance? Size? What tools can we use to find out when dinosaurs lived? How many dinosaurs lived and died? How much oil have we gotten from their remains? How much is left?
Writer:	Where does the word *dinosaur* come from? What do the dinosaur names mean? What legends are there about dinosaurs? Why are they thought of as "monsters"? What is a "monster"? What is a "beast"? Why are dinosaurs considered beasts? What tales are there about beasts and monsters? How are dinosaurs characterized in contemporary stories, films, and television programs? What accounts for people's fascination with dinosaurs?
Economist:	What products do we get from dinosaurs? What is the value of those products? How do they influence trade?

Consider the first big idea about dinosaurs suggested by the question-driven approach to developing topics into themes:

Animals are adapted to their habitats in the ways they feed, move, reproduce, protect themselves, and care for their young.

The big idea is certainly true over space and time; it will be explored through dinosaurs and geologic time. The central concepts of adaptation, habitat, and interdependence are useful for understanding the larger world. The many questions that were formed from different perspectives attest to the interdisciplinary character of the big idea. New questions for investigation are likely to crop up throughout these studies, including questions that continue to be debated: Were dinosaurs warm-blooded or cold-blooded? Are their descendants lizards or birds?

The Significance Approach

In this approach, the central question is "Why is this topic worth studying?" The exploration of this question leads to the development of significant themes that meet the criteria identified above.

When we apply this approach to the same common topic for second graders, *dinosaurs,* we begin by asking the central questions "What makes dinosaurs so interesting to children? Why are dinosaurs worth studying?" Children's questions and discussions might lead to ideas such as:

- ▼ They are mysterious.
- ▼ Some dinosaurs were very large, but others were quite small.
- ▼ Their bodies were adapted to satisfying their needs for food.
- ▼ They had varied defense mechanisms.
- ▼ Their names are etymologically meaningful.

Any of these ideas can be explored further, and developed by asking, "What is the significance of this observation?" or, more briefly, "So what?" Exploring the significance of the observations can lead to the development of sound and meaningful generalizations, principles, and theories.

One line of thinking might go like this: Dinosaurs are like other creatures in their basic needs for food and protection. One hypothesis for their disappearance is that their food sources were no longer available. A major generalization might be that *All creatures have basic needs for food and for protection.* This generalization places the study of dinosaurs in a larger context and makes it more significant.

Another line of thinking could focus upon the adaptation of the dinosaur to its environment. By their size, their teeth, and their defense mechanisms, among other things, dinosaurs were well adapted to survive in their environment. One hypothesis for their extinction is that when the environment changed, the dinosaurs were unable to adapt well enough to survive. This could lead to the generalization that *Survival depends upon adaptation.*

Any one of the observations could lead to a generalization that fits the criteria for significant learning to some extent, for example:

Some dinosaurs were very large. We can measure things using different standard and nonstandard units.

They are mysterious; we are not sure what happened to them. There are scientific means for exploring mysteries that incorporate hypothesis making and testing.

The names of dinosaurs are etymologically meaningful. Words in our language have developed from other languages.

These generalizations fit the criteria for being true over space and over time, for broadening children's understanding of the world, for leading to inquiry, and for providing opportunities for children to make hypotheses and inferences. However, they have limited potential for interdisciplinary study.

For example, the generalization that *We can measure things using different standard and nonstandard units* could lead to an interesting study in mathematics, but lends itself less easily to studies in social studies or science. Similarly, the generalization that *There are scientific means for exploring mysteries that incorporate hypothesis making and testing* is geared more to science than to other areas of the curriculum, while the generalization that *Words in our language have developed from other languages* would lead naturally to a unit on word roots and etymologies, but would be restricted mainly to language arts.

The broader generalization that *Survival depends upon adaptation,* on the other hand, could lead easily to investigations into animal adaptations such as camouflage, plant adaptations to various climates, human adaptation to new areas of settlement, and the wide realm of literature that deals with the theme of survival through adaptation. The concept could also be applied to the ways in which paradigm shifts change our perspectives (Kuhn, 1970).

Generalizations, even those related to the same topic, do vary. Some are broader in scope than others. Some are perhaps more significant than others, or may be especially relevant to a particular group at a particular time. Generalizations that are considered true today may be supplanted or modified as new data are discovered and knowledge is created. Teachers exercise their professional judgment about what is worth knowing when they select themes for study. The choice of a generalization to focus upon depends on a number of variables, such as major goals for student learning, the needs and interests of the children and of the teacher, curriculum requirements, the expected length of the theme study, and so on. It is up to the teacher to determine the major direction that the theme study should take, ensuring that the criteria for significance are met.

The Literature-Based Approach

One aspect of the whole-language approach is its emphasis on the use of sound children's literature to help children learn to read and write. This literature-based curriculum approach is also highly relevant for interdisciplinary curriculum, and the wide realm of children's literature provides a rich resource for topics and themes.

The purposes for using children's literature as a central focus in curriculum and instruction have been clearly defined. One major purpose is to build children's enthusiasm for reading and to strengthen their reading skills (Chatton, 1989; Moss, 1984; Somers & Worthington, 1979). Literature is also seen as a way to provide a new aesthetic dimension to the more content-focused learning found in textbooks; at the same time, content knowledge enriches the child's understanding and enjoyment of literature (Johnson & Louis, 1987; Sebesta, 1989). In addition, the literature-based curriculum promotes the development of higher order thinking: analysis, synthesis, and evaluating, processes that are used across the fields of study (Chatton, 1989; Johnson & Louis, 1987; Moss, 1984; Sebesta, 1989). Furthermore, the themes found in good literature are those that are significant, universal, and worthy of continued exploration.

There are a number of different approaches to using children's and adolescent literature in an interdisciplinary curriculum.

A study of dinosaurs, for example, opens the door to a wealth of children's resource books, such as Aliki's *My Visit to the Dinosaurs, Dinosaurs Are Different,* and *Digging Up Dinosaurs* (1981, 1985a, 1985b), John Bennett Wexo's *Dinosaurs* (1989), and Joyce Milton's *Dinosaur Days* (1985). Dinosaurs are addressed in a variety of genres, including poetry (Jack Prelutsky's *Tyrannosaurus Was a Beast: Dinosaur Poems* [1988]), riddles (David Adler's *The Dinosaur Princess, and Other Prehistoric Riddles* [1988]), and tall tales (Mordecai Richler's *Jacob Two-Two and the Dinosaur* [1987]). Janet Potter's *Dinosaurs,* in the Reading Experiences in Science series (1980), includes poetry, a repetitive story pattern, a play, and cloze-type puzzles. Any of these resources, and many others on this popular topic, could enrich a study of dinosaurs.

Another approach is to use one topic to open the door to an examination of a different topic. For example, Barbara Steiner's *Oliver Dobbs and the Dinosaur Cause* (1986) describes a fifth grade study of dinosaurs, but focuses primarily on the process of getting the stegosaurus adopted as an official state fossil.

A third approach is to identify a universal theme or generalization that can be learned through study of one topic, and examine the theme from other points of view. For example, the generalization that *Survival depends upon adaptation* could be inferred through a study of theories explaining the disappearance of dinosaurs. Many books, such as Wexo's *Dinosaurs* (1989), present a range of scientific theories, while Carol Carrick's *What Happened to Patrick's Dinosaurs?* (1986) addresses the question in a more whimsical fashion.

The theme study might then be expanded to explore other areas of adaptation and survival in animals, plants, and humans. Children might read fables such as *The Town Mouse and the Country Mouse* or *The Ant and the Grasshopper* (Ash & Higton, 1990), and animal stories such as Lydia Dabcovich's *Sleepy Bear* (1985) or Hanna Muschg's *Two Little Bears* (1986). They could explore the interrelationships between plants and animals by examining books such as Jean Craighead George's *One Day in the Woods* (1988) or Miranda MacQuitty's *Side by Side* (1988). They might use Dwight Kuhn's and David Schwartz's (1988a, 1988b, 1988c) books to find out about life in the forest, the meadow, or the pond. They might also explore the theme in human terms through a novel that depicts history, such as Laura Ingalls Wilder's *Little House in the Big Woods* (1932) or one of the other *Little House* books, where a pioneer family learns to adapt to a new environment.

Children's literature must, of course, be selected with care. Norton (1991) identifies standards for evaluating children's fiction that include both literary elements (plot, characterization, setting, theme, style, point of view, and the avoidance of stereotypes) and children's preferences, which may depend upon the accessibility of a wide variety of books, the readability level of the text, and individual interests. In selecting nonfiction, teachers may evaluate their selections by applying standards based upon recommendations made by professional associations concerned with the relevant content area, such as the National Science Teachers Association and the American Association for the Advancement of Science. Norton (1991) identifies the following guidelines:

1. All facts should be accurate.
2. Stereotypes should be eliminated.
3. Illustrations should clarify the text.
4. Analytical thinking should be encouraged.
5. The organization should aid understanding.
6. The style should stimulate interest.

SELECTING APPROPRIATE TOPICS AND THEMES

Earlier in this chapter, we listed 10 possible sources of topics and themes for interdisciplinary theme studies. Here we describe them in more detail.

▼ Children's common interests
▼ Children's and adolescent literature and trade books
▼ Textbook topics
▼ Current events

▼ Local sites and community resources

▼ Cultural heritage

▼ Children's special or temporal interests

▼ Teachers' interests or expertise

▼ Objects and artifacts

▼ Abstract concepts

Children's Common Interests

There are certain topics that all teachers know children love to learn about. Children may demonstrate interest in a topic by talking about it, choosing books related to the subject, bringing in related toys or pictures, or by drawing and writing about the topic. *Dinosaurs* is a topic of fascination for children, particularly at about the second grade level. Another favorite topic is *American Indians.* Too often, a unit on Indians for young children at the prekindergarten or kindergarten level becomes a superficial presentation of selected stories and stereotypes, with attractive but frequently meaningless accompanying art activities.

If the teacher looks for themes rather than topics, however, a study of Native American cultures can become an exploration of significant ideas, such as *satisfying basic needs* (food, shelter, work, community, education, etc.); *adaptation* (to the terrain, the physical environment, the climate, and the ecology of a region); or *communities* (families, tribes, etc.). For example, a teacher working with kindergarten students in a study based upon the 1987 exhibit "Ancient Texans: Rock Art and Life Ways Along the Lower Pecos," at the Witte Museum in San Antonio, Texas, helped the children to explore the generalization that *Human beings all have the same basic needs; the culture and environment in which they live affects the way they meet those needs.*

Children's and Adolescent Literature and Trade Books

A book that is frequently studied at the Grade 3 or Grade 4 level is E. B. White's *Charlotte's Web* (1952). The story can lend itself to fragmented study of spiders, farm life, the geometric patterns in spiders' webs, and so on. Such study becomes more meaningful, however, if it is linked to a theme and if it leads children to discover significant generalizations.

One such theme could be *cycles of life and death.* The studies of spiders, farm life, and geometric patterns take on new meaning, and the study of the book leads to exciting exploration of important ideas. Generalizations related to this study might be that *Life and death are part of the same cycle,* or *Although each life is unique, it follows a common cyclical process of birth, maturity, and death.*

Enabling children to discover significant themes in literature helps them to read and explore other books and other topics in more meaningful ways. As students identify themes of life cycles, friendship, and interdependence in *Charlotte's Web*, they learn to look below the surface in other novels and discover similar or different insights about the world they live in. Chatton (1989) identifies the functions that literature can serve in the elementary curriculum. First and foremost, it entertains but it also extends meaning and helps children raise questions about their world. Literature across the curriculum avoids fragmentation; it enriches brief lessons on specific topics that seem to be isolated bits of information. Literature also makes connections; by using trade books we help children relate what they are learning to what they already know. Literature enhances problem solving ability to recognize analogies, and capacity to visualize and generalize. Children learn to think critically, to evaluate books for their accuracy and develop criteria for making judgments about the quality of what they read. Finally, literature expands horizons and provides students with historical, social and cultural insights. Literature used across the curriculum enriches the life of the classroom and enhances the vicarious experiences of children.

Textbook Topics

Interdisciplinary study should go far beyond the limitations of textbooks, which are usually written to serve vast audiences and to cover large amounts of material. However, textbooks can provide a starting point, a resource for children and teachers, and a reference guide, and can help to meet the special goals, needs, and interests of any particular group of students. A given topic can be developed into a larger study. The teacher's guide often identifies concepts that relate to a particular topic in that subject area. These concepts can be developed or incorporated into a larger theme.

For example, a fifth grade text addresses the topic of the American Revolution. Concepts identified in the teacher's guide include *liberty, democracy,* and *rights of citizenship.* Any one of these could be developed into a theme study, but it would tend to have a strong humanities orientation. A broader theme could be *revolution* itself. This theme applies to physics and biology, to art and literature, to pottery and mechanics, to astronomy and to politics. Each of these can be examined within the study, and the exploration of each contributes to a greater understanding of all the others and of the theme itself.

Current Events

Current events lend themselves to study in classrooms because of their relevance and immediacy. It is easy, though, simply to teach facts about an event rather than exploring the underlying themes that make it significant. Teachers can build on children's expressed interests. They can also develop children's interests in topics, events, and issues. For example, the Columbian quincentenary in 1992 was celebrated in a variety of ways. For a year preceding the anniversary date, televised presentations on Columbus and his New World discoveries were aired on the Public Broadcasting System. Replicas of the *Niña,* the *Pinta,* and the *Santa María* visited several American harbors. A traveling exhibit was created by the Smithsonian Institution, and articles in local newspapers and popular magazines kept the issues of interactions between the Old and New Worlds, from the fifteenth through the twentieth centuries, in the public eye. These events and activities piqued the interest of many children, causing them to bring reports of their experiences to class. Teachers were then able to build on those expressed interests by encouraging classroom discussion and by building lessons around the quincentenary. In some classrooms, where children did not initiate discussion of this anniversary, teachers were able to develop interest in Columbus's voyages by sharing conflicting accounts for their students' reactions. Additionally, through literature, audiovisual presentations, artifact study, and activities in chart and map making, teachers guided children to raise questions. Those questions became starting points for substantive theme studies.

Materials produced by the Smithsonian Institution probed some big ideas about Columbus's voyages of discovery. Using the theme *seeds of change,* these materials guided students to examine the impact of five things that were carried across the Atlantic Ocean by early explorers: corn, potatoes, the horse, sugar, and disease. These studies enabled students to understand not only *what* happened in 1492 and the Age of Exploration but, more important, *why* these voyages were significant, and their impact upon later generations and even upon our own lives.

Local Sites and Community Resources

Like current events, local sites and studies have a particular relevance and immediacy for children and young people. Nearly all schools provide some funds for field trips to local sites. It is important that students know the history and qualities of their own local area. However, it is easy for field trips to become merely a day out, or to limit students' experiences to learning *about* a site. Using a local site as the central point of interest of a study related to a larger theme provides students with a deeper understanding of the site itself, as well as enabling them to explore more universal ideas.

An eighth grade interdisciplinary team at an urban middle school in San Antonio, Texas, selected the San Antonio Missions National Historical Park as a focus for a theme study. Their central question was *Why were the Missions established?* This question led them to explore the theme of *motivation.* As they conducted their inquiries, they discovered a number of universal ideas: Apparent motivations are not always the accurate ones, the design of buildings is related to their purposes, artistic design may emerge from deep conviction and dedication, and religion and politics are often inextricably entangled. At the same time, they became extremely knowledgeable about the Missions themselves. On a highly successful field trip that allowed exploration of scientific, social, and mathematical aspects of the Missions, the students were even able to correct the park rangers, which delighted both parties!

Cultural Heritage

One of the most widely used topics for special school studies that typically incorporate activities in the different areas of the curriculum is *holidays*. A first grade study of Valentine's Day can include reading valentine stories and poems, writing valentine cards, drawing valentine symbols, singing valentine songs, measuring valentine hearts, dramatizing the history of Saint Valentine's Day, and even making valentine cookies, with many and varied measurements. These activities are interesting to the children and can involve them in their use of important reading, writing, and computing skills. Although the children learn about the holiday, the study is somewhat superficial, limited in time and significance. Gamberg, Kwak, Hutchings, and Altheim (1988) make a similar point about a second grade study. If we think about Valentine's Day as the source of big ideas, we can explore its cultural importance. An entirely different kind of study developed when a first grade teacher transformed the topic of Valentine's Day into a special interest to first graders: the theme of *friendship*. A generalization he selected for his students to discover met all the criteria for a big idea:

> *All people use art, music, poetry, and food to celebrate their friendship for one another; the ways may vary with their cultures, but the feelings and meanings are similar.*

A team of sixth grade teachers chose to develop a theme study on *Kwanzaa*, the 7-day holiday between December 26 and January 1 that celebrates the African-American culture and the *nguzo saba*, or seven principles of human life: unity, self-determination, collective work and responsibility, cooperative economics, purpose, creativity, and faith. At this grade level, students are becoming more aware of these abstract principles and how they affect their own lives. The students studied each principle in each of their subject-area classes to better understand the concepts. For example, some questions for study were:

▼ How does mathematics express unity?

▼ What kinds of unifying principles promote community?

▼ How do people express their feelings about unity?

▼ What different kinds of unification have been developed by people in different times and places?

As each concept was studied, the students lighted the candles that symbolize the meanings of Kwanzaa. They performed African-American songs, dances, and chants and read poetry. To culminate the study, the students prepared and enjoyed a feast. According to their teachers, the students demonstrated understanding of these important generalizations:

There are universal principles that transcend ethnic barriers.

All seven principles can be related to our own lives.

Literature also offers extraordinary opportunities to study common elements of cultural heritage. Moss (1984) describes "folk-tale patterns" as a theme for third and fourth grade children: (1) the theft of objects that are magical, (2) ways in which superpowers help heroes, and (3) stories in which greedy characters ultimately ask for too much and gain nothing. Carefully selected examples of folk tales from different cultures can start children on a journey to understanding that

People in all cultures and times share the same hopes, fears, and drives.

Oral traditions are embodied in all cultures, from the beginnings of human experience.

Children's Special and Temporal Interests

When armyworms infested the trees in a community, the curiosity of a group of second grade children was piqued. The boys brought to school as many of these moth larvae as they could carry, not to study them as organisms but to see how the girls in the class would react to the worm-like things. Their teacher saw a potential for theme study in those armyworms because the children were interested in them. Instead of banning them from the classroom, she guided the children to develop questions about the armyworms' physical characteristics and life cycles: Where did they live? What do they eat? Why did they build tent-like webs? Why are they called armyworms, especially if they're not worms? How many armyworms live in one tent? And if they're not worms, what are they? What do they become? How long do they live? Why do people kill them? Observations, interviews, discussions, reading, and other types of data collection led the children to do some serious research. They found answers and formed additional, more probing questions. As the children conducted a serious inquiry into this initially casual and potentially distracting interest, they came to understand the concept of metamorphosis and to infer several big ideas:

Dramatic transformations occur in natural life cycles.

Things are not always what they seem.

Teachers' Interests or Expertise

Teachers know that their enthusiasm for a topic or subject of study can develop the interest of their students. *Railroads* is a topic of special meaning for a fifth grade teacher who remembered playing with model railroads from her childhood. Her enthusiasm for miniature trains and the real thing had been fanned by her father, who had been riding the rails and collecting and making model railroads since his youth. This topic was also of interest to the fifth graders, who were familiar with the freight trains that rolled through their neighborhoods and who enjoyed watching the model trains in holiday displays at the local mall, although few of them had ever ridden on a train. The teacher guided the students' study of the history of railroads in the United States, the geography of railways, the logistics of timetables, the changing use of railroads, railroad folklore and heroes, the ratio and proportion of miniature trains, the geometry of scale, the physics of steam, diesel, and electric engines, and the rhythms and tonalities of the rails, to mention just a few directions of their studies. Each study was chosen to help the fifth graders realize that:

> *Means of transportation change the way people live.*
> *People's needs and technology have influenced means of transportation.*

These big ideas meet all the criteria for determining the value of a theme study. As they were being developed by the children's explorations of the several questions that framed their studies, new questions were generated about the future of transportation and its impact on life in the 21st century.

Objects and Artifacts

Chapter 1 opens with a description of questions children asked about a walking shoe. Objects are tangible starting points for inquiry because you can "read" them. You can see the leather on a shoe, touch the emblem, and find the country of origin stamped in the lining. Each observation suggests a new question. Objects are often commonplace items, so asking questions about them makes us realize how much we take for granted. Think about the questions you could ask to find out about a cup, a shirt, or a pencil.

Artifacts may be even more engaging because they speak to us of times past and people who often are no longer living. Questioning an old bottle someone uncovered in a basement or attic, a great-grandmother's wedding gown, or a rusty nail is like exploring a mystery (see Figure 3.4 for an exploration of a rusty nail). In all cases the inquiries guide the detective to understandings about the world and human experience that reveal universal "truths."

Abstract Concepts

Highly abstract ideas, like *discovery, revolution,* and *relativity,* can be sources of theme studies. In contrast to the other, more specific, stimulators of inquiry that need broadening before they can support substantive theme studies, abstract concepts need to be focused before they can be developed as meaningful curriculum for elementary and middle-school students. In the next chapter, you will see how an abstract concept like *patterns of change* lends itself to several big ideas from which teachers can make selections according to their students' age, developmental levels,

Figure 3.4
Understanding a rusty nail

Aalbert Heine, former director of the Corpus Christi Museum, reminds us that "just one object in a museum, a square nail, rusty and bent, is all that is needed to open up the world, to introduce the flow of knowledge." For instance:

History: to illustrate how houses were built in the old part of town; how the extreme paucity of nails hampered settlement of the prairie states; how important a black-smith shop used to be.

Mechanics: to unravel the forces that bent the nail, the kinetic force of the hammer and the forces of friction that hold it in the lumber; to discuss the electromagnetics.

Chemistry: as an element and an example of oxidation.

Geology: to show the processing of ores to metal.

Anthropology: to discuss the Stone Age and the development of technology into bronze and iron; to discuss societies built without metals.

Astronomy: to discuss meteoric iron and to speculate about the core of the earth.

Economics: the value of nails to railroads and ship building.

Art: as a source of yellow ochre.

According to Heine, the nail can be seen as the center of the universe.

and interests. The richness and versatility of these big ideas make abstract concepts good candidates for schoolwide curriculum. In chapter 4, we tell the story of how teachers and children in an elementary and a middle school used the theme *patterns of change* across the grades to develop interdisciplinary theme studies.

▼ READER INVOLVEMENT

1.   Following are several big ideas that were developed by teams of first, fourth, and seventh grade teachers for theme studies on *patterns of change*. Each can be tested against the criteria for significance presented in this chapter. Apply those questions to each grade level's big idea. To what extent do these meet the criteria?

Grade 1: Growing up leads to changes in independence and interdependence.

Grade 4: Significant changes in communities affect other parts of those communities.

Grade 7: Change in one area is affected by and leads to related changes in other areas.

2.   From the inquiry into a theme that you started in response to the Reader Involvement in chapters 1 and 2, identify several generalizations that meet the criteria for significance. Record them in the inquiry section of your journal.

3.   We encourage you to continue to explore the questions you identified in response to the Reader Involvement section at the end of chapter 1 by consulting resources, collecting data, and formulating new questions. This will provide you with the background knowledge you need to design an interdisciplinary theme study.

REFERENCES

Barber, J., Bergman, L., & Sneider, C. (1991). *To build a house: GEMS and the "thematic approach" to teaching science.* Berkeley, CA: Lawrence Hall of Science. The LHS GEMS series includes nearly 40 teacher's guides for hands-on science and mathematics activities and handbooks on key educational topics. For more information, contact GEMS, Lawrence Hall of Science, University of California, Berkeley, CA 94720, (510) 642-7771.

Chatton, B. (1989). Using literature across the curriculum. In J. Hickman & B. E. Cullinan (Eds.), *Children's literature in the classroom: Weaving Charlotte's web* (pp. 61–70). Needham Heights, MA: Christopher-Gordon.

Gamberg, R., Kwak, W., Hutchings, M., & Altheim, J. (1988). *Learning and loving it: Theme studies in the classroom.* Portsmouth, NH: Heinemann.

Golden, C. (1986). *American history grade 11: Course of study and related learning activities.* New York: New York City Board of Education, Division of Curriculum and Instruction.

Hartoonian, H. M., & Laughlin, M. A. (October, 1989). Designing a social studies scope and sequence for the 21st century. *Social Education, 53(6),* 388–398.

Heine, A. (October, 1984). *Teaching the easy way (the multi-disciplinary approach).* Corpus Christi, TX: Corpus Christi Museum of Science and History.

Jacobs, H. H., & Borland, J. H. (Fall, 1986). The interdisciplinary concept model: Theory and practice. *Gifted Child Quarterly, 30(4),* 159–163.

Johnson, T. D., & Louis, D. R. (1987). *Literacy through literature.* Portsmouth, NH: Heinemann.

Kuhn, T. S. (1970). The structure of scientific revolutions (2nd ed.). Chicago: University of Chicago Press.

Moss, J. F. (1984). *Focus units in literature: A handbook for elementary school teachers.* Urbana, IL: National Council of Teachers of English.

Norton, D. E. (1991). *Through the eyes of a child: An introduction to children's literature* (3rd ed.). New York: Merrill/Macmillan.

Osborne, R., & Freyberg, P. (1985). *Learning in science: The implications of children's science.* Portsmouth, NH: Heinemann.

Philips, W. C. (February, 1991). Earth science misconceptions. *Science Teacher, 58,* 21–23.

Rutherford, F. J., & Ahlgren, A. (1990). *Science for all Americans.* New York: Oxford University Press.

Sebesta, S. L. (1989). Literature across the curriculum. In J. W. Stewig & S. L. Sebesta (Eds.), *Using literature in the elementary classroom* (pp. 110–128). Urbana, IL: National Council of Teachers of English.

Shoemaker, B. J. E. (October, 1989). *Integrative education: A curriculum for the twenty-first century.* Eugene, OR: Oregon School Study Council.

Somers, A. B., & Worthington, J. E. (1979). *Response guides for teaching children's books.* Urbana, IL: National Council of Teachers of English.

Taba, H. (1962). *Curriculum development: Theory and practice.* New York: Harcourt Brace Jovanovich.

References to Children's and Adolescent Literature

Adler, D. (1988). *The dinosaur princess and other prehistoric riddles.* New York: Holiday House.

Aliki (1981). *Digging up dinosaurs.* New York: Thomas Y. Crowell.

Aliki (1985a). *Dinosaurs are different.* New York: Thomas Y. Crowell.

Aliki (1985b). *My visit to the dinosaurs.* New York: Thomas Y. Crowell.

Ash, R., & Higton, B. (Eds.). (1990). *Aesop's fables.* San Francisco: Chronicle Books.

Carrick, C. (1986). *What happened to Patrick's dinosaurs?* New York: Clarion Books.

Dabcovich, L. (1985). *Sleepy bear.* New York: Dutton.

George, J. C. (1988). *One day in the woods.* New York: Thomas Y. Crowell.

Kuhn, D. (photographs), & Schwartz, D. M. (text). (1988a). *The hidden life of the forest.* New York: Crown.

Kuhn, D. (photographs), & Schwartz, D. M. (text). (1988b). *The hidden life of the meadow.* New York: Crown.

Kuhn, D. (photographs), & Schwartz, D. M. (text). (1988c). *The hidden life of the pond.* New York: Crown.

Milton, J. (1985). *Dinosaur days.* New York: Random House.

MacQuitty, M. (Ed.). (1988). *Side by side.* New York: Putnam (Oxford Scientific Films).

Muschg, H. (1986). *Two little bears.* New York: Bradbury Press.

Potter, J. (1980). *Dinosaurs.* Winnipeg, Manitoba: Pegius Publishers.

Prelutsky, J. (1988). *Tyrannosaurus was a beast: Dinosaur poems.* New York: Green-willow Books.

Richler, M. (1987). *Jacob Two-Two and the dinosaur.* New York: Knopf.

Steiner, B. (1986). *Oliver Dobbs and the dinosaur cause.* New York: Four Winds Press.

Wexo, J. B. (1989). *Dinosaurs.* Mankato, MN: Creative Education.

White, E. B. (1952). *Charlotte's web.* New York: Harper & Row.

Wilder, L. I. (1932). *Little house in the big woods.* New York: Harper & Row.

Additional Reading

Holff, K. (April, 1974). AAAS science books: A selection tool. *Library Trends, 22,* 453–462.

Jett-Simpson, M. (Ed.). (1989). *Adventuring with books* (9th ed.). Urbana, IL: National Council of Teachers of English.

National Science Teachers Association. (March, 1986). Outstanding science trade books for children in 1985. *Science and Children, 23(6),* 23–26.

San Antonio Museum Association. (Fall, 1985). *The talisman.* San Antonio, TX: San Antonio Museum Association.

Tanner, D., & Tanner, L. N. (1980). *Curriculum development: Theory into practice.* New York: Macmillan.

Woolsey, K. H., & Cappo, M. (Executive Producers). (1993). *Life story* [CD-ROM disk and teacher's guide]. Apple Computer, Lucas Arts Entertainment, Adrian Malone Productions, and the Smithsonian Institution. Pleasantville, NY: WINGS for Learning/Sunburst.

Chapter Four

Webbing and Questioning

One Tuesday afternoon, the grade-level team leaders assembled in the faculty workroom. They had been selected by their colleagues to begin planning a school-wide interdisciplinary curriculum, and had attended a workshop during the summer to learn about this approach to teaching and learning. They looked at each other expectantly.

"We need to begin by choosing a theme," said Raynetta O'Neal, the fourth grade teacher.

"It needs to be big enough for us all to work on, without too much overlap," commented Pete Martini, the first grade teacher.

"And challenging enough for the fifth graders," added the fifth grade teacher, Bettina Wright.

"But also simple enough for my kindergarteners," added Maria Fernandez, who understood the developmental needs of early childhood.

Joe Piloski, the third grade teacher, was busy looking through a paperback book. "In Science for All Americans, they have identified some big themes. What about one of these: systems, models, patterns of change?" (Rutherford & Ahlgren, 1990)

"Don't you think that those might be too broad?" Mary Wong, the second grade teacher, asked. "We—and the children—could get really lost in trying to find a manageable focus."

"We could always narrow it down," Raynetta suggested. "You know how we have to keep on making choices all through the process of developing theme studies."

"But if it's too broad, we find it really hard to narrow it down enough," Pete complained, "and then it's very easy to just pick some topic out of the web and deal with it in a superficial way."

"Here's an idea," said Joe, still leafing through the book. "What about this: patterns of change. One thing that is common to all of us, and particularly to elementary children, is that they are changing."

There was silence for a few moments as the teachers thought about this idea. Maria Fernandez spoke first. "You know, that's not a bad idea. My five-year-olds are so aware of how their lives change when they go to school."

"And the fifth graders are excited and scared about changes in their lives as they move on to middle school and into adolescence," Bettina remarked.

"What about the middle grades?" Pete asked.

"No problem there," Joe replied. "So much of our curriculum in social studies and science deals with change."

"So does the math curriculum. And my fourth graders enjoy adventure books, and that certainly involves change," Raynetta pointed out. "Where do we go from here?"

"Before we make a firm choice," Bettina suggested, "let's explore the idea in more depth. We can brainstorm on the idea of patterns of change, and see what ideas emerge. That can help us to see if this theme is rich enough for a number of theme studies at the various grade levels."

Pete wrote the words PATTERNS OF CHANGE on a large sheet of butcher paper. The other teachers took small pads of self-stick notes and began to write down their ideas, one idea on each sheet.

"At this stage, anything goes," Raynetta reminded the others. "The more ideas the better."

Soon the table was covered with small slips of paper. The teachers, who had been writing furiously, began to slow down. They looked over each other's shoulders, and sometimes someone else's idea spurred a new flurry of activity.

"I think it's time to start categorizing," Mary suggested. "We can always add new ideas as we think of them."

The teachers began to group the slips of paper. If an idea appeared to belong in more than one category, someone wrote it on a second slip of paper and put one slip in each category. Sometimes the formation of a category led to new ideas, which were added to the grouping.

"I think it's time to label the categories," Bettina said. "Shall we use words or ideas as labels?"

"Whatever seems comfortable," Joe replied. "The main thing is to show what we were thinking about as we grouped them. Sometimes a generalization or a description is more helpful than one word."

As the categories were developed and the labels written on separate cards, the teachers constructed a web, showing where the larger ideas related to each other. Figure 4.1 shows what the web looked like.

▼ READER INVOLVEMENT

Look back at the scenario for the steps in the process.

- ▼ What was the teachers' first task?
- ▼ What were their criteria for the selection of a theme?
- ▼ Why did the teachers decide to brainstorm on the chosen theme?

FLUENT AND FLEXIBLE THINKING

Brainstorming involves thinking fluently and flexibly, habits of mind that are important to productive inquiry. The work of Guilford (1971) and Torrance (1970) on creative thinking defines fluency as the generation of many ideas. Consider the classic example of thinking up uses for a paper clip. The total number of ideas is a measure of fluency, even if they are similar: for example, using the clip to hold up a hem, as a money clip, or as a fastener for a bag of chips. Flexible thinking is evident when the thinker changes classes of ideas. So, for instance, after thinking about the clip as a fastener, we might change our perspective and begin seeing the paper clip as an earring, a lock pick, or even a racetrack for fleas (Parnes and Harding, 1962). Each of those ideas suggests a different point of view on the subject or theme. New perspectives help thinking become more fluent and flexible. See Figure 4.2 for guidelines for brainstorming.

DEVELOPING A WEB

There are many procedures for brainstorming. When we are developing a web, these fluent and flexible ways of thinking can help to redirect the way we look at a theme.

As people brainstorm on their own, they tend to work in categories. For example, Joe began by writing *years;* this led him to write associated words such as *seasons, days, months, hours, minutes,* and *seconds* before he moved to a different set of ideas.

Figure 4.1
Fourth grade web for patterns of change

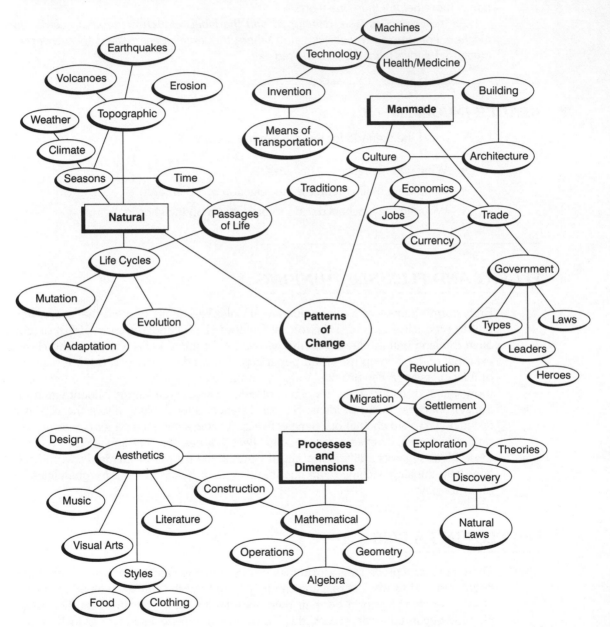

Figure 4.2
Brainstorming

There are many procedures for brainstorming, but there are also some general guidelines:

• Generate as many ideas as possible.

• Accept all ideas.

• Seek clarification, if necessary, but do not edit at this stage.

• Encourage people to brainstorm on their own before contributing to a common pool of ideas. This allows for greater participation and diversity of ideas.

• Remember that brainstorming is an open-ended exercise. At any time, new ideas or directions may be introduced.

• Do not close down the process too soon. Provide enough thinking time.

As people pool their ideas, they tend to share their categories. However, the pooling of ideas can also lead to new categories. For example, Joe's idea of *seasons* led the teachers to develop a whole new category related to *celebration of change* (birthdays, graduation, New Year's, and so forth).

Some of the teachers with whom we have worked web with questions rather than words or phrases. They use an approach that is reminiscent of a computer programmer's authoring program such as HyperCard, Linkway, ToolBook, or AmigaVision. They formulate questions, categorize them by more inclusive questions, and link those categories into interrelated clusters.

The organization of ideas for any theme can take many forms: a web of labels in single words and phrases, a network of question clusters, a collage of graphics, a montage of images, symbols, and words, a storyboard of metaphors, the analysis of an object or artifact, or other combinations of varied expressions of ideas associated with a theme. Such records may be developed from the brainstorming of students, teachers, and students and teachers working collaboratively. Through these records, teachers and students make explicit what they know about a theme at the start of its study and, especially, what they would like to learn about it. This initial collection of ideas lends itself naturally and elegantly to the evaluation of learning. The first web, collage, montage, or storyboard that teachers and their students assemble is a benchmark. When the theme study is done, the development of a similar type of record by teachers and students will testify to what they have learned from their study of the theme.

▼ *READER INVOLVEMENT*

Look back at the web (Figure 4.1). Think flexibly. What new category or categories might you develop around the theme *patterns of change?*

Review the steps the teachers went through in developing the web. Why did they proceed in this way? What did the webbing activity achieve?

The teachers looked at the web. "I think we have got plenty to work with," Raynetta said. "Now we need to take the idea back to the teachers in our grade-level teams, and let them explore the major idea by webbing. We will ask them to take the next step and develop questions for inquiry related to the categories they develop. Then let's come back together and decide on the major focus for each grade level so that there isn't too much overlap. I know that the teachers at each grade level will have a good sense of the required curriculum and the developmental level of their students, and this will affect the choices they make.

▼ *READER INVOLVEMENT*

Read the following scenario and identify the way the fourth grade team used the guidelines in Figure 4.3 for designing theme studies as they continue to develop their interdisciplinary curriculum.

Figure 4.3
Guidelines for designing theme studies

1. Select a theme.
2. Develop a web.
3. Form questions for student inquiry.
4. Identify concepts; formulate generalizations.
5. Check against accepted standards for the curriculum.
6. Map the general sequence.
7. Use resources to explore questions.
8. Develop ideas for learning-activity clusters.
9. Identify content and process objectives.
10. Design learning activities.
11. Choose culminating projects.
12. Organize specific scope and sequence; check for integrity and coherence.
13. Decide on record keeping, reporting, and ongoing assessment.

A week after the grade-level team leaders had begun working with the patterns of change theme, grade-level groups met after early dismissal. Raynetta O'Neal reported what she had learned about interdisciplinary curriculum with her fourth grade colleagues, sharing the initial steps the grade-level team leaders had taken to construct the web she displayed.

Elizabeth West examined the web carefully. Always attentive to detail, she liked to gain a sense of how the pieces of any puzzle fit together. "What are we supposed to do with this web?" she asked.

"Well," Jose Gonzales responded, "according to what Raynetta is telling us, we need to select an emphasis for our grade level."

"For the whole year?" Nicole Gentile asked.

"Maybe," Raynetta answered. "Or, perhaps we'd like to be more limiting. We can't decide until we've worked with the concepts that, in our professional judgment, are most appropriate for our students' instructional program."

"So, what do we do with this web?" Elizabeth was anxious to get on with what she thought might be an academic exercise. She wasn't convinced that theme studies made for the most coherent curriculum. But she was willing to try it.

"Look at the subcategories in the web the team leaders started," Raynetta directed. "Where do you see some areas of interest for our students?"

"Fourth graders love to explore," Jose said. "That's why I like to teach this grade. By nine years of age, the children are beginning to lose some of the egocentrism of earlier childhood."

"Some of them are still babies, though," Elizabeth added.

"Listen to their questions," Jose insisted. "They tell us about their interests."

"The fourth graders I've taught always ask about other people and life styles," Raynetta told the group. "They want to learn about their surroundings too. I never taught a nine-year-old who wasn't fascinated by the living things in their environment, human and nonhuman. Their interests extend to other people and places too. My students would be buried in National Geographic and Ranger Rick all day if I allowed it."

"They're able to imagine beyond their concrete experiences and make inferences," Jose added. "I see that every time we do a science experiment. Most of the children can look at a fossil they've never seen before and infer plausible origins."

"Yes," Nicole Gentile agreed, "our students do seem interested in cause and effect and figuring out how things change. I've noticed that during math lessons when we were examining bar graphs on changes in temperature and rainfall over the years. The children are quick to see interrelationships."

Elizabeth nodded. "They like to build things, too. You know how they love to build models and put together puzzle pieces."

"And play detective with computer games," Raynetta said.

"Well, then," Elizabeth suggested, "do you think that change in community might be an interesting theme for our students?"

"Communities." Jose emphasized the plural. "We can include the study of non-human as well as human communities throughout the world. I think that's consistent with our regular social studies and science curriculum."

"Change in communities," Raynetta repeated. She smiled. It felt right to her. "Change is an inevitable condition of life in communities. What do you think?" she asked the others. They all agreed.

"It suits us," Nicole said.

"All right," Raynetta said. "Now we can brainstorm on that idea and develop our web."

With Raynetta's guidance, the teachers listed their ideas, then formed categories and linked them in a web (Figure 4.4).

FORMULATING QUESTIONS THROUGH THE LENSES OF DIFFERENT DISCIPLINES

The next step in designing interdisciplinary theme studies is to formulate the major questions for student inquiry and the broad generalizations that are to be developed by the students through that inquiry. This process can be done by an individual teacher or by a teacher working with the students; however, if a group of teachers for the same grade level can plan together, particularly when just beginning to develop theme studies, this makes the process more substantive, richer in idea production, and more effective.

"Look at that," Jose directed. "The concepts are jumping out at us: life cycles, adaptations, habitats, ecology, human impact on the environment, natural resources and human uses, time and measurement, historical origins. . . ."

"Remember," Raynetta reminded everyone, "we want this curriculum we're designing to encourage children's inquiry. At the rate that knowledge is multiplying, there's no way that any education can provide students with all the knowledge they will need in adulthood. We must develop in our students skills for self-directive learning."

"And the requisite attitudes," Elizabeth added.

"We know that there are ways of thinking that are used to develop new knowledge in every discipline of study," Jose said. "There are modes of thinking and thinking skills that everyone must develop to do well in any line of work."

"Critical and creative thinking skills," Nicole observed.

"And the attitudes that accompany productive thinking, like risk taking, open-mindedness, perseverance, and cooperation," Elizabeth reminded them.

"Then we have to think about developing concepts through investigative studies. Let's look at each idea in our web through the lenses of different disciplines, and jot down the questions that come to mind. For instance, if you look at life cycles through the eyes of a botanist, what questions come to mind?"

Figure 4.4
Fourth grade web for changes in communities

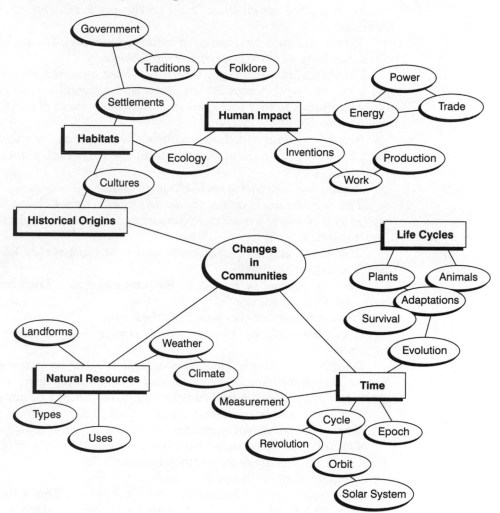

"That's easy," Nicole piped. "I'd want to know how plant life cycles are affected by climate."

"Let's write that as a question," Raynetta suggested. She wrote: How are plant life cycles affected by climate?

"How are they affected by habitat? By droughts and floods? By earthquakes and volcanic eruptions?" Jose added.

"I have another," Elizabeth added. "How are plant life cycles changed by humans?"

"Do changes in plant life cycles affect animal life cycles?" Nicole added.

"How can we restate that question," Raynetta said, *"to make it a deeper investigation?"*

Nicole restated her question: *"How do changes in plant life cycles affect animal life cycles?"*

"We can add questions from other natural science perspectives," Jose said. *"How about the viewpoint of the chemist and the ecologist?"*

"Go ahead," Raynetta urged them. *"Think like a chemist, an ecologist, a zoologist, a microbiologist, a physicist, and from all the natural science perspectives you think appropriate. Record your questions on separate pieces of paper. We'll put them together later."*

"You know," Jose added, *"we shouldn't be limited by the traditional academic disciplines. We can look at our theme in the ways that a doctor might, or a mechanic."*

"What would a mechanic see?" Elizabeth asked.

"The one who works on my car would probably want to know how engines will change as they become more computerized and how that will affect his livelihood," Jose responded.

"That makes you think of inventors and what changes their ideas will make in daily life," Nicole observed.

"Let's try different perspectives," Raynetta suggested. *"Look through the historian's lens. What do you see?"*

"Human settlements over time," Elizabeth said.

"A question could be: How do people change their habitats over time?" Jose suggested.

"A legislator might ask, 'How do people govern their communities? What causes them to change their laws?'" Elizabeth said. *"And a lawyer might wonder about the effects on the exercise of individual rights and on neighboring communities."*

"Boy, that would be interesting to study," Jose said.

Elizabeth looked at him quizzically. *"What's the answer?"*

"I don't know," he answered honestly, *"but I would like to find out—with my students. We could investigate the question together."*

Elizabeth raised her eyebrows.

Raynetta caught the meaning of her expression. *"That's the beautiful side of theme studies,"* she said. *"The teacher can become a coinquirer with the children. You don't need to know all the answers. In fact, sometimes it's better if you don't."*

Nicole caught the spirit of Raynetta's remark. *"If I were a historian, I'd want to find out how women adapted to new settlements,"* she said. *"I have only a smattering of knowledge about that because most of the history books I've read haven't discussed women's experiences. It's said that 'the West was hell on horses and women.' I'd like to study women's changing roles in frontier communities."*

"Think about the geologist's and geographer's perspectives," Jose suggested. *"How do geographic regions affect how people live? And how do natural landforms affect political boundaries?"*

"Write them down. Write them down," Raynetta urged. *After the members of the group had written several, Raynetta urged them to try on the lens that writers might see through.*

"How do people record their changing life styles and traditions?" Elizabeth suggested.

"How does literature tell us about changing heroes?" Nicole added.

"Legends and myths," Raynetta said. *"How do legends and myths reflect and influence change in human communities?"*

"There's no end to the types of questions we could ask about literary art forms in relation to changes in communities," Elizabeth said. *"After all, every literary form is an expression of human experience. So we could explore literature that deals with change in human groups."*

"And animal and plant communities, too," Jose reminded them.

"I have a few questions in mind," Nicole said.

"Jot them down," Raynetta urged everyone, *and allowed a few minutes for the teachers to record their ideas.*

"Now for a hard one," Raynetta told them. *"Try the lens of a mathematician."*

The flurry of question writing that had developed from the earlier perspectives ended abruptly with Raynetta's direction. What would a mathematician see, they wondered. Sensing their stalemate, Raynetta suggested taking the statistician's perspective. That helped.

"How does the trade of a community affect the kinds of jobs people have?" she offered.

"What about monetary systems?" Elizabeth asked. *"How have monetary systems changed over time? An international business executive would want to know how they affect trade among communities. And what are the causes of price fluctuations for different commodities?"*

"A tourist would have a similar question," Nicole added. *In fact, she was planning a trip to Europe and had been meaning to do some research on monetary exchange rates and the cost of food and lodgings in the several countries she thought she might visit. Her findings would influence her choices of places to visit and length of stay in each.*

"We could look at questions of demographics," Jose said. *"How have animal, plant, and human populations in different habitats changed over time? What seems to have caused those changes? What effects have those changes had on the habitats?"*

"A mathematician would also see geometric issues," Raynetta said. *"How are different areas of land use determined by people? What are the areas of migratory patterns of different animals?"*

"That reminds me of ratio and proportion," Nicole said. *"We could investigate the carrying capacity of land; that is, the proportion of land needed to support different animal populations, including the animals that people raise for food."*

"Write them down," Raynetta reminded everyone.

"What would a musician see?" Elizabeth asked.

"Easy," Jose said. *"How does music express changing beliefs and needs?"*

"A dress designer might look at visual design elements. For instance, 'How do clothing styles change over time? What influences their design?'"

"What about colors?" Jose suggested. *"How do visual artists from different cultures use color?"*

"How are animals depicted in the art of different culture groups and what does that tell us about the people's views of those animals?" Raynetta added.

"What is the design of animals that enables their survival?" suggested Elizabeth. *"I think that a visual artist would be very interested in studying design in nature, whether coloration for protection or attraction."*

The teachers now had a sizable collection of questions.

"We can't study all these questions," Raynetta told them. *"One way to narrow the field is to select those explorations that can guide students to discover and to verify the generalizations we want them to form as they analyze the data collected during their inquiries."*

The teachers looked back at the web they had created.

"You know. . . ." Jose paused for a moment, thinking. *The others looked expectantly at him.* *"I can see where the questions fit. Look here."* Jose placed several questions about plants and animals near the category of adaptations. *"And the questions we have about human adaptations to their habitats tell us that we should add that category to our web."*

"I see categories on our web for all our social studies questions," Raynetta said. *"The fit is natural, as you would expect it to be because of the kind of framework the web offers."*

"Some fit in more than one place," Nicole observed. *"See, our questions about ratio and proportion are equally meaningful for the categories of invention, life cycles, and habitats."*

"Can we place all the others?" Elizabeth asked.

"Let's do it!" Raynetta decided to follow the group's interests rather than press for her own agenda. She had hoped to get to deciding on the theme's central generalizations that afternoon, but it was almost five o'clock. The teachers had been working on the theme study for several hours since early dismissal. She felt that they were tiring. Besides, Elizabeth had to pick up her toddler at day care. Nicole had an evening class, and Jose needed to get some reading materials for his students from the library. Raynetta had an ailing mother at home to look after besides reviewing her plans for tomorrow's instruction. We've accomplished a lot, she thought. Even if we don't have our generalizations yet, it's important to see the connections that we're finding between our web and our questions. After all, Raynetta reminded herself,

there are many ways to design theme studies. We shouldn't be slaves to any one model.

By the time they called it quits that afternoon, the fourth grade teachers discovered that some of their categories could include questions asked from different disciplinary perspectives and that some questions were meaningful across several categories.

▼ READER INVOLVEMENT

Figure 4.3 offers guidelines for designing theme studies. Review the scenario of theme planning by the fourth grade teachers, keeping in mind the broad sequence presented in that figure. Can you find evidence in the scenario of how the teachers used each of the steps for planning a theme study? For instance, where and how did they select a theme? Develop a web? Form questions for student inquiry? And use other guidelines? How far did they get? Where are they going? What do they need to do?

QUESTIONS FOR INTERDISCIPLINARY INQUIRY

By formulating questions from diverse perspectives for the study of their theme, *patterns of change in communities,* the fourth grade team was preparing to involve their students in interdisciplinary inquiry. The perspectives the teachers took started with the traditional academic disciplines, such as biology, physics, history, sociology, and statistics. During their brainstorming on ideas for exploration, other perspectives emerged, such as those of the doctor, lawyer, business executive, and mechanic. Other viewpoints would further enrich the interdisciplinary character of the theme study because most occupations use content and skills from several disciplines. So, for example, the questions about a theme that might be raised from the vantage points of banker, salesperson, grocer, or newscaster might be different from those raised by the roles of parent, sibling, patient, or client. The greater the diversity of perspectives from which an idea may be viewed, the more interdisciplinary the studies are likely to become. Consider the Project 2061 (Rutherford & Ahlgren, 1990) theme, *the designed world.* In addition to the perspectives of traditional disciplines of study, other questions might be derived from occupational viewpoints, such as:

Builder: How are structures built to last? What materials are needed? What tools?

Mining engineer: Which resources are most useful for building in different environments? How are they safely extracted from the earth with the least expense?

Highway planner: What are the safest types of highway intersections? How can they be built in the shortest amount of time and with the least disruption to traffic flow?

City manager: How do zoning ordinances affect neighborhoods? How are residential and business areas best connected by a network for streets and sidewalks?

Fashion designer: What fashions are most likely to be popular with particular age groups? What fabrics, textures, and colors are most likely to set trends? At what prices?

Advertiser: What images and patterns will capture the attention of the people who are most likely to buy a product? What methods of persuasion can be used most effectively?

Inventor: What is the easiest and cheapest way to "build a better mousetrap"?

When any one of the questions is played out, the interdisciplinary qualities of the search become even more apparent. For instance, if we develop the builder's question, "How are structures built to last?", the avenues for exploration include, but are certainly not limited to historic, contemporary, and future types, purposes, and construction processes of buildings or bridges, highways, or other constructions. Selecting any one may encourage the study of floor plans and blueprints, building materials, physical principles of construction, construction machinery, tools for carpentry and interior decorating, chemicals and manufacturing processes for paints, wallpapers, and the various interior and exterior trims, human comfort and safety—and the list goes on, defined by learner interests, resources, time, imagination, and, especially, development of knowledge.

Levels of Questions

Our knowledge informs our view of the world. As our knowledge changes, so does our universe (Lynch, 1985). What we know informs the questions we ask. Most inquiries increase in complexity and depth as they proceed because the inquirer becomes more knowledgeable about the subject. Bloom's *Taxonomy of Educational Objectives* (1956) has been used by teachers to develop questions at increasing levels of intellectual abstraction. Theme studies should enable students to move from lower to higher order questioning and from naive to more sophisticated and informed inquiry. Taba (1967) identifies three major cognitive tasks: concept formation, interpretation of data, and application of principles. As students engage in these cognitive tasks in interdisciplinary theme studies, they learn to ask more probing questions and to develop more complex ways of thinking. The teacher's responsibility, then, is to provide opportunities for students to raise a variety of questions that will help them develop the habits of mind associated with creative and critical thinking.

When student inquiries become fragmented and superficial, teachers may need to guide them to rephrase their questions so that the questions themselves suggest the resources that may be consulted for information. (We discuss this further in chapters 7 and 8.) As any exploration proceeds, one question should lead to others that are more profound and more insightful, so that interrelationships become evident among the data each question uncovers. Teachers who have been through the process of formulating directions for interdisciplinary theme studies will be well prepared to guide their students' detective work toward the discovery of meaningful patterns about any theme. Those patterns are usually stated as laws, principles, theories, and generalizations.

CREATIVE AND CRITICAL THINKING

In chapter 1, we presented some ways of thinking or "habits of mind" associated with thinking in all fields of study. Planning interdisciplinary curriculum involves creative and critical thinking at all stages. While there is no one right way to plan theme studies, our experience has shown that the process must include brainstorming to generate a wealth of ideas as well as synthesizing and selecting to develop clear focus. Note that this process incorporates both creative and critical thinking. Creativity is apparent in the fluent and flexible thinking the teachers used as they brainstormed. Movement between creative and critical thinking occurred as they synthesized their ideas to build categories, and then selected the categories they wanted to work with. These same thinking processes are developed in students as teachers guide their generation of ideas for study and the conduct of their inquiries.

We have described the planning that a fourth grade team engaged in as they began to develop interdisciplinary curriculum. The chart in Figure 4.5 indicates the planning conducted by a group of four first grade teachers and by a seventh grade interdisciplinary team that included a teacher from each of these subject areas: mathematics, science, social studies, language arts, and reading. It shows their progression from the first big idea generated by webbing on the theme *patterns of change* toward specific theme studies related to the grade-level curriculum.

After developing their webs from the original idea, *patterns of change,* the teachers looked at the categories they had developed, then generated questions for inquiry. While these questions were couched in adult language, they were related to the developmental level of the students who would be investigating them.

In order to make sure that they had explored the topic as richly as possible, the teachers set themselves the task of adopting the perspective of different fields of study and identifying questions that might be raised by a historian, a scientist, a mathematician, and so on. This helped them to see added possibilities for students' inquiry. Each team developed five or six questions from each perspective, a small sample of which is included in the chart (Figure 4.5). They realized, of course, that not all of the questions would be explored in a single theme study.

This exercise not only gave them many choices but also provided possible avenues for individual study by students who were particularly interested in a viewpoint that might not be included in the formally structured theme study.

Figure 4.5
Planning chart

	Grade 1	Grade 7
<u>Initial Generalization</u>	Growing up means change.	Change in one area is affected by and leads to changes in other areas.
<u>Sample Questions</u> Historian:	How has our country changed as it "grew up"? How did children grow up in other times?	What has caused changes in life styles over the years? How have new inventions and ideas affected history?
Sociologist:	Why do people live in families as they grow up? How do families help people to change?	How do population shifts affect families and cultures?
Writer:	How do people write about growing up (flashback, chronological, critical incident, etc.)?	How might a change in setting affect the plot of a story? How do characters' past history affect their actions?
Mathematician:	How do numbers change as they get larger (place value)? How do we measure change in size?	How does changing the size of one side of a polygon affect the size of its angles?
Scientist:	How do different animals change as they grow? What do living things need as they grow?	In what ways do natural forces such as climate affect landforms? What causes earthquakes?

	Grade 1	Grade 7
Artist:	How can growth be depicted in art? How does art help people to grow (active and passive)?	What effects does a change in perspective have? What causes changes in styles of art or music?
Athlete:	How does the body change as it grows? How can exercise affect growth and development?	What causes sports injuries, and what effects do they have?
<u>Revised Generalization</u>	Growing up leads to changes in independence and interdependence.	Change in one area is affected by and leads to related changes in other areas.
<u>Central Question</u>	How does growing up affect the ways living things depend upon each other?	What leads to change, and how does it lead to other change?
<u>Subquestions</u>	1. How do our senses help us to explore the world and become more independent? 2. How does change and growth affect animals' dependence, independence, and interdependence? 3. In what ways do humans and animals depend upon each other?	1. What are the results of changed perspectives? 2. What causes changes in the topology of an area? How does the topology of an area affect the living things in that area? 3. What effects do weather and climate have? 4. How can the environment be protected during change?

READER INVOLVEMENT

Focus on the theme you have been working on in chapters 1, 2, and 3.

1. Develop a web by brainstorming and building categories.
2. Select one or more categories for further study. Formulate questions for student inquiry using the perspectives of:

   Historian

   Writer

   Mathematician

   Scientist

   Artist

   Diverse occupations

   Any other appropriate vantage points

3. Look back at the generalizations you developed in chapter 3. Are these the ones you want to work with or are there new generalizations that have emerged from your questions? Remember to check selected generalizations against the criteria for significance:

   Is the big idea true over space and time?

   Does it broaden students' understanding of the world or what it means to be human?

   Is the big idea interdisciplinary?

   Does it lead to student inquiry?

4. Reflect on the creative and critical thinking processes that you used. In your journal, list them and give specific examples of each.

REFERENCES

Bloom, B. S. (1956). *Taxonomy of educational objectives: Book 1. Cognitive domain.* New York: McKay.

Guilford, J. P. (1971). *The analysis of intelligence.* New York: McGraw.

Lynch, J. (Producer). (1985). *It started with the Greeks. The day the universe changed: A personal view by James Burke* [Television series]. Los Angeles: Churchill Films.

Parnes, S. J., & Harding, H. F. (Eds.). (1962). *A source book for creative teaching.* New York: Charles Scribner's Sons.

Rutherford, F. J., & Ahlgren, A. (1990). *Science for all Americans.* New York: Oxford University Press.

Taba, H. (1967). Implementing thinking as an objective in social studies. In J. Fair & F. Shaftel (Eds.), *Effective thinking in the social studies.* Washington, DC: National Council for the Social Studies.

Torrance, E. P. (1970). *Creative learning and teaching.* New York: Dodd Mead.

Additional Reading

Gamberg, R., Kwak, W., Hutchings, M., & Altheim, J. (1988). *Learning and loving it: Theme studies in the classroom.* Portsmouth, NH: Heinemann.

Katz, L. G., & Chard, S. C. (1989). *Engaging children's minds: The project approach.* Norwood, NJ: Ablex.

Krogh, S. (1990). *The integrated early childhood curriculum.* New York: McGraw-Hill.

Chapter Five

Meeting Standards and
Mapping the Sequence

*T*he curriculum innovators whose work was described in chapter 2 grappled with the problem of ensuring that students developed requisite concepts and skills while engaging in studies that were relevant, interdisciplinary, and question driven. The same problem is still pertinent today.

Standards are necessary, but minimum requirements may be interpreted as maximum expectations. Interdisciplinary theme studies, if well designed and developed, will enable students to exceed required minimum standards. In addition, teachers who successfully use inquiry-based interdisciplinary approaches can influence state departments of education to move away from lists of specified content and skills toward more process-oriented expectations for student learning.

ADDRESSING THE DIFFERENT
SUBJECT AREAS OF THE CURRICULUM

Teachers are responsible for working within state and district curriculum guidelines, even when they are developing interdisciplinary theme studies. In most schools in the United States, teachers are bound by law to follow the guidelines that have been carefully developed to provide a common course of study for all students in the state or district. This is sound policy. Teachers are usually familiar only with the curriculum for their own grade level or subject area, while students move through the whole system and must have an articulated and sequenced course of study. The state or district curriculum can ensure that essential concepts and skills are presented in developmental sequence.

The traditional textbook-based curriculum frequently has limitations that can interfere with students' learning. It tends to be fragmented. The many textbooks used in the various subject areas can lead to redundancy in some places and gaps in others. Students may fail to make connections among the various subjects, even when the teacher attempts to show how one topic may be related to another.

Because textbooks are necessarily written to serve a large population and to present a great deal of information, there is often more emphasis upon facts than upon concepts or themes. Students typically learn *what* happened rather than *why* it occurred. In addition, textbooks tend to be didactic rather than question-driven, presenting facts and ideas rather than encouraging students to inquire and discover for themselves. And even though textbooks seem to get larger and heavier every year, the amount of material they are expected to contain is so extensive that topics and themes are rarely explored in depth.

Interdisciplinary theme studies can accomplish the major goals of the required curriculum and at the same time avoid the drawbacks of the traditional curriculum. With careful planning, the broad scope and sequence of the state or district curriculum can be followed, but without the redundancy, irrelevancy, and superficiality of the textbook-driven curriculum. (Ways in which textbooks can be used as resources in interdisciplinary theme studies are discussed in chapter 7.)

Education for the 21st century requires new paradigms. The new millennium will call for students who can handle large amounts of new information, who can make connections among a variety of ideas, and who know how to ask significant and relevant questions. At the same time, the complexities of contemporary society call for people who can think in many different ways and who use a variety of learning styles. Different ways of knowing must be understood and brought to bear upon the new challenges and opportunities of the 21st century. And people who may be expected to interact constantly with new ideas and who may change careers several times during their lives must be self-directed learners.

Interdisciplinary curriculum has the potential to develop the higher order critical and creative thinking skills of students, to enable them to see the deep connectedness of the universe and of their own lives, and to become lifelong inquirers and learners. The way in which we conceptualize interdisciplinary theme studies provides opportunities for students to construct meaning through a variety of learning styles and "multiple intelligences" (Gardner, 1983) (see chapter 1). At the same time, they enlarge their repertoire of learning strategies. Students do all this within the broad curriculum guidelines that have been established by those who see the larger picture of a child's education.

It follows, then, that those guidelines must provide a framework for designing interdisciplinary theme studies, so that the expected standards for each grade level are met and that teachers and students are held accountable for maintaining appropriate levels of learning and development. At the same time, theme studies encourage teachers and students to go beyond the narrow confines of the textbook while remaining within the state and district requirements.

How can this be achieved? Let's return to the fourth grade team as they continue their planning.

Feeling satisfied that they had produced a worthwhile framework for curriculum design, the teachers agreed to meet after school in 2 days and to bring their textbooks to the meeting. When they came together again, it was clear that each had done some thinking about how their theme study agreed with the regular curriculum.

"Look at our science text," Jose said excitedly. "The early chapters on flowering plants, animal behavior, food chains and food webs, and animal and plant adaptations are naturals for a theme study on changes in communities."

"The social studies text does too," Raynetta added. "Almost the entire book is devoted to ecological regions: the rain forest, northern forests, mountains, deserts, and grasslands. Take, for instance, the rain forest. We could study questions about location, geography, climate, and weather, plants and animals, life cycles of humans and nonhumans, and the ways human beings use the land, meet their needs, and trade with other groups."

Jose was smiling broadly. "Look at this," he directed, pointing to the section in the science text on changes in landforms and oceans. "We could compare landforms in each of the habitats discussed in the social studies text and their effects on living things."

"Why didn't we see those connections before?" Raynetta wondered aloud. "After all, each of us teaches from both texts."

"I think it's a mindset. You have to think in interdisciplinary ways to do this kind of teaching," Jose responded.

"What do you see as the major advantage of thinking in those ways?" Elizabeth asked.

"Perhaps it encourages you to probe a topic more deeply," Jose answered. "If I plan lessons on life cycles and only explore plants and animals, without reference to humans, I'm not likely to see really important ecological interrelationships. I may not come to understand how habitats influence all life forms, humans included, and how life forms, especially humans, influence habitats."

"But if you learn to look for those connections, you can help kids see them by pointing them out," Elizabeth said. "You don't have to go to all this trouble to develop new curriculum."

"I think that an important key is the concept of a question-driven curriculum, Raynetta added.

"Well," Nicole said. *"There are lots of questions in our science and social studies texts. Just about every chapter contains several."*

"They're useful questions," Raynetta said. *"But they're limited by some constraints. First, when the textbooks pose the question and then give answers, the opportunities for student inquiry are diminished. Second, the questions may not tap all interdisciplinary possibilities. Third, they may be questions that can help students begin thinking about the topic, but they're rarely as probing as the ones we've been asking. Our questions imply subquestions because they are 'meaty.' When each subquestion is answered, students can come to deeper understanding of the main question."*

"I'm not sure I understand your meaning," Nicole said.

"Let's say that our questions are more substantive than the text's questions," Raynetta answered. *"We've said that we don't know the answers to some of the questions we've asked. The text doesn't usually raise a question unless it gives the answer. And because it must cover a lot of information in relatively few pages, many of the questions and their answers give students a taste—a sample—of the topic. I think that fourth graders can handle a 'full course'."*

"Perhaps the best use of texts is to provide resources for student inquiry," Jose observed. *"The students can use them along with trade books and other resources."*

"In some cases." Elizabeth agreed only partially. *"But I see another problem. The only connection I see in the reading text is in the very last unit on changes. There are some stories and poems about the desert, an article about the forest and wetlands, and a poem about spring. There's a mystery that takes place in a marsh. The literature section is E. B. White's* The Trumpet of the Swan *[1970], which would work, I guess, but it's at the very end of the text. Our students won't be ready for that at the beginning of the school year. They need to develop so many skills first!"*

Jose looked through the reader. "What about Unit 2 on 'memories'?" he asks. "There's a tall tale and a ballad on Davy Crockett, an article about the history of the states, and even Tomie De Paola's The Legend of the Bluebonnet *[1983]. Wouldn't that fit with the study of plant life cycles and folkways of culture groups?"*

Raynetta also found some thematic possibilities in the reader. "The study of history is a natural," she told Elizabeth. *"Communities change over time. That's their history. Look at the story here about homesteading in Oklahoma, a family relocating in Alaska, and the recollections of a turn-of-the-century artist living in Georgia. There's even a play about discovering the past in the artifacts stored in an attic."*

Elizabeth nodded. "Maybe some of the section on memories could be studied while the children are working with plant and animal life cycles and adaptations in science. We could connect particular plants and animals indigenous to the locales in the stories. We could also study the effects of weather and climate on people," she added. *"But what about all those reading and language arts skills that we really have to develop in fourth grade? I'm troubled about not teaching the skills."*

"So am I," Nicole said. *"Even though we thought of some good questions from geometric and statistical perspectives to fit our theme studies, math seems to be a misfit in this enterprise. Look at the regular curriculum. We're supposed to study number concepts, place value, multiplication and division, fractions, and decimals. Those operations must be taught. We can't adopt a 'hit or miss' attitude about math skills. Our track record with math achievement isn't good enough for that."* She paused a moment, then suggested, *"Maybe math shouldn't be part of the theme study."*

"Maybe our first theme study shouldn't try to connect all the areas of the curriculum," Elizabeth said, building on Nicole's reservations. *"This one could be a science–social studies theme."*

Raynetta was concerned about the turn in thinking. *"Sometimes themes may connect only two or three areas of the curriculum,"* she acknowledged. *"But they're better when there is more complete integration. Can't we find more complete interdisciplinary possibilities in change in communities?"*

"Wait a minute," Jose answered. *"Skills—skills may suggest a way to get it together. We've said that fourth grade is a time for developing children's competence as learners. We've agreed that an important way to do that is to develop their abilities to inquire. And we're now saying that they need tools in math and language to help them be more critical and creative thinkers."*

"I see where you're headed," Raynetta said. *"We can use content from science and social studies to give the inquiry greater depth. . . ."*

"And draw on the language and math skills we're developing to enhance their explorations," Elizabeth added.

"They'll need to understand place value to study the economic issues of how production affects trade," Nicole observed. *"And multiplication facts and processes to study questions that involve land uses for food production. They'll need to know division facts and operations to figure ratios and proportions when comparing and contrasting demographics. And measurement skills will be important every time the children collect and analyze data."*

Elizabeth spoke about the language arts: *"Any library research they do will require them to use the study skills we teach: following directions, using alphabetical order, using the parts of a book and graphic aids, using the dictionary, encyclopedia, and other library resources. Knowing how to skim and scan the references they consult will be important. Decoding, comprehension, and vocabulary skills are critical, too."*

Nicole nodded. *"It'll work,"* she said, *"so long as we plan the scope and sequence of the various subject areas with care to interrelate them in meaningful ways."*

"That's why we need to have a central emphasis," Raynetta reminded everyone. *"We need to keep the big idea in mind. We sort of agreed that change is inevitable in communities. Do you want to revise that statement?"*

"If we look back at the web, it seems to me we're talking about how everything in a community is interrelated," Jose suggested.

"A change in one may affect a change in another," Elizabeth said.

"Like the 'domino effect,'" Raynetta observed.

"But not all things affect everything else," cautioned Nicole.

"How about this?" Elizabeth asked. *"Significant changes in communities affect other parts of those communities."*

"That's it!" the teachers chorused. *"That's our major generalization, our central idea."*

"Take that back to the team leaders, Raynetta," Nicole directed. *"Tell them that fourth grade wants to develop our theme, emphasizing skills development through the exploration of ecological concepts."*

"Write it down. Write it down," Raynetta said.

Elizabeth wrote the statement on a large sheet of newsprint.

"That's a universal 'truth,'" Nicole observed.

Jose chuckled. *"Then our overarching question is: How does change affect communities?"*

"We'll need to return to our questions, shaping them clearly to promote studies that are true to the central idea," Raynetta said.

"I don't think I can do much more this afternoon," Nicole responded. *"This is hard work."*

The others nodded.

"Let's get together tomorrow to see if we can lay out a preliminary scope and sequence, using the textbooks as an initial resource. Once we know which questions we'll keep for study, we can look to other resources."

"Like those excellent videotapes we can get from the teacher resource center," Elizabeth said.

"And people the children can interview," added Raynetta.

"Not to mention the library and CD-ROM resources," Jose said. *"If we get into historical changes, we have some excellent sources of artifacts in the museum."*

"We need to select and organize our questions next," Nicole said. *"But I'd like to share them with my students first to see what they think."*

"When can we meet again?" Jose asked.

The fourth grade teachers met promptly the next Monday to map out a tentative scope and sequence for the full year (Figure 5.1), using the textbooks as a guide.

This program became a framework for the selection of questions for their students' investigations. They knew, of course, that the program would change as they developed the curriculum with their students and the children suggested new questions for study. "The framework," Jose said, "will keep them on track." Nicole suggested that they needed it to keep them honest.

Figure 5.1
Fourth grade framework scope and sequence

First Six Weeks	Second Six Weeks	Third Six Weeks	Fourth Six Weeks	Fifth Six Weeks	Sixth Six Weeks
Process Themes:					
Focusing and Data gathering	Organizing; Classifying; Hypothesizing	Predicting outcomes	Analyzing; Isolating variables	Inferring; Generalizing	Integrating; Evaluating
Science					
Life cycles Adaptations	Rain forests	Northern forests	Mountains	Deserts	Grasslands
Flowering plants; Animal behavior Food chains and webs	Animal and plant adaptations Human body Measuring weather	Electricity and magnetism	Changes in landforms	Work/energy Light/sound	
Social Studies					
Local community The world: climate/shape/ maps	Location, geography, climate, and weather ————————————————————————————————→				
	Life and life styles/cultures ————————————————————————————————→				
	Land use ————————————————————————————————→				
	Agriculture/economy/products ——————————————————————→				
	History ————————————————————————————————→				
	Borneo Puerto Rico Sierra Leone	Canada Russia	Alps Andes Appalachians	Peru Arabia United States ————→	Africa Argentina

Figure 5.1
continued

First Six Weeks	Second Six Weeks	Third Six Weeks	Fourth Six Weeks	Fifth Six Weeks	Sixth Six Weeks
Language Arts/Reading					
Memories: Historical treatment		"How the forest grew"		Changes: How humans affect environment	
Skills for reading and research -->					
Math					
Basic facts; Number concepts; Place value	Time and measurement; Addition and subtraction	Multiplication----------> Division---------->		Fractions------------> Two-digit divisors Decimals Statistics Probability Graphing	
		Geometry ----------> Measurement ---------->			

▼ READER INVOLVEMENT

1. Look back over the fourth grade team planning. How did they go about developing their theme study within the framework of the given curriculum?

2. Now look at the description of the first and seventh grade teams as they developed their theme studies. How were the processes alike? How were they different?

3. What are some next steps for the fourth grade team to take as they develop their theme study?

At this point, the teachers in the first and seventh grade teams turned to their required district or school curriculum guidelines and the texts that they already had for each content area. They knew that the texts would serve as only one resource among many others, but they also realized that the texts were closely related to the state and district guidelines, and thought that since they already had a class set of each text, they could use the books as a useful resource, especially for whole-group or small-group work.

As they had suspected from their previous knowledge of the curriculum, the initial generalization that they had selected could be supported by the curriculum guidelines and the texts. Now they began to select those areas of the curriculum that were clearly related to the theme.

The first grade teachers decided to develop an extended theme study for each 6-week marking period. They felt that the theme was rich enough to engage the students for most of their instructional time, and to encompass all the subject areas. They selected three major generalizations for exploration, one for each 6-week period in the first part of the year. They decided not to plan any further ahead, since they did not really know their children very well at this early stage of the school year, and they wanted to leave plenty of flexibility for later planning with the students. They did, however, want to have a common broad curriculum for all of the classes at that grade level. Figure 5.2 shows the result of their planning thus far.

The seventh grade team also developed their own web related to the initial generalization, and brainstormed on the types of questions that could be explored, using varied perspectives to enrich the pool of questions. Since the school was departmentalized, and each teacher felt responsible for addressing specialized content and skills, the teachers decided to develop four separate theme studies during the year, each of which would use a different perspective to help students develop the major generalization. The first theme study, on *perspectives,* allowed the science and social studies teachers to team-teach a unit on map and globe skills, which was represented in the science and the social studies textbooks, while the math teacher saw this as an opportunity to review the concepts of ratio, proportion, and area as the students worked with maps of different scale, projection, and scope. The language arts and reading teachers agreed to provide the social studies and science teachers with some selections from the reading text that dealt with flight and the new perspec-

Figure 5.2
Grade 1 overview of year

Generalization: Growing up leads to changes in dependence and interdependence.				
Six-Week Periods	Reading	Math	Social Studies	Science
1 Our senses help us to explore the world.	pp. 12–18: "Our Five Senses"	Ch. 1: Classification, patterns, counting 1–9	Unit 1: "About You"	Ch. 1: "Our Senses"
2 Animals change and grow in different ways.	p. 22: "The Frog"; p. 42: "A Secret"; p. 95: "Little Mouse Goes Exploring"; p.141: "Animal Tracks and Trails"	Ch. 2: Counting to 20; graphing (Meal worms); graphing (Animal tracks); introduction to measurement (informal)	Unit 4: "Changes Around Us", esp. p. 105: "The Changing Seasons"	Ch. 4: "Animal Lives"; Ch. 8: "The Weather and Seasons"
3 We depend upon each other.	Unit 2: "Helping Each Other"	Ch. 7: Measurement (continued work on Chs. 3–6: Addition and subtraction)	Unit 2: "Families"; Unit 3: "Our Needs and Wants"; Unit 5: "Our Country"	Ch. 4, Lesson 2: "Caring for a Pet"; Ch. 9: "Working" (continued work related to major generalization)
4–6 (to be planned)				

tives of the world that came from these adventures. For their major contribution to the study, however, they decided to examine the theme of *perspectives* from a more human and aesthetic viewpoint, examining styles of art, music, literature, and writing.

The second and third studies linked science and social studies in an examination of landforms and of weather and climate, and their effects upon human life and existence. For this theme study, they decided that the students could select particular topographic and regional areas of the United States and Canada and of the world for intensive study related to general scientific and social studies concepts. The language arts and reading teachers decided to support this individual or group study by helping the students to use their reading and writing skills in their inquiry studies. The math teacher agreed to provide specialized instruction that would help the students with map reading, scale drawings, measurement, graphs, and statistics.

The final theme study was to be a fully integrated unit on the environment, with each teacher working with the students to raise and explore questions about the protection of the environment. They felt that by late in the year the students would know the teachers well enough to be able to seek them out for special assistance with individual and group studies. Like the first grade teachers, the seventh grade team decided not to plan in too much detail for the second semester of the year until they knew their students and understood their special interests, strengths, and needs. Figure 5.3 shows the broad scope and sequence for the seventh grade.

Open-Ended, Learner-Centered Approaches to Theme Development

As we have indicated earlier, there are many approaches to the development of interdisciplinary theme studies. The direction selected by an individual teacher or teaching team depends on many factors, including district requirements, teacher comfort levels, and availability of resources. The teachers in the fourth grade team decided to work closely with the textbooks they were using because those resources defined their curriculum standards. Teachers who have greater latitude in designing curriculum often like to develop theme studies in more open, learner-centered ways.

Some of the most challenging theme studies derive from student-initiated questions. James Beane (1990) advocates theme studies that are planned with students and that draw on their special interests and concerns. Krough (1990) sees children as quite capable of generating themes for study that are both inherently interesting and substantive. Vars (1987) believes that the skillful teacher can guide students toward probing explorations from almost any starting point of interest. The concept of an inquiry-oriented curriculum encourages this open-ended learner-centered approach to theme development. Teachers who listen to their students' questions and expressions of interest will know where to begin. Most will start with students' ideas or

Figure 5.3
Grade 7 overview of year

Generalization: *Changes in one area result from and lead to changes in other areas.*

Six-Week Periods	Reading	Math	Social Studies	Science
1 Perspectives	Unit 1: "Surprises"	Ch. 2: Review ratio, prop, area	Chs. 1, 2: Map and globe skills (2 weeks)	Chs. 1, 3: Map and globe skills (2 weeks)
2 (no theme study)	Unit 2	Chs. 5, 6	Basic geography, U.S. and Canada	Unit 2
3 Landforms	Unit 3: "Human Settlement"	Ch. 4: Geometry; Ch. 6: Fractions; Ch. 7: Measurement	Unit 2: U.S. and Canada: group research	Units 5 and 6: "The Surface of the Earth"; "The History of the Earth"
4 Living on the Earth	Unit 4: "Survival"	Ch. 8: Scale; Ch. 9: Percent; Ch. 10: Geometry and Measurement; Ch. 11: Statistics	Units 3–10: World Geography: Group and individual study (first)	Unit 3: "Air and Water"
5 (no theme study)	Unit 6	Chs. 13, 14, 15	Group and individual study (second)	Unit 4
6 Protecting the Environment	Unit 5: "Living in the Future"	Ch. 12: Probability Applying all skills learned	Review all units from environmental perspective	Unit 7: "Natural Resources"

queries—things they are wondering about. The teacher serves as guide and mentor by helping students refine their questions and by drawing additional, researchable questions from the group. Teachers become coinquirers as they participate in organizing the search, finding resources, uncovering clues, and making discoveries.

Open-ended inquiry may occur at any point in the development of theme studies. Some theme studies may be initiated by learner interests. Others, introduced by the teacher, may be directed and extended by student questions as the study develops. Invariably, student-initiated studies have the potential to extend learning beyond conventional expectations for any age group or grade level because they free students and teachers to explore their own questions to the degree they wish, and in the directions they choose. The open-ended, learner-centered approach to theme studies respects the integrity of students' interests and the human drive to learn.

SEARCHING FOR PATTERNS

In designing interdisciplinary theme studies, teachers and students use the same processes. "Searching for patterns," one of the habits of mind described in chapter 1, occurs when the general sequence for interdisciplinary theme studies is developed, connecting ideas from across the subject areas. This requires organizational thinking as topics are integrated into themes and as associations are articulated among separate units to build the larger framework of a cohesive curriculum.

This process of searching for patterns involves teachers and students in information gathering, decision making, remembering, comparing and contrasting, organizing, analyzing, and synthesizing. These cognitive operations have been identified as important for students to develop by authorities such as Beyer, Marzano, Gubbins, and Bloom, and are found in the California and Oregon skills lists (Willis, 1992) and in the Texas "Essential Elements" (Texas Education Agency, 1991).

DETERMINING THE SCOPE AND ORGANIZATION OF THE THEME STUDY

When teachers determine the extent of a theme study, they make a number of choices. These choices can depend upon the age and developmental level of the students, the educational goals the teachers have for their students, the given curriculum, time limitations and constraints, and other factors that emerge in the complexity of schooling.

Configuration

Figure 5.4 provides some guidelines that teachers can use as they decide how to organize a theme study. Teachers make choices along various continuums as they ask themselves the following questions:

1. *Should we include all the disciplines or subject areas, or does the theme study lend itself to working in one or two major areas?* The seventh grade team in the earlier example determined that map and globe study should be a central focus for science and social studies, with some support from the mathematics teacher, while the first grade team decided to incorporate all the subject areas in their planned theme studies for the first half of the year.

2. *How long should the theme study last?* The first grade team expected that each theme study would take about 6 weeks. The seventh grade team began the year with a 2-week study of map and globe skills, and ended the year with a 6-week unit on the environment. Theme studies can be limited to a week, or may extend over an entire year, depending upon such variables as student interest, scope and significance of the theme study, and how it fits the required curriculum.

3. *Should the classroom organization be primarily whole group, small group, or individual?* Of course, there is opportunity for all types of grouping within any study. However, there may be more emphasis on whole-group exploration of a topic, as in the first grade unit on the five senses, or there may be a deliberate effort to enable the students to conduct small-group or individual inquiry, as in the seventh grade unit on "Living on the Earth," where the students each selected two areas of the world to research in depth over an extended period of time.

4. *Should the study be mainly concentrated, with a clear beginning, middle, and end to the study, as in the first grade theme study on "Animals"; or should it be expansive, where the students share in common experiences and then select separate areas for further exploration and research?* In the seventh grade study on "Landforms," after a whole-group study of the geography of the United States and Canada, the students each selected one area, such as the Central Plains or the Pacific Coast, for individual and group study.

Figure 5.4
Configuration of choices teachers make as they organize a theme study

```
Selected content areas <----------------> All content areas
Short-term <----------------------------------> Long-term
Whole group <---------> Small group <---------> Individual
Concentrated <------------------------------> Expansive
```

None of these questions is intended to force an either/or choice, or to limit teachers' flexibility. Rather, they are designed to provide a framework within which to plan unique theme studies related clearly to instructional purposes, the strengths and needs of the learners, and the opportunities and demands of the instructional environment.

Emphasis

Another important set of choices is related to the emphasis of the study, as depicted in Figure 5.5. Depending upon the particular needs and goals of a group of students at a given time, the emphasis of the study may be upon *concepts, factual content,* or *processes and skills,* or may encompass all of these emphases equally. Naturally, any theme study should be designed to teach concepts, factual content, and processes (including skills), but the emphasis may be shifted among them. For example, the seventh grade team decided to spend the first part of the year exploring the *concept* of *perspectives.* The social studies and science teachers chose to explore this concept through a brief study of maps and globes. They were teaching processes and skills, but the major focus was on the idea that maps and globes provide varied perspectives through which to view the world. During the same time period, the language arts and reading teachers decided to teach the concept of *perspectives* by involving the students in the reading and writing of works that clearly showed varied perspectives on events and on human behavior.

Content is an important part of any education. While concepts and processes are more universal in character, concepts and processes cannot be separated from factual content. Content knowledge is an inevitable and essential part of inquiry. We do not inquire in a vacuum. Furthermore, content knowledge enables the inquirer to move forward in the processes of inquiry. Some theme studies therefore need to focus on factual content. For example, the first grade theme study on "Animals" was designed to help children acquire a great deal of information about the animal world

Figure 5.5
Emphasis

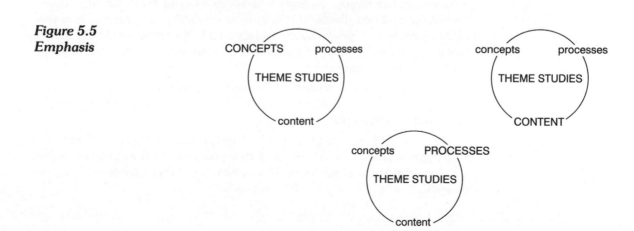

and how animals grow and change. This knowledge enabled the children to understand the concept of growth in a way that would not have been possible if they had examined only their own growth and had relied only upon their own prior experiences.

Another emphasis may be on *processes*. While the general content of the fourth grade and seventh grade curriculums in social studies and science is very similar, the approach to learning this content is different at each grade level. Fourth grade students are at a stage where the conscious development of higher order thinking skills is of particular significance. At this stage, for example, children are often required to shift from reading simple stories to coping with the more complicated and demanding structure and concepts of subject-area textbooks (Anderson, Hiebert, Scott, & Wilkinson, 1985). The fourth grade study of "Northern Forests" therefore focused on the processes of *predicting outcomes* and *hypothesizing*. At the seventh grade level, the students need to expand their abilities to think more abstractly and to develop individual research strategies. Their study of "Landforms" therefore involved the students in individual and group study of abstract concepts.

All theme studies are designed to help the student learn concepts, content, and processes and skills. It is up to the teacher to select the major emphasis for any particular theme study, dependent upon student interests, needs, and developmental stages, and, at the same time, to make sure that these interlocking entities are all addressed.

▼ READER INVOLVEMENT

1. Select one or more of the generalizations that you checked for significance in chapter 4. Look carefully at the textbooks and the curriculum guidelines for your grade level to see if your generalization can be taught through the major concepts and topics identified in these resources.

2. Develop a *broad* scope and sequence for interdisciplinary theme studies that incorporate the major concepts and ideas of your required curriculum. Remember that your theme studies can be of varying lengths, and that they do not have to incorporate *every* subject area to the same extent. Be sure to provide enough flexibility for students to play an active part in the development of the theme study.

3. Examine the questions related to *configuration* and the different *emphases* identified in this chapter. Where does your scope and sequence fit in terms of *configuration* and *emphasis?*

4. In the section of your journal reserved for personal reflection, identify the thinking processes or habits of mind that you employed as you developed your broad scope and sequence. In what ways did they enable you to complete this task?

REFERENCES

Anderson, R. C., Hiebert, E. H., Scott, J. A., & Wilkinson, I. A. G. (1985). *Becoming a nation of readers.* Washington, DC: The National Institute of Education, U.S. Department of Education.

Beane, J. A. (1990). *Middle school curriculum: From rhetoric to reality.* Columbus, OH: National Middle School Association.

De Paola, Tomie (1983) *The legend of the bluebonnet: An old tale of Texas.* New York: Putnam

Gardner, H. (1983). *Frames of mind: The theory of multiple intelligences.* New York: Basic Books.

Krough, S. (1990). *The integrated early childhood curriculum.* New York: McGraw-Hill.

Texas Education Agency. (1991). *State Board of Education rules for curriculum: Essential elements.* Austin, TX: Author.

Vars, G. F. (1987). *Interdisciplinary teaching in the middle grades.* Columbus, OH: National Middle School Association.

White, E. B. (1970). *The trumpet of the swan.* New York: Harper & Row.

Willis, S. (June, 1992). Teaching thinking. *ASCD Curriculum Update 34(5),* 1–8.

Chapter Six

Designing Learning Activities

Any curriculum presents a vision for student learning that is based on philosophical premises for education and perceptions of learning. Interdisciplinary theme studies are designed from the beliefs that the most meaningful education, especially for life in the 21st century, is

- ▼ Integrated, finding meaning in the ways that the content of the several fields of study is interrelated;

- ▼ Holistic, focusing on principles, theories, laws, issues, and questions that have universal significance;

- ▼ Inquiry-oriented, inviting students to explore questions through varied types of research, to use diverse resources, and to develop their thinking processes; and

- ▼ Constructivist, enabling students to derive their own meanings through the studies they are given and those they are encouraged to develop for themselves.

The construct of any interdisciplinary theme study should be true to the vision for student learning derived from these premises. We can determine a theme study's consistency with these premises by examining its anatomy.

We have been tracing the way in which a theme study on *patterns of change* was begun with a committee of grade-level representatives and developed differently by teacher teams in grades 1, 4, and 7. The seventh grade team stated its big idea as follows: *Patterns of change: Changes in one area result from and lead to changes in other areas.* That big idea meets the four criteria for significance discussed in chapter 3:

1. It is true over space and time;
2. It can broaden the students' understanding of the world and what it means to be human;
3. It is interdisciplinary; and
4. It can lead to student inquiry.

UNIT STUDIES

The team selected several *unit studies* to develop this big idea during one school year: "Perspectives," "Landforms," "Living on the Earth," and "Protecting the Environment." Each meets the criteria for unit studies:

1. Is the unit interdisciplinary?
2. Does it fit a definable time frame?
3. Does it meet established curriculum requirements?
4. Does it address one or more aspects of the big idea?

The design process now turns to developing the unit studies in more detail. In a question-driven, inquiry-oriented curriculum, these units are headed by questions. The Eugene School District 4J in Oregon demonstrates how *focus questions* can define and develop the units in its *Education 2000 Elementary Integrated Curriculum* (1991). Our seventh grade example uses *central questions* and *subquestions* in similar ways, for compiling sets of activities or *activity clusters*.

The seventh grade English, math, science, social studies, and reading teachers shared ideas on how they might develop the unit, "Living on the Earth," so that it would permit them to meet the required curriculum, use their available resources, contribute to the students' understanding of the big idea they had selected, and involve students in exploration. They worked with students to formulate several questions that they considered central to the unit's study (Figure 6.1). Each central question became the source of subquestions for investigative activities that could meet the learning styles and needs of their students.

Figure 6.1
Anatomy of the seventh grade team's theme study

Big Idea: Patterns of Change: Changes in one area result from and lead to changes in other areas.

Unit Study: Living on the Earth

<u>Unit Concepts</u>

Concept 1	Concept 2	Concept *n*
Food production in natural environments is affected by weather and climate.	Human survival requires adaptations capable of meeting different needs and responding to different conditions.	

<u>Central Questions</u>

1. How do weather and climate affect food production in different regions of the world?	2. How do humans adapt to meet the challenges in their lives?	*n*

<u>Subquestions</u>

a, b, c, *n*	a, b, c, *n*	a, b, c, *n*
a. How are weather and climate interrelated? b. In what ways do weather and climate affect food production?	a. What kinds of challenges do human face? b. In what ways do humans adapt?	

ACTIVITY CLUSTERS

With central questions and subquestions in place, the seventh grade teaching team could begin to define sets of learning activities to help students explore each of the subquestions. These clusters became the bases for several lessons during the unit study and offered teachers options for lesson planning. The teachers used the format shown in Figure 6.2 for learning activity clusters that helped them to keep in mind several guidelines for interdisciplinary instruction:

1. Providing for different ways of knowing and thinking
2. Maximizing interdisciplinary connections among the subjects
3. Staying true to the standards of the regular curriculum
4. Using diverse resources for student inquiry

Figure 6.2
Activity clusters

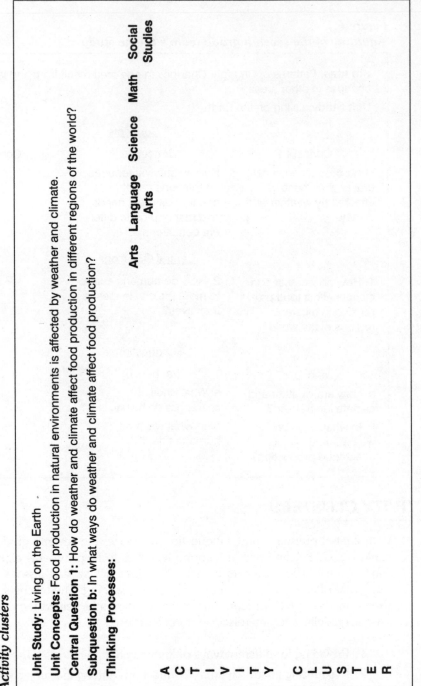

Unit Study: Living on the Earth

Unit Concepts: Food production in natural environments is affected by weather and climate.

Central Question 1: How do weather and climate affect food production in different regions of the world?

Subquestion b: In what ways do weather and climate affect food production?

Thinking Processes:

	Arts	Language Arts	Science	Math	Social Studies

A
C
T
I
V
I
T
Y

C
L
U
S
T
E
R

Modes of Inquiry

In chapter 1, we discussed three major categories of thinking modalities: symbolic, imagic, and affective. These represent different ways of constructing and expressing meanings. Individuals differ in how they use these modes. In *The Unschooled Mind*, Gardner (1991) underscores the importance of planning instruction that engages special intelligences to maximize learning. When teachers consider the types of activities to include among sets of options for students' exploration of any subquestions, they must consider how well these options promote student use of the different modalities.

For students who prefer symbolic modes, teachers must ask, *What types of learning activities require thinking with words, numbers, or other symbol systems?*

For primarily imagic thinkers, teachers must ask, *What types of learning activities require visual, spatial, tonal, or kinesthetic–sensate thinking?*

For students who have strong affective tendencies in learning, teachers must ask, *What types of learning activities engage students with feelings and emotions that can color, direct, and drive an investigation?*

The role of these modalities should be considered in every phase of planning for interdisciplinary theme learning.

Habits of Mind

In chapter 1, we also described the habits of mind that appear to be shared by inquirers in all fields of study. They include:

1. Finding and keeping focus
2. Simplifying questions and problems
3. Attentiveness
4. Thinking fluently and flexibly
5. Forming hunches
6. Designing tests and experimenting
7. Searching for patterns
8. Using models and metaphors
9. Finding elegant solutions
10. Risk taking
11. Cooperating and collaborating
12. Competing
13. Perseverance and self-discipline

These intellectual habits incorporate the processes that are often called "thinking skills" in the educational literature and that appear in state and district curriculum standards as process objectives for student achievement. Any curriculum that intends to develop students' learning-to-learn skills must attend to these habits of mind.

Working with the subquestion *In what ways do weather and climate affect food production?*, the seventh grade teachers in our example thought about the kinds of explorations their students could do to research the questions. They noted that several regions of the world were included in the social studies texts: Latin America, South America, Africa, the Middle East, southern Asia, Southeast Asia, eastern Asia, Western Europe, Eastern Europe, Australia, and the Pacific Islands. The science text had sections on the measurement of weather conditions (e.g., pressure, temperature, relative humidity, and wind direction) and cause of weather (e.g., fronts, winds, ocean currents, and the hydrologic cycle). In mathematics, the regular curriculum called for study of ratios and proportions, geometric concepts and the calculation of areas, statistical computations and interpretations, including means, medians, and modes, and drawing to scale. The literary selections in the seventh grade reading text did not address interrelationships of weather and food production but had several selections about human responses to hardship. The teachers decided that these stories could be explored through Central Question 2, *How do humans adapt to meet the challenges in their lives?*, and that the language arts components of studies of Central Question 1, *How do weather and climate affect food production in different regions of the world?*, would develop note-taking and writing skills and the ability to read graphics such as tables, graphs, and maps. The students would also read varied reference texts on the geographic regions selected for study. The reading teacher offered to look for an appropriate novel to read with the students. There seemed to be no substantive applications to the fine arts through the study of this question about the effects of weather and climate on food production. The teachers were resistant to the temptation to insert some drawing activities into the studies. If the students chose to draw or photograph weather conditions to record and illustrate some of their research findings, they would provide needed guidance, but the teachers felt that this would be more accidental than integral to the exploration. They reminded one another that not every activity or activity cluster had to be totally interdisciplinary. The important objective was to maintain a balance across the curriculum throughout the several activity clusters of each unit study. They were satisfied with their determinations. Later, another teacher would help them see new possibilities in the learning activities in that cluster.

The teachers agreed on several activities for student exploration of Subquestion b under Central Question 1, *In what ways do weather and climate affect food production?*, recording them on the activity cluster form. They determined which areas of the curriculum were represented by each. They researched resources that could be brought into the classroom and that students could access in the school and community. Teachers of each of the subject areas would develop their specific lessons using this range of resources, including appropriate sections of their textbooks. In looking over the activity clusters, they noted that several thinking processes would be developed. These would be detailed in the objectives for specific lesson plans. In this activity cluster, they agreed to focus on the habit of mind that seemed central and critical.

▼ READER INVOLVEMENT

Read the activity clusters in Figure 6.3, described for the study of Subquestion b of Central Question 1, *In what ways do weather and climate affect food production? Which habits of mind would you select as central and critical to these activities?*

Student Inquiry Across the Fields of Study

At this point in the planning, it is important to check the activity clusters to find opportunities for student inquiry in the different subject areas. For example, the seventh grade science teacher in our scenario found ways for the students to apply the knowledge and skills they had developed during their study of Subquestion a, *How are weather and climate interrelated?*, by gathering data on climate and weather conditions in the respective regions. These data could be found in international indexes, atlases, and almanacs. The social studies teacher thought that political and topographic maps would be useful for student study of relationships between population densities and physical features and political boundaries. Using some of the same data, with appropriate additional raw data, the math teacher saw opportunities for calculations of ratios and proportions, and varied statistical treatments of quantitative information about populations and food production, and, perhaps, price indexes for traded produce. The language arts teacher saw clear opportunities for students to learn how to record data in written form. Discussions about alternative ways of recording data led the teachers to consult the art teacher. Citing, among other sources, Tufte's (1983) *The Visual Display of Quantitative Information,* the art teacher explained how students could make pictorial maps and graphs that use symbol, shading, color, visual metaphors, representational and abstract designs, black-and-white and color drawings and photographs, and two- and three-dimensional images of aesthetic presentations of numerical data. When the art teacher talked about the theory and aesthetics of graphics, the others saw how his contribution would add special distinction to their interdisciplinary theme study. They immediately noted the connection with fine arts on their record of activity clusters and, as they considered ways of thinking that could be developed through this activity cluster, they noted the centrality of one particular habit of mind: using models and metaphors. The importance of direct experience and personal involvement for student learning caused the teachers to consider another possibility for an activity cluster. They added to their set one that would encourage students' individual investigation of local food production sites and the people and conditions that exist there (Figure 6.4). They thought that this might serve as a transition to the second central question in the unit study: *How do humans adapt to meet the challenges in their lives?* (Figure 6.1).

Figure 6.3
Activity clusters

Unit Study: Living on the Earth

Unit Concepts: Food production in natural environments is affected by weather and climate.

Central Question 1: How do weather and climate affect food production in different regions of the world?

Subquestion b: In what ways do weather and climate affect food production?

Thinking Processes:

	Arts	Language Arts	Science	Math	Social Studies
A C T I V I T Y Group Activities 1. Study each geographic region to discover its characteristics for food production: location and physical area; land area and proportion; quantities of food produced. Use resources such as topographical and product maps, and data tables regarding food production.		✓	✓	✓	✓
C L U S T E R 2. Investigate natural factors that affect food production in each area: e.g., topographic features, rainfall, temperature, wind patterns, ocean currents, and other factors such as volcanic eruptions, floods, and earthquakes. Consult varied resources including maps, weather data, and videotapes of natural events in each region.			✓	✓	
3. Investigate the lives of people involved in food production in specific regions, searching for evidence of the effects of climate and weather. Examine evidence such as personal testimonies in written and recorded forms and newspaper reports of events associated with food production.		✓			✓

Figure 6.4
Activity clusters

Unit Study: Living on the Earth

Unit Concepts: Food production in natural environments is affected by weather and climate.

Central Question 1: How do weather and climate affect food production in different regions of the world?

Subquestion b: In what ways do weather and climate affect food production?

Thinking Processes: Using Models and Metaphors

ACTIVITY — Group Activities	Arts	Language Arts	Science	Math	Social Studies
1. Study each geographic region to discover its characteristics for food production: location and physical area; land area and proportion; quantities of food produced.	✓	✓	✓	✓	✓
2. Investigate natural factors that affect food production in each area: e.g., topographic features, rainfall, temperature, wind patterns, ocean currents, and other factors such as volcanic eruptions, floods, and earthquakes.	✓	✓	✓		
3. Investigate the lives of people involved in food production in specific regions, searching for evidence of the effects of climate and weather.	✓	✓	✓	✓	
4. Visit local sites for food production and explore their historical records to compare former and contemporary character of the site. Link older and contemporary character to influences of weather and climate and to any human challenges the research uncovers.	✓	✓		✓	✓

▼ READER INVOLVEMENT

Select a central question for the interdisciplinary theme study you are planning. Identify several subquestions under that central question. Using the form for designing learning activity clusters (Figure 6.5), determine the resources available for student explorations. Develop activity clusters for your selected grade level that would help students discover answers to the questions and guide them to develop the big idea of your interdisciplinary theme study. For each activity cluster, ask yourself these questions:

1. In what ways does the generalization (big idea) meet the criteria for significance? In what ways can you adjust the statement of the generalization (big idea) to better meet the criteria? Does it address questions of *why* and *how*?

2. In what ways does the main question help the children *discover* the generalization (big idea)? In what ways can you adjust the question?

3. In what ways do the subquestions help the children explore the main question? In what ways can you make a clearer connection?

LEARNING ACTIVITIES

Once activity clusters are in place, teachers can begin to plan more detailed learning activities. There are elements that should be included in the planning of any learning activity, and making a written record of these elements preserves the integrity of the activity, facilitates communication among different teachers or between teachers and administration, and provides for accountability and evaluation.

Plans for learning activities may take various forms, depending upon the requirements of the school or district and the preferences of the individual teacher or the grade-level team. It is possible that several lesson plans may be in operation at the same time with different individuals or groups. The format presented in Figure 6.6 includes the elements that teachers need to keep in mind.

Introduction

The introduction section in the Learning Activity Plan shows clearly its place in the interdisciplinary unit study. This section includes:

Grade level/developmental level: While it may not be necessary to indicate the grade level on each plan, it may be useful to note the developmental level of the students. In the primary grades, this might include some indication of the reading level, motor abilities, or numerical proficiency of the group. In all grades, this section might indicate prior learnings students are expected to bring to the activity. This section also allows for the identification of students with special abilities or needs.

Figure 6.5
Activity cluster plan

Unit Study:

Unit Concepts:

Central Question _____ :

Subquestion _____ :

Thinking Processes:

	Arts	Language Arts	Science	Math	Social Studies
A C T I V I T Y C L U S T E R					

Figure 6.6
Learning activity plan

Introduction
Grade Level/Developmental Level: _____
Interdisciplinary Unit Study:
_____

Central Question:
_____

Subquestion:
_____

Objectives:
The students will know that:
_____

_____

The students will use these cognitive processes:
_____

The students will develop these affective abilities:
_____

Materials and Resources: (including primary and community resources)
_____

_____

Description of Learning Activity:

Means of Evaluation:
_____

Subject Areas and Curriculum Standards:

Visual Arts	Music	Language	Mathematics	P.E./Health	Science	Social Studies	Other
_____	____	_____	_____	_____	____	_____	____

Interdisciplinary unit study: This is taken from the Activity Clusters form (Figure 6.2), and indicates the major focus of the unit.

Central question: This is the broad question for this part of the unit.

Subquestion: This is the specific question, related to the central question, that will be directly explored through the learning activity.

Objectives

The objectives indicate clearly the learning that the teacher expects to occur through completion of the learning activity. Objectives cannot, of course, delineate all the learning that occurs, nor should they. Any learning activity has boundless possibilities for individual learning by students, depending upon their prior experience, their developmental level, their abilities, and their interests and aptitudes. However, teachers are accountable for knowing what students are expected to learn, and objectives help to provide direction and criteria for the learning activity. As the theme study develops, student inquiry will indicate new directions for exploration. These emergent objectives need to be recognized by the teacher, who will then select and relate them to the major focus of the study.

There are three main types of objectives that address

▼ The factual content to be learned,

▼ The processes to be developed, and

▼ The affective abilities to be nurtured.

Each of these is closely interrelated in any activity. It is unlikely that students will learn content without using cognitive processes or experiencing the impact of attitudes, interests, and appreciations. However, for the purpose of accountability and clarity, it is helpful for the teacher to articulate the specific projected learning in each category.

Notice that these objectives are not written in terms of exactly what the students will *do*, as is the case in some behavioral objectives. This difference arises from the philosophical and pedagogical basis of the inquiry-driven curriculum. The focus is upon the students' understanding of

▼ Concepts and significant "big ideas,"

▼ Cognitive processes, and

▼ Attitudes that lead to continued exploration and investigation.

The students will know that: This phrase is important. Note that the teacher is required to state with precision the content that will be learned. For example, a content objective for one of the learning activities in the activity cluster described above might be: *The students will know that people adapt to geographic challenges by relo-*

cating, by diversifying, and by using technology. Note that this is more specific than saying *Students will know* how *people adapt to geographic challenges.*

The amount of detail depends upon the scope of the learning activity. Content objectives may be very specific, e.g.: *The students will know that there are twelve inches in a linear foot.* Or, they may be broader, e.g.: *Students will know that objects may be measured using standard or nonstandard units.*

The scope of the content objective is related to the scope of the learning activity.

The students will use these cognitive processes: It is sometimes difficult to put names to the types of cognitive processes that are the objectives of a learning activity. Kovalik and Olsen (1991) developed an "Inquiry-Builder Chart" (Figure 6.7) that incorporates and synthesizes several models of thinking:

▼ Bloom's (1984) taxonomy of cognitive objectives: knowledge, comprehension, application, analysis, evaluation, and synthesis;

▼ Five of Gardner's (1983) "frames of mind": logico-mathematical, linguistic, musical, bodily–kinesthetic, and spatial; and

▼ The "scientific thinking processes" described in the California Department of Education's (1990) *Science Framework for California Public Schools: Kindergarten Through Grade Twelve:* observing, communicating, comparing, organizing (ordering and categorizing), relating, inferring, and applying.

This synthesis provides a model for identifying cognitive processes to be taught. It is impossible to identify all the cognitive processes that may be learned through an activity. The objective should identify those processes that are the major focus of the activity. Thus, an activity that involves students in open-ended research might be designed to help students *identify, locate,* and *describe,* while the compiling of a report might require students to *organize, compose,* and *assemble.*

The students will develop these affective abilities: As we have indicated in chapter 1, the productive thinkers of the world seem to have developed "habits of mind" that include both cognitive and affective processes. The affective processes include: finding and keeping a focus, attentiveness, risk taking, cooperating and collaborating, competing, persevering, and self-discipline. As students engage in inquiry, it is important that they, as well as their teachers, experience the feelings and emotions that make inquiry possible and rewarding. Not all of these will be learned in a single activity or even in one activity cluster. However, over the course of a theme study, there should be opportunities for students to develop affectively as well as cognitively.

Description of Learning Activity

The format and the amount of detail required by an individual teacher for a specific learning activity depends on a large number of factors. For example, the less familiar the learning activity, the more detail the teacher may wish to include. Some teachers can do much of their planning in their heads and like to record a brief summary of

Figure 6.7
Inquiry-builder chart

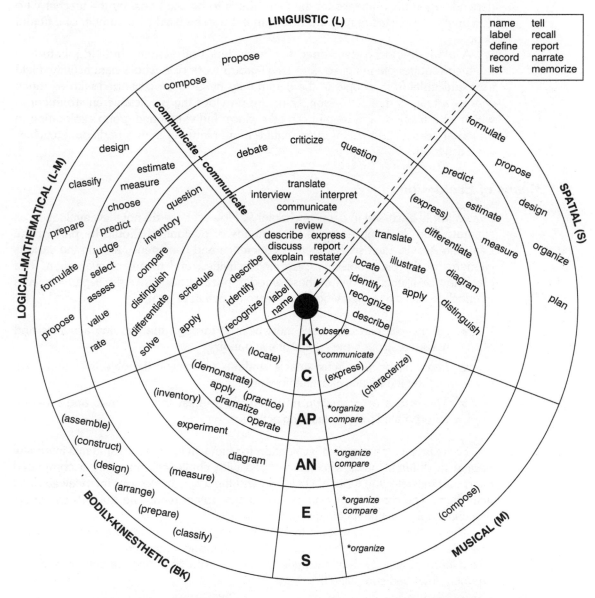

name	tell
label	recall
define	report
record	narrate
list	memorize

*science thinking processes

( ) indicates verbs that would be appropriate for this intelligence if specifically designed to be

Source: S. J. Kovalik & K. D. Olsen. (1991). *Kid's eye view of science: A teacher's handbook for implementing an integrated approach to teaching science, K–6*. Village of Oak Creek, AZ: Center for the Future of Public Education.

major points; other teachers find that the process of writing out a detailed plan helps them to clarify their thinking and planning. Sometimes the amount of detail needed depends upon the audience for the plan. If it is to be used only by the teacher who designed it, less detail may be needed than if it is to be used by a number of different people.

A plan should be developed for *every* learning activity. Individual student research requires planning; so does small-group work or a whole-class activity. Field trips and visits from people in the community need to be organized with as much care as a teacher-directed lesson. Structure provides the predictable environment in which investigations and inquiry can take place. Individual and group exploration in an inquiry-driven curriculum often require more planning than a traditional teacher-led discussion.

Means of Evaluation

Evaluation is discussed in detail in chapter 9. However, we do not view evaluation as separate from learning activities. The means of evaluation should be part of the Learning Activity Plan so that there is coherence and consistency among the various elements of the plan: objectives, learning activities, and means of evaluation. The plan may be likened to one of those wooden puzzle balls where the separate pieces interlock to make a unified whole. In a learning activities plan,

▼ All the planned *objectives* must be met through the learning activities and assessed through the means of evaluation;

▼ *Learning activities* must enable students to achieve the objectives and must include the means of evaluation; and

▼ The *means of evaluation* must directly address the objectives and must be incorporated into the learning activities.

For example, the means of evaluation for the activity in which students interview people in different fields who have coped with challenges might be a completed chart that indicates the types of challenge and the ways the persons interviewed dealt with them. The content objective in such a case might read: *The students will know that challenges may be met in a variety of ways.*

The process objective would include the processes of *comparing* and *organizing*. The affective objective might include *collaboration* and *attentiveness*. The description of the learning activity should include the process of comparing the data from different interviews and compiling the chart.

Materials and Resources

Resources are essential in any inquiry. Like researchers in other fields, teachers will sometimes determine resources for inquiry before they formulate questions for their students' studies. We devote two chapters to resources because we believe that some of the most valuable are often overlooked and undervalued in learning. In chapters 7 and 8, we discuss in detail some of the primary, secondary, and community resources that can support interdisciplinary theme study. These resources include:

1. Objects and artifacts
2. Audiovisuals
3. Print resources, including textbooks, libraries, and documents
4. Interviews with people
5. Experiments
6. Field sites
7. Technology

It is useful to list all resources that will be used in a learning activity, so that the materials are prepared and available.

Subject Areas and Curriculum Standards

The Activity Cluster form provides opportunities to note the various subject areas addressed in each activity (Figure 6.5). These should be transferred to the Learning Activity Plan (Figure 6.6). If there are specific curriculum requirements that must be met in each subject area, such as the "Essential Elements" in Texas (Texas Education Agency, 1991), these requirements may be referenced here. Alternatively, this area might be used to indicate sections of a curriculum guide or even pages in a required text. In this way, the Learning Activity Plan clearly shows the required concepts, content, and processes that are being addressed in this particular learning activity, and provides evidence for accountability. As noted earlier, several Learning Activity Plans may be in use at the same time. Ways of scheduling these are discussed later in this chapter.

▼ READER INVOLVEMENT

Select a learning activity from the activity cluster for your theme study. Using the Learning Activity Plan outline, develop a detailed plan in which the objectives, learning activities, and means of evaluation are clearly interrelated. These questions are offered to guide the development of your learning activity plan:

1. What *specific* databases are available for the children to explore? How do these databases help the children find clues that lead to answers to the sub-question? How will the children access the databases?
2. What will the children do in order to use the databases to uncover clues that may answer the question?

3. How will the children put the clues together to explore the question and arrive at their findings?

4. What grouping patterns will be used by the children (whole class, cooperative learning groups, informal groups, individual work, etc.)?

5. What thinking processes will the children use as they explore the data (observation, comparison, prediction, inference, analysis, synthesis, etc.)?

6. How will the children record and/or share their findings?

CULMINATING ACTIVITIES

A culminating activity is one that allows the students to synthesize their learning in an interdisciplinary theme unit and to present this synthesis to an audience. The culminating activity enables the student to shift from recording data to the next important step of reporting learning. Every unit should have some type of a culminating activity:

▼ To bring closure to the unit,

▼ To provide opportunities for students to reflect on their learning, and

▼ To enable them to share their products with a real audience.

Bringing Closure to the Unit

Inquiry has no end. An investigation can open up new questions that lead to new investigations. This does not mean, however, that there should not be closure to a unit. The length of units is determined by a number of variables, including the school calendar, with its reporting periods; students' interests; availability of resources; and the necessity to address other aspects of the larger theme. As human beings, we look for beginnings and endings: the week, the year, the seasons, the stages and cycles of our lives. Students and teachers gain a sense of satisfaction from experiencing the beginnings and endings of units of study.

Reflecting on Learning

Dewey was an advocate of reflection as a significant and integral part of learning. In schools, we often deny students opportunities to engage in reflection. To bring closure to a lesson, we may reiterate the objectives, or ask students to tell what they learned, but we seldom allow students the time or opportunity to think deeply about the concepts they have internalized, the processes and skills they have developed, or the attitudes they have adopted. A culminating activity can provide students with that opportunity.

Sharing Products with a Real Audience

It is becoming increasingly evident to educators that if learning is to be meaningful and long-lasting, it cannot be divorced from real life. Curriculum developments in all of the subject areas stress the importance of relevance and of real experiences. Students read literature, create real mathematics problems, conduct scientific experiments, and investigate social issues. How they report their new knowledge, however, often tends to take the traditional forms—essays, book reports, pages of practice exercises, and tests—designed primarily for one audience, the teacher. When students engage in real investigations, they need to report their results in ways that are true to the spirit of inquiry and that can be shared with wider audiences.

Types of Culminating Activities

Students growing up in contemporary society are constantly exposed to sophisticated methods of sharing news, ideas, and entertainment. They learn from an early age to use symbolic, imagic, and affective modes of thought to understand the world and to express themselves. As we have seen in chapter 1, these are the same modes of thought that are used by thinkers in the various fields of study.

Culminating activities can be designed to use these modes of thought as students synthesize their learning and present it for new audiences. Culminating activities can encourage students to contribute in different individual ways. A variety of means of presentation should be used, so that all modes of thinking are represented.

Symbolic Modes of Thought.   These include thinking with words, numbers, or other symbol systems. Culminating activities that use this mode of thought include:

▼ Writing and publishing books: class books, group books, individual books

▼ Producing dramatic works

▼ Making oral presentations

▼ Creating new mathematics problems and solving them

▼ Writing reports, letters, diaries, and so forth

▼ Designing timelines, charts, and maps

The symbolic modes of thought are those most commonly represented in traditional schoolwork. Care must therefore be taken that the culminating project does involve the students in meaningful and relevant uses of symbolic thought.

Imagic Thinking.   This includes visual, spatial, tonal, and kinesthetic–sensate thinking and representation. Many students are very comfortable with these ways of thinking and enjoy using them. Students can use these preferred ways of thinking to create products such as:

▼ Murals and pictorial displays

▼ Models, dioramas, and other three-dimensional artifacts

▼ Movement and dance

▼ Musical productions

▼ Videotapes, audiotapes, and films

For students who are raised in environments rich in imagic stimulation, including television and computer technology, this type of culminating project is particularly meaningful.

Affective Modes of Thought.   Much schoolwork depends heavily upon rational thinking. Investigations tend to follow a sequential, reasoned, scientific process. We teach students to use models and strategies. Intuitive thought, the largely unconscious processes that lead to flashes of inspiration, is rarely acknowledged or encouraged in schools. Yet all great thinkers, scientists and artists alike, pay tribute to the significant role that intuition plays in their work.

Most culminating projects are rational, ordered, organized syntheses of student learning. Yet synthesis can also be an intuitive flash of understanding, a vision that makes sense of unrelated ideas. Students should be encouraged to use and value intuition as one mode of thought. Culminating projects that incorporate intuitive thinking might include:

▼ Inventing new ways of solving problems

▼ Creating models or visuals out of unconventional materials or media

▼ Presenting data in imaginative ways, e.g., poetry, comic strips, songs, and skits.

▼ Developing surrealistic ways of writing or drawing or moving

Children and young people are much more comfortable with intuitive thinking than are many adults. Interdisciplinary theme studies can provide many opportunities for students to use this rich mode of thought.

Multimodal Presentations.   Culminating projects should allow for the use of many modes of thought, both by the students and by their audience. Students are very creative in thinking of ways to share their learning with others. Multimodal projects may include:

▼ A fair, in which stalls present the learned material in a variety of ways, and in which live presentations play an important role;

▼ A multimedia presentation, possibly using computer technology to combine text, images, and sound through hypermedia so that there are many ways to access the material;

▼ A classroom or school museum-like exhibition, with words, objects, pictures, music, and audiovisual presentations;

▼ A tour, where information about different regions is presented in many modes to the "traveler";

▼ A "shopping mall" where students "sell" their products through a variety of different marketing approaches.

Notice that all of these multimodal presentations incorporate audience participation. This is congruent with some of the beliefs about learning that underlie the interdisciplinary theme approach:

▼ Learning occurs when the learner is engaged with what is to be learned and the media through which it is learned;

▼ Learning is an active process;

▼ Learning involves the investigation of meaningful questions;

▼ Learning can occur through a variety of modes of thought.

Members of the audience are perceived not as passive onlookers but as active participants who will come away from the experience changed and enriched, and with new questions to explore.

SCHEDULING

It is not easy or wise to plan learning activities without taking into account the time frame that can be allotted to each activity. This involves some scheduling.

In a self-contained elementary classroom, the individual teacher often has some freedom to decide how to schedule the activities. In some schools, part of every day is allotted to interdisciplinary theme studies. In others, there are time allotments for the different subject areas, but the teacher can determine how these requirements are met. Some schools like to maintain a fairly structured time schedule, with all classes at a certain grade level engaged in the same subject area at the same time. Such a situation calls for careful team planning to ensure that the interdisciplinary theme unit is appropriately incorporated into the curriculum.

For example, an extensive activity that incorporates mathematics, science, social studies, and language might be scheduled for an entire morning or a whole day. This will allow students to get involved in their own inquiry without constant interruptions and changes of focus. An activity such as journal writing related to the study might be scheduled for thirty minutes each morning, perhaps during the time allotted for language arts. Of course, activities that are taught across the school by specialists, such as physical education and music, must be honored; where possible, these specialists should participate in the planning of the interdisciplinary theme study, and develop learning activities related to its "big ideas."

In a departmentalized situation, especially in the middle school, schedules may be less flexible, and the individual teachers may focus particularly on activities related to their own specialization. Team-teaching and flexible grouping of the students within a grade level can allow for joint planning and teaching when the learning activities require the expert guidance of more than one specialist. For example, in the seventh grade activity cluster that explored the question *In what ways do weather and climate affect food production?* (Figure 6.1), the teachers found that one activity, 1b.1, involved the students in language arts, science, math, social studies, and fine arts as they investigated types of food production across the world. They decided that for 1 week they would keep the students in their homeroom groups during the time allotted for math, science, social studies, language arts, and fine arts, and would allow the small groups studying each major area of the world to visit the subject-area specialists whenever they had particular problems related to that subject area.

There are many possibilities for flexible scheduling to meet the major goals and specific objectives of the interdisciplinary theme study. The major consideration is, of course, to provide the best possible learning situation for the students, bearing in mind that students learn in many different ways.

Three sample schedules present alternative ways of organizing theme studies in the classroom (Figures 6.8, 6.9, and 6.10). These are merely suggestions, of course. There is virtually no limit to the ways in which theme studies may be integrated into the regular curriculum. Teachers may wish to begin with one type of schedule and then modify it as they and the students develop the theme study.

Figure 6.8 illustrates a time schedule for 1 day built around the extensive use of a theme. Students are working individually and in groups on theme-related explorations, and the teacher plans carefully to work with different individuals and groups over the course of the day. Sometimes groups may join with other groups; at other times a group may split up for the students to work individually or in pairs. The class comes together for common experiences.

Figure 6.9 presents a time schedule for 1 week in which the teacher has allocated several blocks of time to work on theme studies. These may be expanded or adapted as needs arise and as the theme study develops. The Tuesday and Thursday schedules allow for a 2½-hour block of time for theme studies, with a break for lunch. The specific subject-area slots may be used to reinforce and teach particular concepts and skills as the teacher deems appropriate, or may be used for work related to the theme study.

Figure 6.10 demonstrates a more traditional schedule, where a 1½-hour block of time each day is allocated to theme studies. During the rest of the time, students follow the regular curriculum, although connections with the theme are made wherever possible.

Planning for instruction is a complex, interactive, and dynamic process in which the teacher always takes into account a wide variety of factors. Within the broad scope of the curriculum guidelines established by the school, district, state, and other local requirements or conditions, the teacher works to meet the instructional needs of students and to enable them to develop as self-directed learners.

Figure 6.8
Time schedule for 1 day

8:00–9:00	* Work with whole group to discuss new ideas ⟶		
9:00–10:00	Susie and Jose read and prepare for report	*Groups 3 and 6 work on measuring	Groups 1, 2, and 5 view film on animal adaptation	Mike and Gloria work on model habitat
10:00–11:00	⟶	Share results with each other	*Discuss film and continue individual work	⟶
11:00–12:00	* Reading aloud to whole class	LUNCH		
12:00–1:30	*Groups 2, 3, and 4 work on science experiments	Groups 1 and 5 work on research about animal adaptation	Pete and Maria prepare questions for interview with Mr. Li	Marilyn and Sergio finish their letters to Ms. Wilson and write their interview report
1:30–2:15	P.E. *Conference period: meet with grade-level team			
2:15–3:00	Groups 2, 3, and 4 write up science experiments	*Groups 1 and 5 share research findings and decide how to record them	Group 6 works on measuring and cutting paper for the model	⟶

*Indicates with whom the teacher is working directly.

141

Figure 6.9
Time schedule for 1 week

	Monday	Tuesday	Wednesday	Thursday	Friday
8:00–10:00	Theme Studies	Language Arts	Theme Studies	Language Arts	Theme Studies
10:00–11:00	Mathematics	Theme Studies	Mathematics	Theme Studies	Mathematics
11:00–12:00	Lunch				
	Reading aloud to whole class →				
12:00–1:30	Social Studies	Theme Studies	Social Studies	Theme Studies	Social Studies
1:30–2:15	P.E.	Music	P.E.	Music	P.E.
2:15–3:00	Theme Studies	Science/Health	Theme Studies	Science/Health	Theme Studies

Figure 6.10
Time schedule for 1 week

	Monday	Tuesday	Wednesday	Thursday	Friday
8:00–10:00	Language Arts				
10:00–11:00	Mathematics				
11:00–12:00	Lunch				
	Reading aloud to whole class →				
12:00–1:30	Theme Studies				
1:30–2:15	P.E.	Music	P.E.	Music	P.E.
2:15–3:00	Science/Health	Social Studies	Science/Health	Social Studies	Science/Health

REFERENCES

Bloom, B. S. (Ed.). (1984). *Taxonomy of educational objectives: Book 1. Cognitive domain.* New York: Longman.

California Department of Education. (1990). *Science framework for California Public Schools: Kindergarten through grade twelve.* Sacramento, CA: Author.

Eugene School District 4J. (1991). *Education 2000 elementary integrated curriculum K–5.* Eugene, OR: Eugene Public Schools.

Gardner, H. (1983). *Frames of mind: Theory of multiple intelligences.* New York: Basic Books.

Gardner, H. (1991). *The unschooled mind.* New York: Basic Books.

Kovalik, S. J., & Olsen, K. D. (1991). *Kid's eye view of science: A teacher's handbook for implementing an integrated thematic approach to teaching science, K–6.* Village of Oak Creek, AZ: Center for the Future of Public Education.

Texas Education Agency. (1991). *State Board of Education rules for curriculum: Essential elements.* Austin, TX: Author.

Tufte, E. R. (1983). *The visual display of quantitative information.* Cheshire, CT: Graphics Press.

Chapter Seven

Using Resources for Interdisciplinary Theme Studies

*W*ithout the right resources, there can be no substantive study. Even the most conventional curriculum, implemented through didactic instructional methods, is supported by textbooks, dictionaries, and encyclopedias. Any single-subject curriculum that is organized around questions requires at least teacher access to several data sources for students' exploration of those given questions. Question-driven interdisciplinary theme studies demand much more. They require many and varied resources to support students' detective-like searches for answers to questions that cross conventional disciplinary boundaries. The abundance and diversity of resources is often discovered during planning for theme studies because the interdisciplinary perspective allows teachers to see the potential for investigation in any source, no matter how closely it may be associated with a particular field of study. We present in this and the following chapter several common categories of resources that are important contributors to children's exploration of interdisciplinary themes:

1. Objects and artifacts
2. Audiovisuals
3. Print resources
4. Interviews with people

5. Experiments

6. Field sites

7. Technology

RESOURCES AND MODES OF LEARNING

Each category of the resources listed above appeals to one or more of the symbolic, imagic, and affective modes of inquiry that differentiate our preferences and options for learning. For example, the many print resources that are available for instruction within and outside the classroom engage learners with linguistic symbol systems. The pictorial contents of books, individual drawings, photographs, motion pictures and video, two- and three-dimensional artworks, and objects and artifacts have special significance for the visual learner. Experiments appeal to those who find special meaning in the language of numbers and symbolic representations and who appreciate the kinesthetic experience of the physical presence of ideas, including handling realia and making models. This kinesthetic–sensate modality is also called into play in the exploration of objects and artifacts. Audiovisual resources hold special value for visual, spatial, tonal, and affective learners. People are the ultimate in multimodal appeal. This "flesh-and-blood" resource can be experienced simultaneously in symbolic, imagic, and affective ways.

Resources and Learning to Learn

The thematic teacher finds resources that are appropriate to student inquiries and guides students to interact with them by exploring them with thoroughness and creativity. In this way, one of the most important purposes of interdisciplinary theme studies is advanced: to develop students' learning-to-learn skills.

Each of the habits of mind presented in chapter 1 is associated with thinking processes commonly found in lists of cognitive operations such as one compiled in the Association for Supervision and Curriculum Development's *Curriculum Update* (June, 1992): predicting, hypothesizing, information gathering, decision making, problem solving, remembering, comparing and contrasting, organizing, analyzing, inferring, and evaluating. These associations are presented in Figure 7.1 (pp.147-148). Some of the processes involve primarily analytical thinking; others intuitive reasoning; most require both.

Every interaction with a resource can develop students' prowess in thinking so that they may continue to ask questions, search for relevant data, and construct their own answers. The thematic teacher is instrumental in providing opportunities for students to learn how to do this for the rest of their lives.

Figure 7.1
Habits of mind and thinking processes

Finding and keeping focus includes knowing *how* and *when* to ask questions and define problems in ways that can narrow or broaden the search for information. Comparing and contrasting and organizing or categorizing are important "skills" here.

Simplifying questions and problems refers to skill in using symbol systems (words, numbers, or other symbols) to clarify the intent of questions and problems by isolating variables and stating predictions and hypotheses.

Attentiveness is a habit of mind that modulates the way we observe details, how we see wholes, and how we remember and imagine concrete and abstract images, sensations, and symbols. This habit of mind influences how we perceive and gather information.

Thinking fluently and flexibly is open-mindedness in creative thinking that permits variations on the theme and paradigm shifts. Like the character of attentiveness, this habit of mind also influences abilities to look through different lenses to see from different perspectives.

Forming hunches is clearly concerned with predicting and hypothesizing, and sensing cause–effect relationships. This "if–then" anticipatory reasoning is mandatory in successful problem solving and decision making.

Designing tests and experimenting cannot be done without the ability to isolate and to test possible influences in physical events, in human performances, and in our thoughts. The act of "experimenting" in any medium involves data collection and analysis. It also enables the verification and evaluation of "findings."

USING VARIED TYPES OF RESOURCES FOR STUDENT INQUIRY

There are several questions about resources that teachers must ask as they design interdisciplinary theme studies:

1. Where can I find the most appropriate resources for the theme study?
2. How do I prepare my students to use them? What questions can I pose? What are the logistics that I must consider?
3. How can I involve my students with those resources? How will they be involved in data collection?

Figure 7.1
continued

Searching for patterns is the drive to see relationships, to find associations and to categorize, to infer and to generalize, and even to see the whole as more than the sum of its parts. Synthesis is an especially important process in this effort.

Using models and metaphors uses imagic modes of inquiry to communicate and to explain the intangible or the incompletely understood. Associational and analogic thinking are processes that figure prominently in designing models and using metaphors.

Finding elegant solutions also demands the ability to synthesize and evaluate ideas in order to break through artificial complexities. This habit of mind values the aesthetic in thinking.

Risk taking undergirds problem solving, decision making, and inventing, among a host of human activities too numerous to list. This affective dimension of thinking is present in all thought, to lesser and greater degrees, depending on the circumstances.

Cooperating and collaborating, and competing, move to and fro in human thinking activities. Like risk taking, these emotional habits of mind can influence the way any thinking process or skill is used.

Perseverance/self-discipline is at the heart of learning to learn. Without the exercise of these, a search cannot proceed far; only accidental learning is likely to occur.

---

4. What types of follow-up activities are most meaningful? How will the students analyze the data they collect? What methods of recording their findings should be used? What new questions may develop from using the resources?

These questions suggest the steps presented in Figure 7.2.

There are three important considerations in selecting resources:

1. The resource must suggest researchable questions.

2. The resource should contain enough clues so that at least a few questions can be answered by gathering data from the object; it should permit students to make informed inferences or hypotheses that suggest meaningful patterns.

3. The resource should be able to be combined with other resources to support student investigation of the theme study's big ideas and to extend and expand student inquiry.

Figure 7.2
Steps in using resources for theme studies

1. Locate the resources.
2. Prepare for their use.
3. Involve students in using the resources.
4. Follow up in applying the findings.

In chapter 5, we presented an overview of a year's theme studies that had been planned by a team of first grade teachers to develop a big idea: *Growing up leads to changes in dependence and independence.* The second 6-week period was designed to explore the idea that *Animals vary in their degree of dependency on their parents according to their species.*

The teachers selected a main question for that unit: *In what ways do different species of animals grow and develop?* They had read Joyce Pope's *Do Animals Dream?* (1986), a collection of questions asked most often at the Natural History Museum in London, and noted that several of those questions were similar to ones their students asked: Are newborn baby animals as helpless as human babies? Do animals feed their young? Are animal families like ours? With these specific questions in mind, the teachers set out to find resources to support their first grade children's exploration of this theme study on *animal species' growth and development.* They turned first to the category of objects and artifacts because young children are intrigued by concrete things and learn best through sensory experiences.

OBJECTS AND ARTIFACTS

Aalbert Heine's elegant discussion of the interdisciplinary significance of a rusty nail, reproduced in chapter 3, illustrates the power of objects and artifacts to spark inquiry. For decades now, museum educators have been encouraging people to learn how to "read" objects and artifacts to *detect* the information they hold. In the search for the story of an early 20th century German-Texan farm woman's life, *The Search for Emma's Story* (Martinello, 1987), the author examined several *signpost* artifacts; the term denotes an artifact that guides a study by suggesting new directions for the inquiry. Several signpost artifacts in *The Search for Emma's Story* were interpreted: a wedding portrait, an empty medicine bottle, a list of home furnishings handwritten by Emma, and the house in which she lived. Each of these artifacts holds clues to understanding the woman, her community, her times, and her way of life. By attending to details, searching for patterns, and forming hunches, the inquirer was able to tease out those clues, form questions that led to other sources, and find interrelationships among the data found in the several sources. The habits of mind we term *attentiveness, searching for patterns,* and *forming hunches* are critical to this process.

We can ask questions about a walking shoe, as we did in the section that began our discussion of inquiry in chapter 1, or about a butterfly that lights on a flower bordering our path. Objects and artifacts include just about anything that is tangible. Many people associate artifacts with times past. An old chair is an artifact, but so is one made by a living carpenter. Artifacts are generally defined as simple objects that show signs of workmanship or modification by humans, as opposed to natural objects. Whether natural or man-made, the things of our world hold clues to nonhuman and human life. They need not be old. A contemporary coin can tell as much about the culture in which it is used as an ancient coin tells about earlier people and their times. As we have seen in earlier chapters, artifacts are particularly valuable as starting points for theme studies.

An old road can spark inquiry into its origins, the settlements along its route, its history of trade and transportation, the engineering that determined its construction, and about the people who traveled its pathways or lived along the route, among a myriad of other factors that influence and are influenced by the built environment. For instance, a middle-school theme study developed from inquiry into Los Caminos Reales in Texas, a network of Indian trails that became important routes for transportation and commerce during the Spanish Colonial period and have since merged with contemporary public highways. Some questions asked about that "King's Highway" include: Why was our community settled along the Camino Real and how did it become linked to others along the route? What was the Camino Real used for? What types of commerce and communication did it enable? What caused changes in modes of transportation and in the routes taken? What alternate routes were there? How did their presence influence what occurred along the main highway? Who were the people who settled our Camino Real community? How did the groups earn their living? What businesses developed along the Camino Real? What was the terrain and natural environment of the area like when the first settlers arrived? How did they adapt to it, use it, and change it? How did the availability of resources affect the community? What effect has our area's climate had on its economy? How has the ecology of our area been altered by commerce along the road? How did different groups interact for economic reasons? What conflicts have occurred when economic or cultural values clashed? How are these reflected in the myths and folklore of the cultures along the Camino Real?

The clues that surface as the search proceeds lead to new questions, and each new question can impel inquirers to explore beyond the known and to consult additional sources.

Selection and Focus

There is a wealth of objects and artifacts available to teachers for student inquiry. In addition to natural life and manufactured items that surround us, there are objects in attics, closets, and flea markets, among the most obvious places, that can be used as artifacts. Replicas of artifacts can be purchased from museum shops and commercial distributors. Natural objects can be collected from the outdoors and obtained in quantities from scientific supply houses. Availability is not the issue—usefulness for inquiry is! This means that teachers themselves must thoroughly interact with the resource as inquirers before they introduce it to their students.

Consider the following example of the use of objects in the first grade theme study.

What better way to begin a study of animal growth and development in first grade than with living animals, the teachers thought. They wanted the children to discover that there are differences among species in patterns of growth and development and that not all newborn baby animals are as helpless as human babies, the focus of one of the questions asked frequently by their students. The science textbook suggested observing mealworms to study the life cycle of the meal beetle, Tenebrio molitor, illustrating metamorphosis. Mealworms can be obtained from pet stores and biological supply houses. The teachers had access to class quantities through their local teaching resource center.

The reading textbook contained a story about frogs, another example of metamorphosis, and one about mice. Mice are a good example of live-bearing mammals, relatively easy to get from teacher resource centers or pet stores, and good examples of young that require maternal nurturing for a short time. The teachers also planned to include egg-bearing guppies in a shared aquarium as illustrations of a nonmetamorphic life cycle in which the young need to be separated from their parents to survive. Other species would be examined through different resources.

The first grade teachers decided that the children would observe the life cycle of the meal beetle and contrast it with the growth and development of baby mice. By setting up colonies of mealworms and a cage containing a female mouse with her newborns, they would encourage the children's observation and interpretation of animal characteristics and behaviors. They would start with mealworms as the catalyst for the study.

The teachers studied the mealworm's potential for observation by the children, gathering information about the insect and its life cycle from the textbook, from personnel in the pet stores that sold mealworms as food for pet birds and lizards, from literature provided by biological supply houses, from professional sources of ideas for science teaching, and from other teachers who had used mealworms for instruction. The teachers found an excellent source of ideas for using mealworms in the Elementary Science Study teacher manual and kit entitled The Behavior of Mealworms *(1966). They filled large mayonnaise jars three-quarters full of bran, with apple or potato slices as moisture sources to encourage the mealworms to complete their metamorphic life cycle. They wanted the children to observe the exoskeletons that would pile on the surface of the bran as the mealworms shed them from 9 to 20 times during their larval stage. They arranged to get mealworms that were still active,* so the children could observe their movements and reactions to stimuli. They also wanted mealworms that were several months old so that the children would not have to wait long for the mealworm to form a pupae from which, in 2 or 3 weeks, the adult beetles would emerge, products of complete metamorphosis. To avoid problems that could occur with mealworm mortality and delays in their movement through the stages of the life cycle, the teachers set up several mealworm colonies and obtained some samples of pupae in addition to the larvae.

The teachers obtained a female mouse who was about to give birth. After the children had begun the mealworm observations, they would introduce the female mouse and her young. On the advice of a local veterinarian, they prepared a large cage for the mice to be placed on a table in the classroom. Several additional cages were prepared so that the young mice could be separated from their mother at the appropriate time and placed on tables for the children's observations in each of the first grade classrooms.

The teachers anticipated that they would need to talk with the children about how people can learn about animals by watching them and about the importance of treating all living things with care and respect.

Learning to Learn through Objects and Artifacts

Mealworms are wonderful objects for observation because they have distinguishable parts and because they move in interesting ways. In this example, the teachers planned to guide the children's observations with questions such as:

▼ How many parts can you see in the mealworm's body?

▼ How many legs does it have? (The mealworm's six legs would later be introduced as a clue to its categorization as an insect.)

▼ Which is the head, with its antennae?

▼ How is the head clearly different from the mealworm's rear segment?

As the children examined the mealworm, they asked:

▼ How does the mealworm move? How does it use its segmented body to move and its legs to walk? (Careful observation will show that the front pair of legs moves first, followed by the rear pair, and then the middle pair moves forward.)

▼ What makes it turn around?

▼ Why does it head toward dark places and burrow into a pile of meal?

All observations would be recorded on a class chart for regular reference and for checking as observations continued over time.

Then the teachers guided the children to think about how mealworms change as they grow. They entertained predictions about what would happen and encouraged the children to make regular observations of the mealworm colonies in the mayonnaise jars to discover when pupae appeared, how this dormant form behaved, how beetle forms became visible through the translucent pupal covering, and then how white beetles were "born" fully grown, turning brown and then black in a few hours. From *Ranger Rick's Naturescope* edition, *Amazing Mammals* (1986), the teachers got the idea to have the children make "baby announcements" for the newborns. The children's drawings and descriptions of the birth of meal beetles would develop their vocabulary and recording skills and provide a means for comparing the young of several animals the children would study during the unit.

The recorded baby announcements would make it possible for the children to compare the life-cycle differences among meal beetles, mice, and guppies, with special attention to the different relationships between babies and their parents that each illustrates. From these comparisons, new questions for extended study would emerge about how different animals care for their young. Those questions would demand additional resources.

Artifacts are appropriate resources at any age. For example, after reading a story in their literature text about people who were trailblazers, some of the seventh grade students wondered about the people who had been the early leaders in their community. Their teacher suggested that they start in the cemetery, where tombstones might hold clues to local heroes and heroines.

Fourth graders who were studying food production in different countries and regions found that kitchen implements provided important clues to food production and to available resources in the local environment.

AUDIOVISUALS

Still and moving images, with and without sound, are easy to get and to use in the classroom. High-resolution still color images are abundant in magazines, books, and posters. For decades photographs, maps, drawings, and filmstrips have been recognized as useful and inexpensive resources for teaching and learning. Additionally, videotapes offer moving images for student study. CD-ROM disks and videodiscs store great quantities of information in visual, audio, and audiovisual format.

Visuals are so prominent in our communication media that we tend to take them for granted, and do not always evaluate carefully the ones we use for instruction. The same criteria that we suggest for any resource are applicable to visuals. In addition, visuals should

▼ Be unambiguous in their presentation of information

▼ Be large enough to be seen in the physical situation in which they will be studied

▼ Be rich in detail, displaying primary and secondary information

▼ Have aesthetic appeal

▼ Engage the viewer's imagic thinking

Arnheim (1969) explains how visual thinking enables ways of knowing that are different from ways derived from thinking with words. McKim (1972) describes images as vehicles for thinking that allow the solution of problems that cannot be solved with linguistic or numeric symbol systems. A CD-ROM program in the Living Books series produced by Brøderbund Software in 1992, *Just Grandma and Me,* by Mercer Mayer, is presented as a way to help students learn how to read between the lines of the text by "reading" and interpreting the moving images of the characters in the story's different scenes. Arnheim, McKim, and the Brøderbund programmers understand that visual thinking is a learning-to-learn process that requires early development along with the skills of reading text.

For dyslexic students and those with hearing disabilities, visuals take on added importance in learning. They, in particular, need to develop the skills for probing the details and the full character of images. Children can learn how to use images for inquiry only when the visuals are good enough to support investigation.

Selection and Focus

When the first grade children asked about animal babies that could not be brought live into the classroom, their teachers immediately thought of still pictures and video. Sources of images on animals are abundant in nature magazines such as *Audubon,* in children's materials such as *Your Big Backyard* and *Ranger Rick,* published by the National Wildlife Federation, in the many trade books on animals for children, and in posters and other oversized images that are readily available through catalogs, museum shops, and specialty stores. The first grade teachers went through back issues of *Ranger Rick* for pictures of animal babies the children had asked about. They also asked the librarian to pull books about animal babies that contained many pictures so they could stock the library shelves in the children's classrooms. When all the sources had been compiled, the teachers selected the images that were richest in visual information to encourage children's attention to detail and search for patterns.

Transparencies for overhead projection can now be made in color and 35-mm slides make clear and colorful large images when projected. Almost anyone can use a 35-mm camera to produce slides that are usable in the classroom. One of the first grade teachers was an amateur photographer who enjoyed visiting the zoo, her camera loaded with 35-mm color transparency (slide) film, to take pictures of young animals and their parents.

Some of the most useful images are made by the students, because they photograph subjects of study from their own perspectives. For example, a field trip to the desert conservatory of the local botanical gardens was scheduled during the fourth grade study of deserts. The children used automatic 35-mm cameras to make color slides of desert plants with observable adaptations for life in arid environments. Those images were later compared with pictures of desert plants in the trade books the teachers had borrowed from the library to search for commonalities and differences. The children discovered variations in the characteristics of spines on succulents that generated new directions for inquiry that the teachers had not anticipated. New sources, including Audubon Society videos, supplied some answers.

Videocassettes of nature films contain information about animals in their natural habitats. The first grade teachers found several in the Audubon Society library. But the films had been prepared for a general audience and only short segments were particularly relevant to the children's questions. The teachers did not want to use the video programs for entertainment; they wanted to help the children gather information from them. Fortunately, the same programs were available on videodiscs, and their school had a videodisc player with a bar-code scanner. This allowed them to select those video segments most relevant to the theme study.

The seventh grade teachers found a videotape produced by the National Geographic Society on causes of climate in several illustrative regions of the world. The images were outstanding and the narration was clear. Because not all of the regions the students were studying were represented, the teachers decided to have only those groups whose climatic regions were represented actually view the videotape. They reviewed with the students questions about climate to keep in mind during the viewing and reminded them to record information that was pertinent to each question.

Audio recordings of various types of natural and manufactured sounds in our environment, musical forms, and the spoken word are also valuable resources. They have particular relevance for students who are visually impaired or who learn best through tonal modalities. The same types of considerations that apply to selecting visuals apply to audio recordings. They should

- ▼ Be unambiguous in their presentation of information
- ▼ Have auditory quality appropriate for hearing in the physical situation in which they will be studied
- ▼ Be rich in detail, offering primary and secondary information
- ▼ Have aesthetic appeal
- ▼ Engage the viewer's imagic thinking

Audio recordings and photographs are valuable ways for teachers and students to collect data for their inquiries. Where camcorders are available, student-made videotapes that document a trip or an interview are invaluable for reviewing and verifying the data collected.

Learning to Learn Through Audiovisuals

Visual literacy refers, in part, to the skills of observing and interpreting images. The best way to interpret a visual is to look at more than the subject of the image; the idea is to view the image as the image maker might have perceived it and to look beyond the subject to explore its depicted surroundings and the environment in which it was made.

During the fourth grade study of deserts, special emphasis was given to exploring changes that humans have caused in the environment. One group of students had access to dated photographs of similar locations in several desert environments. The photographs offered opportunities to compare and contrast observable changes in those locations over time. The population densities in one area had grown substantially more than in another, and the impact of human population growth had dramatically affected the natural environment. The students asked questions of these photographs that led them to understand what had happened in each location and why. By examining the details of each picture, the students were also able to infer why, when, and how the photographs had been made. Some of those inferences raised questions that led them to search the library for demographic and topographic maps and of the regions and newspaper accounts of events in the areas when the photographs had been made. By the time they were done, the students had discovered many of the changes that accompany the economic development of an area.

More than just observing and interpreting visual images, being visually literate means knowing and using the language of vision. Kyvig and Marty (1982) describe the expressions of visual language as light and shadow; color and texture; line, shape, and pattern; similarities and contrasts; and movement.

As the first grade students continued their study of animal babies and their relationships to their parents, they were able to visit a local art museum where they could view a special exhibit on paintings, photographs, and sculptures of wildlife. The teachers guided the children to gather information about the characteristics of each depicted animal. They also guided them to view the artworks in terms of the artists' use of light and shadow, color and texture, line, shape, and pattern, similarities and contrasts, and movement.

In addition to visual language, the language of sound influences our ways of learning and knowing. Audiovisuals are as much an auditory medium as a visual one. Listening for pitch, volume, and timbre can heighten our sensitivity to a piece of music. Sensitivity to those tonal elements in a movie's background music can heighten our understanding of the meanings the music contributes to the images it accompanies. Attentiveness to nuances in spoken language helps us to detect the implied as well as the explicit meanings of human talk.

PRINT RESOURCES

Textbooks

For many years, textbooks have been the primary resource for student learning in classrooms. More recently, there has been a strong move to supplement or even replace class sets of textbooks with children's and adolescent literature, trade books, and other print and nonprint materials.

In interdisciplinary theme studies, textbooks are used as one important resource among many. Textbooks have many advantages:

▼ They present a large amount of material

▼ Artwork and production is usually of high quality

▼ The text is written for a specific developmental and reading level

▼ They contain a wide variety of suggested activities for teachers and students

▼ Supplementary materials are designed to accompany the text

However, they also have disadvantages:

▼ Concepts and topics are often not explored in depth or detail

▼ They do not usually engage students in inquiry

▼ They are written for a very broad audience, and therefore may not meet the needs or build on the experiences of specific groups of students

▼ Supplementary materials such as worksheets frequently test rather than teach

How may textbooks be used to facilitate and enrich student inquiry? With careful selection and focus, teachers can make textbooks a valuable and rich resource.

Selection and Focus. In many states and districts, certain textbooks are adopted for use in schools, and although teachers usually participate at some stage in the selection process, individual classroom teachers seldom have much choice in determining what textbooks will be available to them.

Teachers can, however, make choices as to how to use the textbooks. As we have seen in previous chapters, teachers can select and organize materials from textbooks according to the main questions to be explored and the major generalizations to be learned by students.

For example, the first grade team in our earlier examples selected for the second 6 weeks an interdisciplinary theme study on *animals,* in which the major generalization was that *Animals change and grow in different ways.* The big question that they wanted their students to investigate was: *How does change and growth affect ani-*

mals' dependence, independence, and interdependence? As they examined the required textbooks for their grade level, they found that there were sections of each textbook that could be a resource for children's examination of these questions. In the science text, they decided to use chapter 4, "Animal Lives," and chapter 8, "The Weather and Seasons." As they looked at these chapters, they checked carefully to see if changing the sequence of the lessons in the text would cause difficulties. These chapters seemed to stand alone, and therefore could be taken out of context. The mathematics text, on the other hand, was carefully sequenced, and taking chapters out of order would be problematic. The teachers therefore decided to focus on the math skills of counting to 20, the subject of chapter 2, and teach these skills through a variety of investigative activities that could involve the children in counting real things. They also looked ahead to see what would be taught in later chapters, and decided that in the unit on *animals* they would informally introduce simple measurement and graphing as a means of collecting data and recording learning.

While the reading program was highly individualized, with children working in small groups or even on their own at their reading levels, the teachers found that two sections of one of the first grade reading textbooks could be used by the whole class: a section on animal tracks and trails, and another section on animal families. While the text would be too difficult for some first grade readers and too easy for others, the pictures could be used for investigation, and the text could be read by the able readers or by the teacher as needed. The children also used a variety of trade books written at different levels to supplement the textbooks.

One section of the social studies text seemed particularly appropriate for the theme study, though it did not directly address the subject of animals. This was a short selection about the seasons and the changes that they brought. The teachers realized that the selection complemented the science chapter on the weather and seasons, and could provide added information on this topic.

They decided to use these two pieces of information at the same time. They also decided that the four pictures of a farm at different seasons of the year could help the children to think about how farm animals grew and changed during the year. They encouraged the children who showed special interest in this topic to look for other books about the seasons.

They decided not to use some sections of the text because the concepts and skills were being addressed in other parts of the curriculum.

Learning to Learn Through Textbooks.   Textbooks can be both exciting and daunting to young children. Children are eager to explore this resource, but they may find it difficult to navigate their way through the books. Teachers need to spend some time in helping children learn how a textbook is organized, how to follow the page numbers, how to use the table of contents, and how to access information from pictures and text. These skills should not be taught separately. As students need information from textbooks, with the help of the teacher they will learn how to find it.

In the first grade theme unit on animals, after the students had developed questions they wanted to explore, the teacher encouraged them to look at the table of contents in the science textbook and find the section entitled "Animal Lives." Children who already knew how to count to 90 located the first page of this section, and then helped others to find the page in their own books. When the teacher wanted a less advanced group to count the sea creatures in a picture on page 16 in the math textbook, she had the children turn the pages together and read the number of each page aloud from page 1 to page 16 so that the students could understand the concept of sequential page numeration. This helped the children to work more effectively with their individual resources.

Documents

Documents have been defined as "a written or printed paper furnishing information or evidence" (*Webster's,* 1989). In interdisciplinary theme studies, documents are an important primary resource that can complement and provide verification for secondary sources such as textbooks, encyclopedias, and trade books.

Documents fall into several categories:

Personal documents: Letters, accounts, bills of sale, diaries, certificates, and so forth

Government documents: Census reports, records, laws, rules and regulations, announcements, certificates

Business documents: Advertisements, catalogs, day books, accounts, correspondence, employment records

Church records: Baptismal, marriage, and death certificates, vestry minutes

Educational documents: Children's magazines such as *Ranger Rick* and National Geographic Society publications, informational leaflets, guides

Directories: Telephone directories, city directories

Newspapers and journals

Documents may contain verbal, visual, and numerical information that students can use in their investigations.

Selection and Focus. The teacher's responsibility is to identify the sources for documents. This requires open-mindedness and creativity. Documents may be found in homes, schools, and businesses, in churches and hospitals, in stores and flea markets, in government offices and service organizations. Some textbooks contain lists of resources that include documents. There are publications such as the *Educator's*

Guide to Free Social Studies Materials (Suttles & Suttles, 1990) that list a wide range of resources, including documents. Libraries often have vertical files or special sections for documents. Often the best resource for locating documents is a willingness to look for information in likely and unlikely places.

The first grade teachers in our example looked for resources that could help the children explore the question *How do animals change and grow?* They easily found excellent pictures of animals in magazines such as *Ranger Rick,* and also in literature distributed by organizations such as the American Society for the Prevention of Cruelty to Animals (ASPCA), the National Wildlife Federation, the World Wildlife Fund, the American Humane Society, and Greenpeace. A local wildlife park provided illustrated leaflets, and a local pet store was willing to contribute pamphlets on the care of various kinds of pets.

The seventh grade students found a wealth of documents pertaining to the countries they were investigating, not only from foreign embassies and tourist offices but also from less likely sources such as the United States Department of Agriculture. In their study of farming, they contacted food manufacturing and distribution firms that provided factual information about imports and exports and about food processing. Even the local supermarket was able to provide some written information about fruits and vegetables from different parts of the world, which contributed to the students' understanding of the relationships between climate and crops.

Learning to Learn Through Documents.   Documents are usually written in adult language, and this can interfere with children's access to them. Teachers can address this in several ways:

1. Read the document to the students. This may be useful as a short-term strategy, but it does not help students learn how to use documents.

2. Select parts of documents that are particularly relevant to the theme study, and provide additional supportive resources such as visual aids to help the students understand and use them.

3. Provide structured directions or study guides to enable students to find their way around the documents.

4. Teach students how to find information in documents. This should be taught in real situations where the students want to use the information to answer real questions. This is probably the most valuable approach in the long run, because students can apply these strategies to other sources as they conduct their own individual or group inquiry.

First grade students were unable to read the text in the documents the teachers found for them. However, they could cut out the pictures and develop a picture bank that was used later for categorizing types of animals and for making inferences about them.

Seventh grade students were impressed by the number of official-looking documents they received in answer to their letters to foreign embassies and tourist offices. They were also somewhat overwhelmed by some of the technical language and the statistics. The language arts teacher used these real problems to teach the students some word roots and suffixes that would help them to decode and comprehend unfamiliar vocabulary, and reviewed strategies for using dictionaries effectively. The math teacher, meanwhile, used the documents as real data to be explored in the required study of statistics.

Libraries

Print sources other than textbooks are usually stored in some type of library. This may be as small as a class library or a teacher's personal library. It may be a public library in the community, a government library, or a library attached to an institution such as a college or university, museum, historical site, or hospital. It may be part of a factory or business enterprise. It may be a national or international library, which is frequently accessed through some type of electronic network.

Selection and Focus.   Most classrooms have a limited class library, which often includes books from the teacher's personal library. Such a library is seldom adequate for a full interdisciplinary theme study. These resources need to be augmented either by bringing more resources into the classroom or by enabling the students to visit other libraries.

Many public libraries have a policy whereby teachers can take out 30 or 40 books for a limited time for classroom use. The first grade teachers in our example found that the children's librarian at their local branch library was willing to identify and collect 40 books on animals, with a special emphasis on animal families.

Meanwhile, the teachers also searched for other sources for print materials that could be brought into their classrooms. One teacher attended the local university. Although the main university library was most useful for supplying the teachers with reference materials at the adult level, the curriculum library, designed primarily for students in the teacher education program, provided some extra children's books and other print and nonprint materials. Another source was the local educational resource center, which had an extensive collection of print and nonprint materials and would deliver them to the school.

It is not enough to bring books into the classroom. For one thing, the scope of the resources is necessarily limited by space and availability. More important, students who find all their information in teacher-provided books do not learn how to find their way around libraries.

For many children, the school library is often the first large library that they encounter, though families may introduce their young children to the public library as soon as they can enjoy books. The school librarian is an important member of the team for interdisciplinary theme study. It is a good idea to include the librarian in early planning stages whenever possible, or at least to give the librarian a copy of the broad scope and sequence of the theme study. Apart from anything else, the librarian can make sure that different grade levels do not need the same books at the same time. School librarians might also be invited to attend the classes when the students brainstorm on themes and identify the questions they wish to investigate, so that they can identify appropriate library sources for the study. Some library books may be housed temporarily in the classroom for the duration of the theme study. Whenever possible, however, the students should go to the school library and learn how to locate the information they need.

Learning to Learn Through Libraries.   All libraries contain large amounts of information, usually cataloged in a variety of ways. Like any resource, it is necessary to learn how to use a library in order to retrieve information. These skills are best taught not in isolation but as part of student research.

When working with students, the teacher can help the students to use libraries in various ways:

- ▼ By looking up material with students
- ▼ By collecting a limited number of books related to the focus of the theme study
- ▼ By taking students to the relevant part of a library
- ▼ By teaching students how to use catalogs and indexes
- ▼ By working with students in a library situation and helping them to find specific information
- ▼ By teaching students how to get help in a library

On occasion, it is valuable for students to go to libraries outside the school. When a seventh grade class was engaged in a study of different areas of the world, some of the students found a great deal of information at the public library, while one enterprising group contacted a local foreign-embassy official and gained access to the embassy library. During a fourth grade study of deserts, the students visited a local natural history museum where the book room and the bookstore provided resources unavailable elsewhere.

Any of these approaches may be appropriate at different times. The main goal of the teacher should be, in the short term, to enable students to find the materials they need to conduct their inquiries as efficiently as possible and, in the long term, to learn how to use libraries effectively.

The resources discussed in this chapter are rich databases for students' explorations primarily through symbolic or imagic modes of inquiry. In the next chapter, we examine resources that engage the students in multimodal interactions.

REFERENCES

Association for Supervision and Curriculum Development (June, 1992). *Curriculum update.* Alexandria, VA: Author.

Arnheim, R. (1969). *Visual thinking.* Berkeley, CA: University of California Press.

Elementary Science Study. (1966). *The behavior of mealworms.* Nashua, NH: Delta Education.

Kyvig, D., & Marty, M. A. (1982). *Nearby history: Exploring the past around you.* Nashville, TN: American Association for State and Local History.

Martinello, M. L. (1987). *The search for Emma's story: A model for humanities detective work.* Fort Worth: Texas Christian University Press.

Mayer, M. (1992). *Just Grandma and me. Living books series.* San Rafael, CA: Brøderbund Software, Inc.

McKim, R. H. (1972). *Experiences in visual thinking.* Monterey, CA: Brooks Cole.

Pope, J. (1986). *Do animals dream?* New York: Viking Kestrel.

Ranger Rick's Naturescope. (1986). Pt. 1: *Amazing mammals.* Washington, DC: National Wildlife Federation.

Suttles, S. A., & Suttles, S. F. (Eds.). (1990). *Educator's guide to free social studies materials* (30th ed.). Randolph, NH: Educators Progress Service.

Webster's encyclopedic unabridged dictionary of the English language. (1989). New York: Portland House.

Additional Reading

Chendall, R. G. (1978). *Nomenclature for museum cataloguing: A system for classifying man-made objects.* Nashville, TN: American Association for State and Local History.

Chapter Eight

Interacting with Resources for Interdisciplinary Theme Studies

*I*nterdisciplinary inquiries accommodate different learning styles because their search for meanings encourages students to use many and varied resources. Students whose preferred learning modality is primarily symbolic, imagic, or affective may enjoy using the resources discussed in chapter 7. The several categories of resources that we discuss there appeal to one or more of the modes that differentiate our preferences and options for learning. While it is important to appeal to students' individual learning styles, a high-quality education guarantees that students enlarge their repertoire for learning. People should be able to direct their own learning in a wide variety of contexts and through widely different content. This is an inherent advantage of the interdisciplinary question-focused approach to curriculum development. Exploratory studies require students to search for clues in many sources, piecing them together to find meaningful patterns, moving students beyond the limiting goal of only finding specific answers to particular questions. These discoveries can give momentum to the continuing learning cycle described by Bredekamp and Rosegrant (1992) by developing new interests, suggesting extended explorations, prompting additional and even more insightful questions, and encouraging innovative ways to utilize learning that in turn lead to further awareness, exploration, inquiry, and application. The process of learning from diverse resources can encourage students to use many more than their preferred modalities. It is likely that students will enlarge their repertoires for learning as they interact with resources that invite multimodal learning. The following are described in this chapter:

Interviews with people

Experiments

Field sites

Technology

For students who learn best through combined modalities, these resources have special value. Their regular use can develop any student's ability to access information through aural, oral, visual, and tactile stimuli.

People are wonderful resources for students who relate well to others, who like to work with one stimulus at a time, and who learn best by listening and by talking about their ideas and questions. Field sites appeal to highly observant students, who are adept at gathering information through several senses at one time. The term *hands-on* speaks to the kinesthetic–sensate orientation of learners who like to "touch" ideas and phenomena in concrete representation. These learners also enjoy the focused discipline of designing and conducting experiments. For those who benefit from multisensory stimulation, the developing computer technology uses print, sound, and still and moving images in gray tone and color, with two- and three-dimensional visual effects. These tools may be selected and combined to meet the special developmental needs and preferences of any learner.

INTERVIEWS WITH PEOPLE

People in all walks of life are usually willing to share their knowledge and their ideas with others. This human resource is, perhaps, the most readily available and least well used of all resources for inquiry.

Human sources on almost any subject include:

Professional experts

Serious amateurs

People who have casual experiences with aspects of the subject

Professional experts may be found in the Yellow Pages of the telephone directory, through local chambers of commerce, museums, reference libraries, and universities. Serious amateurs are usually located through clubs and volunteer organizations. People who have had casual experiences with many and varied subjects of interest for theme studies are all around us, in our communities, our neighborhoods, and our homes.

Selection and Focus

A key to finding human resources for an inquiry is found in the specific questions asked. The questions usually contain references to concepts. Those concept labels are clues to categories of human resources. For instance, when the seventh grade students wanted to explore how climate affects food production, one of the questions they posed was: *How are climate and weather interrelated?* The concept labels *climate* and *weather* are clearly associated with meteorologists. The students contacted the local weather broadcaster and she agreed to be interviewed.

The fourth grade teachers included the study of statistics in their unit on deserts. The process theme they selected for that unit was inferring and generalizing. One question for study became: What can we infer from demographics about how people live in deserts? *They wondered who in their community could speak to fourth graders about life and demographics in deserts. By asking around the school, they found an exchange student from Saudi Arabia who was staying with a local family. He agreed to speak about the character of life in his native land. To deal with interpreting demographics, the teachers asked a locally based insurance firm to send a statistician who could explain to fourth graders how population data is analyzed to find answers to demographic questions. One teacher from the team visited with each resource person before they met with the children. She gave them a list of questions that the teachers and children wanted to make sure they addressed during their interview. The teacher also discussed with the resource people ways in which they could make their statements most meaningful to fourth grade children.*

When we have difficulty finding human resources for theme studies, it may be because:

▼ We tend to take one another for granted and not to think of ordinary people as sources of information.

▼ Most people have poorly developed interviewing skills.

The first problem prevents us from thinking about ordinary people as resources for study. The second prevents us from learning from one another.

The first grade teachers were aware of these problems and were determined to help their students learn to interact with people as resources. So they asked their young students to name some people who could be consulted about the animals they were studying. A list was formed that included:

1. Friends and neighbors who were known to keep small animals as pets (for instance, gerbils and hamsters, and birds);
2. Veterinarians the children visited with their pets;
3. Pet shop personnel;
4. Curators at the zoo.

They added one another to the list because the children realized that they had personal knowledge of how animals grow and develop. With their teachers' help, the children selected several people to interview. One of them was a fifth grade boy who was an expert on metamorphosis. The children wrote an invitation to the older student, asking him to visit their classroom for the purpose of the interview. One of the teachers met with the student to prepare him for being interviewed by the entire first grade class.

Learning to Learn Through Interviews with People

The teachers worked with the children to draft a list of questions to ask their guest. The children were helped to keep the purpose of their interview in mind: to find out which animals undergo metamorphosis and to determine if there are differences in the stages of their life cycles. Before the date of the interview, the teachers worked with the children on interviewing skills. They included discussion of how to ask questions, how to listen to responses, and how to make note of the information for future use. The teachers took the role of the respondent so the children could practice asking their questions and following up with additional questions. Then the teachers gave the children opportunities to practice interviewing one another about themselves in pairs, in small groups, and in large groups.

After trying their interview techniques on the fifth grade respondent, the children talked about the experience with their teachers, evaluating their questions and the ways in which they interacted with their expert on metamorphosis and summarizing what they had learned. They then prepared for another interview, this time with one of the children's mothers who had a new baby. They decided on their focus, listed their questions, determined who would ask which questions, and how the interview would be recorded. Their teachers were helping the children learn how to focus their questions and gather comparative data. Additionally, they were learning how to collaborate in doing research.

While visiting the local botanical gardens, some of the fourth grade students interviewed the curator of desert plants with the intent of gathering information to verify what they had discerned from an Audubon Society videotape they had viewed. The students recorded the interview on videotape. They were then able to compare the information gathered from the curator with similar types of information contained in commercial videos. The discrepancies they found caused them to follow up the interview with a telephone call. The curator put the students in touch with a botanist to explore questions that the curator could not answer. The students had begun to ask increasingly challenging questions. Their learning exceeded the standards of the regular curriculum.

Less formal interviews can be done by individuals or small groups of children who can talk with parents and other family members and neighbors in their homes. This encourages the student to develop skills of "visiting." To uncover the story of the life of a Texas farm woman, Martinello (1987) found informal interviews useful:

> The people I interviewed preferred a conversational style, a style more appropriate to "visiting." Often, the person I was visiting would serve me food, and conversation would continue over the table. Paper and pencil were my best ally for maintaining records of those conversations. The notes I made while conversing were cryptic, but as soon as I got home, I transcribed them. Then, to be sure that those notes were accurate, I sent the informant copies of the transcription with a self-addressed, stamped envelope and a request to review what I had written, make corrections and even additions as necessary, and return the notes to me. This proved to be a good way both to verify my understanding of what they had said and my recollection of how they had said it. It also sparked recollections that had not come to mind during our conversations. Several sets of notes were returned to me with significant additions. (p. 211)

Teachers who assign interviews for homework are pleased when students return to class with a sheaf of notes in hand. The notes are evidence of their ability to obtain information from human resources. Just as significant is the appreciation they express for the resource when they state, with the gleefulness of a brand-new realization and appreciation, "I didn't know my grandmother knew so much. I didn't think that she had so much to share."

EXPERIMENTS

Many experiments that are done in the elementary and middle school are usually done in science class as outlined by the textbook. Too often the answer is supplied, rendering the "experiment" an exercise and not a real investigation. Experiments can be done in social studies, the visual and literary arts, and in mathematics, just as they are done in science studies.

Some experiments *test* the effects of isolating, manipulating, and controlling specified variables. Experiments in physics and chemistry are often associated with this approach to inquiry. When the purpose is to *identify* variables for later testing, more open-ended experiments are conducted. This type of investigation tends to be associated with qualitative studies in disciplines such as history and education. Qualitative experiments are also done in the arts, not with languages of numbers or words, but with the language of visual and tonal forms, designs, and styles.

Experiments in elementary and middle-school classrooms typically appeal to students who learn well from the manipulation of equipment and the sensory experience of physical variables. Experiments are also meaningful to students who enjoy creating models and designing and testing inventions. These are often learners who prefer imagic modes of thinking.

Selection and Focus

Questions determine the type of experiment teachers choose to help their students complete. Sometimes teachers need to help students restate the question they want to research so that it is possible to gather meaningful data. For instance, the question *Why does a plant form fruit?* needs to be focused through subquestions before answers can be discovered. As stated, the question offers no direction for the isolation of variables and the collection of data. When asked in a more operational way, the question becomes researchable through direct experimentation. Some possibilities are:

▼ Which plants form fruits?

▼ Where does the fruit come from?

▼ What influences the size, shape, and condition of the fruit produced by a peach tree, a blackberry bush, or a tomato plant?

▼ How does the amount and type of water affect fruit production in different plants? The amount and band of light? The amount and type of nutrients supplied to the plant?

These questions direct the inquirer to look at specific characteristics of plants and fruits. They can observe the plants they choose to study as they grow and form fruits; they can compare and contrast the fruit-bearing parts of each plant; and they can test the influence of the named variables on fruit production in different plants, with increasingly sophisticated and controlled experiments.

Experiments that teachers demonstrate can produce data to help students answer their questions. Sometimes, a teacher demonstration is the most efficient and safest way of gathering good data. But there is no substitute for students' active and personal involvement in experiments, where they take the role of experimenter.

After the first graders had completed their open-ended observations of the physical characteristics and behavioral tendencies of the mealworms, they began to ask questions based on what they had seen. One that intrigued a group of children was Why does the mealworm stay in the pile of bran if you don't take it out? This question was a natural lead-in to an experiment that helped the students discover that mealworms are light sensitive. The teachers realized that the children needed to phrase the question in more specific terms before they could discover the answer. They helped them work with the idea until the question more clearly addressed the relationship between mealworm behavior and the presence of light. They guided the children to state the question this way: What does the mealworm do when we put it in light? *Now the teachers were able to help the children set up a simple experimental situation in which light was the controlled variable. They discussed the importance of testing many mealworms in situations with bright light, dim light, and no light and of controlling heat in all three conditions. They also discussed the need to offer the mealworms an escape from the light if they so desired. The children suggested putting a pile of bran in each environment. With a clear plan in mind, the children set up the three conditions and placed the mealworms in each. Then they made observations and recorded their own data on mealworm behavior. The children discovered that mealworms in both lighted conditions tended to remain burrowed in the bran; those in the dark were less likely to stay in the bran pile all the time. The children interpreted their data to suggest that mealworms like the dark better than the light. Now they began to ask about mealworm food preferences:* Would they burrow in flour as well as bran? What about sugar? *These questions opened up possibilities for new experiments.*

Teachers must also be aware of those experimental situations that require special precautions, skills, and equipment. When seventh grade students were involved in a theme study about the germ theory of disease in a microbiology laboratory course, the teachers had to prepare them to use the microscope. Special skills sessions were conducted in using this tool. The students also had to learn the skills of sterile technique, slide preparation, staining procedures, and general precautions for working with living microbes. Protective gear is needed even in the regular classroom during science studies. Teachers need to prepare students to use protective clothing when necessary. Whether the gear includes goggles and lab coats for science experiments or smocks for experiments with art media, learning how and when to use them is prerequisite to inquiry that can proceed without distracting and potentially harmful accidents.

Learning to Learn Through Experiments

Many of the ways of thinking that are most readily associated with inquiry are developed through experimentation. Almost every experiment requires students to:

▼ Formulate questions
▼ Make observations
▼ Compare and contrast

▼ Form hunches that will suggest predictions and become formalized as hypotheses

▼ Build models and use metaphors

▼ Isolate variables and, in some experiments, control and manipulate them

▼ Collect, record, and organize data

▼ Interpret data, making inferences from observations

▼ Evaluate hypotheses and form generalizations

▼ Report findings

▼ Formulate new questions

For example, the fourth grade use of probabilities, during the desert unit, led to one group posing the question *What are the chances of rainfall increasing in a desert area during the next decade?* The math teacher helped them use the data on conditions associated with rainfall in deserts and other areas and weather conditions in the desert during each month of the year during the past 10 years to make informed predictions.

The stories the seventh grade students had been reading about how human beings deal with hardships caused one group to ask *What kinds of hardships do students in our school have to cope with?* The group consulted the math and social studies teachers about ways to gather this information. The teachers suggested doing an experiment by conducting a survey on hardships experienced by their peers. The group set to work to develop a survey instrument that would provide quantitative and qualitative data. They trial-tested the instrument with their classmates. Their findings uncovered interesting information about hardships and also about flaws in their instrument. They redesigned the survey and trial-tested it again. When they were satisfied that it would gather the type of information they wanted, the students asked permission from the principal to administer the survey to all students in the school who were willing to complete it. The volume of data they collected was impressive and kept the students busy finding the most efficient ways of collating, analyzing, and reporting their findings. Their report revealed a number of severe hardship cases in the school that needed attention.

FIELD SITES

Field sites offer rich opportunities for students to conduct investigations across the curriculum. At field sites, students can trace the history of a community, observe scientific principles in action, follow the workings of government, learn about the natural world, or develop an appreciation for art or music.

Field sites abound in any community. Think about the possibilities in your own community in each of these categories:

1. Sites designed to be used for educational purposes:

    Museums

    Nature and wildlife centers, including zoos

2. Sites that include an educational component:

    Public services, e.g., fire station, police station, courthouse, bus system

    Businesses that have tours for schoolchildren

    Military bases

3. Sites designed primarily for recreation:

    Parks, including theme parks

    Sports facilities

4. Sites not primarily designed for educational purposes:

    Businesses, e.g., grocery stores, corner stores, specialty stores, department stores, offices, factories, farms and ranches

    Neighborhoods, e.g., streets, houses, public buildings, recreation areas

    Services, e.g., restaurants, medical services, auto repairs

    Artisans, e.g., artists, musicians, potters, weavers, dancers

Selection and Focus

As teachers plan field studies for their students, there are a number of important questions that should be considered:

1. *How do we plan for the field visit?* Any field study requires careful preparation. Chicago's Field Museum of Natural History (Voris, Sedzielarz, & Blackmon, 1986) suggests the following steps in planning:

    Get to know museums [or other field sites] in your area.

    Decide why and where you are going.

    Visit the [field site] before your field trip.

    Make advance arrangements.

    Introduce museums [or field sites] before the trip.

    Practice perceptual skills.

    Introduce field-trip subject.

    Plan field-trip activities.

    Review field-trip plans with chaperones.

2. *Where shall we go?* The amount of choice and autonomy that a teacher has in selecting a field site varies from school to school. Some schools specify the field trip

for each grade level: the zoo for first grade, a local industry for second grade, a museum for third grade, and so on. This can make it difficult to use the field site for an investigative learning experience, but if teachers know in advance which field site they are required to visit, they can design interdisciplinary unit studies that incorporate the field site as a learning laboratory.

In other schools, teachers have more choice, though choices are rarely unlimited. Early planning for the year allows for the selection of field sites that are the most appropriate resources for the theme study. In addition, popular field sites may become booked up early in the school year. Some field sites, such as local stores or nearby parks, can be used with minimum prior planning. They also have the advantages that there are no travel expenses and that the visits can be arranged on short notice to meet the needs of the students.

3. *When should the field visit take place?* In some schools, there is an unfortunate tradition of scheduling field trips at the end of the school year. This may provide a pleasant day out, but minimizes the possibility of substantive learning. Field studies should be organized to take place within a theme unit. It is particularly desirable that the field visit be scheduled far enough into the study for students to have sufficient background information and preparation to use the field site wisely, but early enough for the students to be able to use the information learned at the field site to illuminate and enrich other aspects of the study. The exact timing of a field visit within the theme study depends upon its purpose. Sometimes a field study can come fairly early in the theme study, to provide a starting point for investigation. Alternatively, a field visit later in the theme study affords opportunities for synthesis, extension, and application of earlier learnings. Of course, any theme study should probably incorporate several field visits.

4. *Who should go on a field study?* Anyone for whom it will be an appropriate learning experience. Frequently, all the students in a class or grade level go to the same field site at the same time. This may not be the best use of the students' time. Where teachers work in teams, it may be more rewarding to take selected groups of students to a variety of field sites, even if limited time and money restrict each student to a single field visit. First grade students were divided according to interest so that one group visited the zoo to compare babies of different species, another group explored an exhibit of baby grouse at the natural history museum, and a third group attended a veterinary's office to learn about the care of abandoned baby animals.

Sometimes, particularly in the upper grades and middle school, students are excluded from field visits because of behavior problems. Care should be taken to ensure that such students get other opportunities for field study, perhaps in more structured environments, and that while their fellow students are on the field visit, these students are engaged in rewarding and meaningful investigations at the school site.

5. *How do we get there?* This often depends upon district policies. Sometimes school buses are chartered; at other times, students and teachers travel by public transportation. Some field sites may be within walking distance. It is important to remember that the travel time itself should be an important learning time for the students as they go through an unfamiliar part of town or look at familiar sites through new "lenses" that provide different perspectives and added significance.

Learning to Learn Through Field Visits

Field trips are probably one of the most popular and most misused activities in schools. While field study provides wonderful opportunities for students to engage in real research and relevant learning, a field trip is often perceived as passive entertainment, with learning being incidental.

Students need to be prepared so that a field visit becomes an interactive learning experience. This includes two types of preparation, which may be termed *logistical* and *educational*.

Logistical preparation includes setting rules and expectations so that the students know how to behave at the field site and on the way to it. When children are in unfamiliar settings, they feel insecure, and this insecurity often is displayed in inappropriate behavior. Students should be very clear about what to expect, what they will see, the schedule for the day, and how refreshments and bathroom breaks will be provided. Appropriate behavior should be discussed, and with younger children may be practiced in a simulated setting. First graders, for example, might spend class time "playing" at getting on the bus, going into the field site, and carrying out their investigations. Students can be encouraged to develop their own standards for behavior.

Educational preparation is part of the interdisciplinary theme unit. Before the students reach the field site, each individual or group should know clearly what questions they are investigating, how to conduct the investigation, and how to record their data.

TECHNOLOGY

By the age of 16, most children will have been entertained by television for more than 15,000 hours. The entertainment continues through their exposure to the sights and sounds of the movies, video games, videotapes, and audio recordings. Children who have such multimodal experiences from their earliest days develop receptivity to audio and visual stimuli that prepares them for learning in dynamic and multidimensional ways. These ways are dramatically different from the linear and print-oriented learning styles of earlier generations. Although the impact of audiovisual technology on children's cognitive development is often discussed and recognized by teachers, schooling continues to rely on use of the printed text almost exclusively as a resource for student learning.

Perhaps because television and its audiovisual presentation is associated with entertainment, its use in the classroom has tended to be tangential—an add-on to the "regular" lesson. Whether in the classroom or living room, students have been invited to *witness* broadcasts or videotapes rather than to interact with their content, to ask questions of their presentations, to discover patterns that enlarge concepts, and to critically explore their assertions. In this chapter, we suggest ways to use some of the readily available audiovisuals in theme studies: audiotapes, compact discs, still images, filmstrips, movies, and videotapes.

A persistent instructional problem has been the unchanging sequential form of these ubiquitous audiovisual materials. It is usually more difficult to access a section of a videotape than a page in a book. It is often harder to obtain a sustained and repeating view of a moving image than to examine a printed graphic in a textbook. But developing technology is changing that. Enter the personal computer as a powerful tool for learning.

Computer-assisted instruction (CAI) has many and varied applications and forms. In this chapter, we discuss only a few of the technological tools that have special significance for students' interdisciplinary theme inquiries. Each tool is examined in broad contexts on the assumption that their particular forms will change dramatically as research and development efforts succeed in producing more efficient, more powerful, and more economical resources based on intuitive and user-friendly design principles that substantially simplify the interface between the user and the machine. These qualities of the computer should make them particularly valuable learning tools for intuitive learners. CAI may be able to engage students who have been disadvantaged by their intuitive preferences (notably girls) with the study of subject matter such as mathematics and the physical sciences that traditionally are not taught in ways that appeal to the intuiting mind. The tools we believe will have continuing relevance for interdisciplinary theme studies include word processing and spreadsheet programs, CD-ROM, multimedia and interactive multimedia, and networking.

Selection and Focus

The type of technology that teachers and students use during theme studies depends on their needs and the availability of equipment. Following are some suggestions and examples.

Audiovisuals.   In our earlier discussion of documents and objects and artifacts, we referred to the use of maps and 35-mm slides and photographs as sources of visual information about a subject of study. When a living plant or animal or an inanimate object cannot be brought into the classroom, students can gain considerable information about the subject by studying its photograph or other graphic representation. The same is true of sounds and music, and of moving images of dynamic actions and events that students cannot experience directly. Audiotapes, compact discs, films, videotapes, and laser discs bring exotic sounds and images to the student. These materials are frequently experienced in their entirety, partly because graphics, audio recordings, and audiovisuals are associated with entertainment. Most of us usually view photographs superficially, focusing on their central subject. People prefer to listen to an entire musical performance and to view a movie from beginning to end; the stage and movie theater continue in the age of television partly because they provide for relatively uninterrupted performances. Likewise, at home we can mute the commercial intrusions into the sequence of events we are viewing. Rarely do people *study* parts of a recording, an image, or a selection from a film. The "entertainment" way of experiencing resources is inconsistent with education, in general, and for interdisciplinary inquiry, in particular.

An image may be full of details that contain clues to understanding its subject's context. Photographs, maps, diagrams, and other graphics can be studied for their background content as well as their obvious subject. For instance, a photograph of a picnic at the beach in the 1920s may contain visual information about the condition of the beach and its ecosystem and the ways people of the time dressed for swimming and played on the beach, in addition to information about who attended the picnic. Students should be helped to look beyond the obvious and to attend to details in any graphic. They also need time to read still images; the time needed to read a graphic may be substantially more than that needed to read a page of print.

At some point in the process of inquiry, audio recordings and audiovisuals need to be studied in segments. But some may prefer to hear and view them first in their entirety. The access style will be influenced by the learner's tendency toward analytic or holistic perception, as well as by the material itself. But all inquiry requires attention to details within their larger context. The use of audiovisuals as resources for inquiry is no exception. At some point, the inquirer must search for clues that address particular questions and examine the most relevant parts of the resource. Laser discs with bar codes and bar-code readers facilitate the process of selecting sections of audio recordings and videodiscs in the same way that indexes for print materials allow readers to find the sections of texts that are most pertinent to their interests.

Third grade children were investigating the question How alike or different are the calls of birds of similar species who nest in different areas of the world? *When discussing ways to gather the necessary data, the children realized that they could record the calls of birds nesting in their own environment. The issue of how to hear the calls of birds nesting in distant areas of the globe required special reference material. Their school librarian found sources of audio recordings and videotapes that presented the types of birds the children were studying. Small groups assumed responsibility for selecting those parts of the audio- and videotapes that contained the sounds the class wanted to compare. They were able to access some with the bar-code index, recording the appropriate reference for quick retrieval. During several whole-class sessions, each group presented its selection and the teacher helped the class develop a comparative chart, recording the children's descriptions of the distinguishing characteristics of the bird calls they heard.*

Children who are visually or hearing impaired are especially well served by audio or visual resources, respectively. Often, people with sensory handicaps have developed sharpened abilities to collect information through other senses. During theme studies that require the use of detailed audio or visual data, handicapped children may make valuable and unique contributions when asked to use their strongest sensory abilities to gather data for their classmates.

Bilingual students can make invaluable contributions to class inquiries that need information from non-English sources. For instance, when seventh grade students were studying similarities and differences among Spanish and Mexican cultures, they obtained documentaries on life styles in Spain and Mexico from Spanish and Mexican television stations. The English-speaking students were able to gather some data from the visual presentation, but their comparative study could go no further without Spanish interpreters. Bilingual Hispanic students in their class assumed responsibility for this; an important by-product was peer-group recognition of the bilingual students' special expertise.

Computer Tools and Multimedia.   Several decades ago, word processing, graphics, and spreadsheet programs, CD-ROM, multimedia and interactive multimedia, and networking were recognized as opening new vistas for learning. The possibilities for their development in the 21st century could drastically change schooling and, unquestionably, enhance and expand the processes of inquiry. These remarkable resources can connect students with the larger world to make their explorations more substantive and more challenging. The tools offered by personal computing, if used with imagination, can even help students exceed many of the curriculum standards that have been formulated in times of more limited resources for teaching and learning.

Word processing programs encourage different ways of composing. Most people who do "electronic" writing differentiate the "feel" of composing on the computer from writing with paper and pencil or with the typewriter. Format preferences, multiple fonts and print styles, layout and editing options, and spell-check programs offer the writer a full desktop of tools, easily found and used. Their availability frees the writer to concentrate on the expression of ideas. Students can make many drafts of their written work, saving each to floppy disks for editorial review and comments by many different readers, such as peers, parents, and teachers. Word processing programs make it possible for students to keep, organize, collate, and share notes on their explorations, create several drafts of their writing, and produce clean and professional-looking final copies of individual and group work. When combined with graphics programs, students may add their own illustrations and clip art to enhance the presentation of their findings. Spreadsheets offer students ways to do the same things with quantitative data and its graphic expression. The implications for learning to learn are many, as discussed in the section below, "Learning to Learn with Technology."

The enormous reserves of print and visual information that are contained on CD-ROM literally bring the libraries of the world into the classroom, including many archives of special collections that were once reserved for use by scholars. Students conducting an inquiry into almost any theme can gather information from diverse primary and secondary sources through the technology of CD-ROM.

When a group of eighth grade students who were studying World War II wanted to know the different points of view about the war, they asked their school librarian to help them find resources. The librarian first acquainted the students with CD-ROM encyclopedias to help them focus their search and frame their questions. As the students phrased researchable questions, they asked: How did the people in different parts of the United States view the reasons for the impending war in 1939? How did this compare with people in Germany? Great Britain? France? How did attitudes change in 1942? What changes in opinion were occurring in 1945? What about today? The librarian was able to obtain CD-ROM collections of American newspapers from major metropolitan areas for the years the students had selected. He also began searching for similar resources for British, German, and French populations. As the students' inquiry continued, other resources were found in audiovisuals, extending the exploration to other groups in the class; the inquiry continued for the full school year.

A particular value of CD-ROM resources is their combination of audio, visual, and print data. Technology makes it possible to experience phenomena on demand. CD-ROM encyclopedias can present movie clips, including cross-section and x-ray views, that illustrate the written text.

Patrick Lynch (1991), of the Yale University School of Medicine, makes a case for the computer's abilities to meet individual learning needs because students interact with the applications, directing each according to their unique interests and preferences. Lynch refers to the terms *hypertext* and *hypermedia,* coined by Nelson in 1974 (Nelson, 1987), as "nonsequential documents," containing audio, print, and visual material that the computer can search for, retrieve, and interlink to form a "web of information." Interactive hypermedia programs invite students to select foci for study from arrays of questions. Through a system of linked "cards," students may access print, graphic, and audiovisual resources for their study in any combination and sequence they choose. Students may add resource options as they discover them, enhancing the program during their inquiries. There is a striking parallel here to our concept of interdisciplinary theme studies. The interdisciplinary inquiries that we are recommending are specifically designed to guide students through the exploration of questions and ideas in nonsequential ways, by consulting diverse resources through varied learning modalities. Throughout the process, students should discover meaningful patterns in the webs of information they construct and interpret. Computer technology can aid this process, helping students develop the habits of mind we describe as critical to self-directed, lifelong learning.

An increasing variety of commercially produced interactive multimedia programs can allow students to interact with persons, places, things, and phenomena that are not typically available to ordinary people. Some multimedia programs invite students to conduct experiments that formerly were done only in uniquely outfitted research laboratories having highly sophisticated and costly prototype equipment. For instance, interactive multimedia programs permit students to explore the action of an object in zero gravity, alter the variables in an ecosystem to determine their effects on the inhabitants and the habitat, test proofs of mathematical theorems, apply principles of design to invent solutions to problems such as architectural and mechanical challenges, perform simulated dissection and surgical procedures, experiment with models of dangerous substances, and even experience some characteristics of life in different places during past, present, and future eras. Many of these programs invite students to take the role of detective to research questions about human experience, all forms of life, and the physical world.

Sally Narodick and the Education Team of the Edmark Corporation (1992) offer a clear set of criteria for selecting software for students that they compiled from studies of educational software for young children. The criteria have equal relevance for older students and, indeed, for all people who use educational software for learning.

1. *Can the individual use the software easily and independently?* Narodick and her associates prefer graphic and spoken instructions for children so that reading skill is not a prerequisite for computer-assisted learning.

2. *Is the software open-ended and exploratory?* The idea here is that the user should be able to control the software's pace and path. Further, the software should invite students to experiment and to think creatively about what they are doing.

3. *Can the software "grow" with the student?* Software programs that are developmentally appropriate permit students to explore varied concepts in different ways and on different levels of complexity.

4. *Does the software provide quick reactions to selections?* Students should be able to use the entire screen, exploring different components of the visual presentation and receiving responses that are immediate.

5.   *Is the software technically sophisticated?* Programs should appeal to students' multisensory ways of learning. The computer's capabilities to make presentations in print, sound, still graphics, and moving images should be used fully to capture and hold the user's attention.

6.   *Is the software appropriately challenging?* Programs that are worth using invite sustained exploration. Ideally, they should impose no ceiling on the potential for learning through their use.

7.   *Is the program lively and entertaining?* This criterion refers to the program's ability to encourage students "to use their imaginations, to explore, and to laugh" (Narodick et al., 1992, p. 7).

8.   *Does the program build self-esteem?* All learners need to feel successful and to experience empowerment through learning. The best programs *guide* students to find answers to questions rather than giving them the answers, and always meet student responses with positive and constructive feedback.

The hypertext and hypermedia authoring tools that commercial producers use to create the types of multimedia programs referred to above are also available to the teacher and student. They are becoming increasingly easy to create and to use. Their special value is their ability to make resources accessible in forms that students can understand. When teachers create hypertext and hypermedia programs for their students, they select and focus the presentation of resources to reduce student frustration in dealing with quantities of data that may be overwhelming to the novice researcher, while still providing enough challenge to motivate the students' drive to wade through extraneous information. For instance, in an eighth grade theme study of *ethnic conflict* in the United States during World War I, a well-designed hypermedia program might offer students several articles about German-Americans from different newspapers around the country circa 1917–1918, a selection of letters and diaries written by German-Americans during that time, and film clips from audiovisual documentaries about the U.S. involvement in World War I that deal with issues of distrust of Germans (e.g., the official renaming of German measles as "liberty measles" and dachshunds as "liberty pups"). The same type of selection and focus would present accessible primary sources to students searching for patterns of ethnic distrust in the treatment of Japanese-Americans during World War II.

Teachers who want students to consult sources on a theme like *migration* might construct a HyperCard stack that includes some of the main questions and subquestions that they and the students have identified, with access to resource files including film clips, maps, data tables, oral histories, legends, and drawings, and other resources that contain clues to the migratory patterns of the people or animals under study. In effect, hypermedia allows teachers and students to compile and access any of the resource types discussed here and in chapter 7.

Virtual reality further expands the opportunities for extraordinary experiences that are available to ordinary people. Students may visit places that once were reserved for the most affluent and elite, or were unapproachable by human beings, entering those environments with full sensory stimulation. So, for instance, students may walk through a technological simulation of the Palace of Versailles or the Taj Mahal; they may visit a Brazilian rain forest or the Sahara Desert; they may enter the human circulatory system, moving through arteries, veins, and vital organs with the blood flow; or they may look inside an erupting volcano or experience an earthquake. Immersion in these simulated environments can effectively offset the limitations imposed by learning disabilities or physical handicaps.

There is, of course, no substitute for students' direct experience with a resource in real time. But by bringing distant, unique, and precious resources within the reach of every student, technology can effectively equalize the opportunities of all students to use resources that once were not available to even the wealthiest and most privileged.

Networking connects people electronically across large distances around the world. Technology makes it possible for students in villages, towns, cities, the barrios and ghettos of large metropolitan areas, and even remote areas of the world to communicate instantaneously and over time with others. The implications of interstate, interregional, and international networking for interdisciplinary theme studies are enormous. Networked students can collaborate, contributing their questions, resources, and ideas to one another's theme studies. Through their "electronic conversations," participants can share their knowledge, resources, questions, and perspectives with one another. The use of technology to link people for collaborative learning in this way may serve to develop multicultural insights, values, and appreciations as a natural outgrowth of students' shared experiences during that search for knowledge, information, and truth that is the process of inquiry.

If intelligently used, according to the highest ethical standards, computer technology can become an aid to the democratization of educational opportunity. As a resource for interdisciplinary inquiries, this increasingly sophisticated technology can increase the depth of students' interdisciplinary inquiries.

Learning to Learn with Technology

As indicated in the preceding section, technology has the ability to appeal to symbolic, imagic, and affective modes of thinking. Its multimodal qualities allow the student to determine which mode to use; it also enlarges the learner's opportunities to develop other modalities. Technology can help us "see" sound by presenting tonalities in graphic representation and "hear" visuals through the electronic representation of sounds associated with still or moving visual images. Virtual reality enables kinesthetic–sensory and audiovisual stimulation. "Electronic conversations" across political and cultural boundaries cannot fail to involve the affective dimensions of cooperation, competition, interpersonal relationships, and cultural interactions. The very character of computer technology appeals to and encourages intuitive thinking, even when the content may be presented in analytic ways. As all these abilities develop, the learner becomes more proficient and, in many ways, "smarter."

As mentioned earlier in this chapter, word processing programs empower students to create many drafts of their written work, editing them with one another's help as the writing process proceeds. In networked situations, students share their creative productions with others and serve as critics for one another, offering reactions and raising questions for constructive feedback.

Graphing programs allow students to enter data from direct experimentation or secondary sources that are instantly converted to graphs and charts that would take considerable time to construct by hand. The clear advantage is the reduction in time between the actual collection of data and an opportunity for its interpretation.

Perhaps the most long-lasting contribution that technology can make to students' ability to learn derives from its invitation to create. Animations may be made and edited by individuals or small groups working cooperatively. Photographs and graphics may be scanned into a printed text. Moving video clips can be imported into hypertexts. The possibilities that technology offers for creative production and use are boundless. The Santa Ana Kids' Project (1992) is a case in point.

The students and a teacher of McFadden Intermediate School in Santa Ana, California, collaborated with the Wells Fargo Bank to conduct an inquiry into their city's history, culture, and heritage. The students gathered information from local archives on the personalities, places, and events that were special to their community. They took trips to local sites to explore businesses and occupations in their environment. They interviewed local people, making audiovisual and print records of their findings. As they gathered this wealth of data, the students and their teacher developed an interactive multimedia program, using hypertext and hypermedia, through which they imported video and graphics into HyperCard stacks to enhance the formal text and the story narratives they wrote about the many topics and subtopics that composed their theme. They added musical selections, artwork, and dramatizations about Santa Ana. Their program allows users to choose optional ways to explore the Santa Ana story that the children created.

This extensive inquiry involved 223 students with one classroom teacher in gathering and organizing their findings to share in multidimensional formats. By so doing, these young learners were using all of the habits of mind discussed in chapter 1 at the levels and degrees appropriate to their widely varying developmental abilities.

Whether students make audio recordings of an interview, take snapshots of an event, videotape an experiment, construct a hypertext, or use any combination of technological tools to collect data during their inquiry or to synthesize and present their findings through a culminating project, they will be using increasingly complex thinking processes. Student use of technology to construct materials that communicate their learning requires them to plan as teachers do, bearing in mind the needs of their audience while they work with the language and ideas of their selected content. When well done, student products have a professional, "high-tech" appearance that can be a reward in itself for the producers.

A group of first grade students had enjoyed talking with an author of picture books they had read with their teacher. One of the parents recorded those conversations with a camcorder and showed the children the videotapes. Excited by these images, the children asked for help in making a "movie" of their "Talks with Writers." One child thought that most people wouldn't know what the talks were about unless they had read the books. She suggested that the interviews be added to a presentation of the stories themselves. Another child recalled the storybook programs they had been using, in which particular illustrations serve as "buttons" to reveal additional contextual information. So, with the help of several fifth graders who had created multimedia programs, the children and their teacher created their own version of living books. They scanned selected illustrations from the books themselves, then decided which segments of the illustration to program, created additional illustrations to enlarge the text, and added video clips from the children's interviews with the author. As one child observed, the program looked like the ones he had seen on TV, where the author talks about the story after the story is told. These first graders shared the completed program with other children in their school. Its presentation, with large-screen projection, was the highlight of a local school board meeting.

Projects that use the electronic tools of technology to present student work need not be as ambitious as those described above. The key to learning to learn through technology is its use to construct and communicate meanings. It makes little sense to improperly use electronic equipment to do what a paper and pencil or chalkboard does sufficiently well. But when instantaneous, multidimensional, and multimodal service is needed to clarify varying types of data, large quantities of information, complex content, or abstract ideas, technology offers instruments with special advantages for teaching and learning.

DATA COLLECTION

Resources provide the raw data for inquiry. Data collection incorporates two major steps: identifying the questions that will guide the search, and recording the results of that search. These are processes that must be learned by students as they engage in inquiry.

Identifying Questions

The students and the teacher can begin a theme study by brainstorming about the major theme to help the students identify what they already know, what they want to know, and where they will go to find out. This can be recorded in chart form (Figure 8.1), and the charts can provide an organizational structure for the theme study. The chart can be displayed on a bulletin board for reference and can be further developed as students discover answers to some of their questions. Older students can develop their own charts and keep them in their theme-study journals.

As the questions are developed, they must be checked to see if they are operational—if they can be investigated. It is often difficult for students to identify a clear focus that pinpoints the specific questions that will help them to explore a larger one. For example, first grade students wanted to know how animals cared for their babies. In the class library, they found a book called *Animal Mothers* (Kumori, 1979), but this gave them only limited information. However, once they had looked at this more general book, they were able to develop questions such as *How long do elephants look after their babies?* and *How does a baby kangaroo get into its mother's pouch?*

In this case, rethinking the original question enabled the students to develop researchable questions. However, a question may not be researchable for a certain grade level or a specific theme unit, for a variety of reasons. It may be too general. For example, a fourth grader may want to know "all about mountains," a question that needs to be refined. It may be too specific. A first grader might ask, *How many legs does this bug have?* This interest might be developed into a broader, more researchable question, such as *How many legs do insects, spiders, or mammals have?* The way a question is phrased determines how much you can find out.

Figure 8.1
Data collection chart

What we know	What we want to find out	Where we can find out	What we found out

A question may require investigation that requires too much prior knowledge. A seventh grader might want to investigate the mathematical probability of a farmer in Java being able to double the size of his farm. While this is an intriguing question, the amount of information needed and the mathematical skills involved are probably too extensive and sophisticated for the student to handle within the scope of the unit.

A question may seem irrelevant. One of the challenges of inquiry is to balance focus with open-mindedness. Students need the freedom and encouragement to follow their special interests and to raise new questions, yet the unit should maintain a common focus. One way to check for this focus is to review the "big idea" for the unit and judge whether exploring the question will lead students to a deeper understanding of that idea.

Another challenge for students is to know where to begin looking. It is tempting to rely upon the encyclopedia for all information. However, students can learn how to expand their search, to use bibliographic references in the encyclopedia to find other sources, to gain access to information through catalogs, and to know how to access a variety of resources such as those discussed above. A class might brainstorm on the types of institutions that would be likely to have needed resources.

The first grade students had no difficulty in predicting that the zoo might have information about animal development in its library. However, students did need help in going beyond the obvious. When one child had a question about the development of a particular type of local hawk, the teacher helped her to locate an authority in the community whom another child had seen on local television news.

Many students (and teachers) expect that information comes only from expository text. Stories, poems, and drama can also provide information about themes and generalizations, and can help to answer significant questions. Including appropriate novels, books of poetry, and other genres among the resources for a theme study can encourage students to look for other similar resources.

The amount of structure needed to enable students to get information from a given source depends upon the complexity of the task. Complex tasks require more structure; simple tasks using the same material require less structure.

For fourth grade students, calculating population density from data of the area of a region and the size of the population would be a complex task that needed careful organization and structure by the teacher, with opportunities for the whole class to work together at times. A simpler task, such as inferring major topographical and geographic features from pamphlets, travel brochures, and children's magazines, could be completed with little structure or direction and could be handled by individuals or small groups.

Recording

When beginning theme studies, it is tempting to structure the inquiry by having students complete worksheets that help them all to collect the same data, particularly when using textbooks that provide a common source of information. This is appropriate only if it is essential for all students to record the same basic facts. However, if the focus is on discovering generalizations and answering broad questions, all students will seldom need to have the same data.

For example, to teach skills of counting from 1 to 20 in first grade, instead of completing a common worksheet with pictures of animals, students can more appropriately apply the concepts and skills presented in the textbook as they individually count the number of adult and baby animals in pictures of a herd of cows, a flock of sheep, and a pride of lions, and compare these numbers to learn about animals and patterns of raising their young.

A seventh grade class was learning about ocean currents in science, and instead of each student completing identical maps to show the location of these currents, they explored the currents that affected a particular part of the world they were studying. From that perspective they learned how to map warm and cold currents and their directionality.

As students collect data in response to their questions, they have to record it in some fashion. Traditionally, this has been done primarily through the completion of structured worksheets, written responses to given questions, and note taking.

In chapter 1, we described several modes of thought, which fall into three categories: symbolic, imagic, and affective. The traditional approaches to recording data tend to be limited to one type of symbolic thought, verbal thinking. We know that people use many modes of thought, and that verbal thinking is not necessarily the preferred mode. Children are often much more comfortable with the imagic modes than with the symbolic modes of reading and writing.

There is no compelling reason why the recording of data should be limited to writing. Indeed, across the fields of study, researchers use a variety of modes to record information and ideas: drawing, model making, music, choreography, and so on. Students, too, can be encouraged to use verbal, visual, spatial, tonal, and kinesthetic–sensate modes of expression in order to record their learning. Such records can take various forms:

Written notes: Sequential reports, lab notebooks, responses to open-ended questions, structured note taking

Schematic representations: Maps, charts

Mathematical records: Formulas, diagrams, graphs

Oral recordings: Interviews, dialogues, descriptions of phenomena, observations

Visual records: Drawings, photographs, videotapes, computer graphics

Musical records (written or taped): Songs, musical themes

Spatial representations: Models, sculpture

Kinesthetic records: Dance, exercise routines, sports strategies

As they collect data, students have to organize it. They have to learn to identify the main ideas and the information that supports those ideas. This is a difficult and abstract task. In order to help students organize their data, it is useful to think about the processes that are used in data collection and use them to structure student thinking. Such processes include:

Categorizing: What ideas go together?

Comparing and contrasting: Which ideas are the same? Which are different?

Sequencing: What happened first? Next?

Cause and effect: Why did this happen?

Predicting: What is likely to happen next? What will be discussed next?

Determining fact and opinion: What is presented as fact? What are the author's ideas or opinions?

These processes are basic to all thinking and are taught across the curriculum. They help us to make sense of our world.

REPORTING AND COMMUNICATING

Students who have learned to organize the search for information have already begun to analyze their findings. The next step is to be able to report and present their findings and to identify new questions. Whatever sources of information students consult during their theme studies, they will be developing the habits of mind that were discussed in chapter 1. As they examine their data and try to make sense of it, students will be using the intuitive and analytic processes of predicting and hypothesizing that are components of *forming hunches*. They will be *searching for patterns* as they organize their findings, then will infer and generalize from them. They will use *models* and *metaphors* to clarify, explain, and communicate the meanings they have constructed during their inquiries.

There are significant differences between and among recording and reporting the findings of investigations and communicating one's understandings of a theme study through a culminating project.

In chapter 9, we explore in detail some alternative methods of assessing and evaluating student learning. Here we distinguish between the formative evaluation that occurs when students are recording their findings and the summative evaluation that occurs when they report their findings.

During and after consultation of resources to find answers to their questions, students compile and organize their data and put their findings into some tangible form in order to articulate their findings. This permits verification, which is an important and necessary part of all inquiry. Feedback from other students and the teacher helps students find the gaps in their work and the holes in their reasoning. The responses students get from others offers them direction for revising, editing, and further developing their analyses and their ideas about how to synthesize their findings. This process guides students in interpreting the factual content they have found, in defining the concepts they have been studying, in formulating the generalizations that are best supported by their data, and in selecting the forms they will use to express their syntheses. The recording process permits several "drafts" and much editing and revising.

When students express their syntheses, in whatever ways they choose, they are demonstrating what they have learned. Evaluation here is summative; it assesses what has been accomplished and learned. The work products that signal the formal end of a theme study may result from individual or group effort. Some students may wish to explore the theme beyond its completion by the class, but that is usually an individual choice.

Some of the methods students select for reporting their syntheses may contribute to the culminating project. For any class or grade level, the culminating project is a special collection of the very best that each student can share. Some students will report their findings by producing models. Others may create different types of texts, including expository, narrative, and poetic forms. Books are frequently products of students' syntheses. Oral presentations permit the student with linguistic capabilities to share most effectively. Visual thinkers may find films and audiovisual productions comfortable ways to share their knowledge. Even young children can prepare exhibits of objects and artifacts that tell the story of their investigations. Experiments that are described in the fashion of science-fair entries may be added to those that are more like hands-on exhibits, leading the visitor to discover a main idea or formulate an inference or generalization. The creation of Hypercard Stacks for interactive multimedia productions can be developed by an individual, small group, or whole class, or can even be a sophisticated project like the Santa Ana Kids' Project (Santa Ana Kids' Project, 1991).

The culminating project is a showcase of learning that was developed through individual theme units and long-term interdisciplinary theme studies. The culminating project may be designed for other students, parents, and all members of the school community to experience. Its major purposes are:

▼ To define the theme study

▼ To explain what was learned and how that learning was achieved

▼ To illustrate the integrity of the questions and problems the students have explored and the elegance of their solutions

▼ READER INVOLVEMENT

Look back at the activity cluster you developed in chapter 6. Determine what kinds of resources can be used to explore the subquestion for the activity cluster. Revise your activity cluster to incorporate the resources. Develop learning activities that include the use of as many resources as possible.

REFERENCES

Bredekamp, S., & Rosegrant, T. (Eds.). (1992). *Reaching potential: Appropriate curriculum and assessment for young children* (Vol. 1). Washington, DC: National Association for the Education of Young Children.

Kumori, A. (1979). *Animal mothers.* New York: Philomel Books.

Lynch, P. (1991). *Multimedia: Getting started.* Sunnyvale, CA: PUBLIX Information Products for Apple Computer.

Martinello, M. L. (1987). *The search for Emma's story: A model for humanities detective work.* Fort Worth: Texas Christian University Press.

Narodick, S., & the Education Team. (1992). *Parent's guide to educational software for young children.* Redmond, WA: Edmark Corporation.

Nelson, T. (1987). *Dream machine/computer lib.* Redmond, WA: Tempus Books.

Santa Ana Kids' Project [Unpublished computer program]. (1991). McFadden Intermediate School, Santa Ana, CA.

Voris, H. H., Sedzielarz, M., & Blackmon, C. P. (1986). *Teach the mind, touch the spirit: A guide to focussed field trips.* Chicago: Department of Education, Field Museum of Natural History.

Part Three

Evaluation and Implementation

Chapter Nine

Evaluation and Thematic Inquiry

*I*n 1975, the North Dakota Study Group on Evaluation, under the leadership of Vito Perrone, published a handbook on documentation of children's learning (Engel, 1975). The purposes of documentation were defined as follows:

1. To "know" the event more closely.
2. To order and objectify materials for analysis and evaluation, for purposes of improvement.
3. To present the materials for general interest, communication, funding, etc. (p. 3)

These purposes, which may be summarized as knowledge and understanding, analysis and interpretation, and presentation and communication, are clearly applicable to the documentation and assessment of children's learning through interdisciplinary inquiry. In this chapter, we explore approaches to evaluation that are particularly appropriate for student inquiry through interdisciplinary theme studies.

ASSESSMENT PROCESSES AND PROCEDURES

The next time the fourth grade team met, everyone was pleased with the scope and sequence they had outlined, and with the learning activity plans they had developed.

"Boy, we sure got a lot done at our last meeting!" exclaimed Jose. "I can see how the resources I've found fit the activities we've developed. The students are about ready to find some resources to begin their explorations."

"We're ready, too," said Elizabeth. "I have found some books and poetry selections for the students to use as we discuss memories."

"We've really come a long way in our planning," Raynetta interjected, "but we still need to decide how to evaluate the students' achievements and learning during the thematic study."

"Hm-m-m," Nicole mused. "I guess we could use the end-of-the-chapter tests from the math textbook, just as we have always done."

"I've been giving literature and poetry tests at the end of each unit. I have those ready for use," Elizabeth added.

"Yes, but it seems to me that those types of evaluation may not work anymore," Jose suggested.

"What do you mean?" asked Nicole.

"Well, think about it," he continued. "If our students are collecting oral histories and using their math skills in reading and making maps, for example, they are learning content and thinking processes that are not assessed by our traditional testing materials."

"I agree," Raynetta said. "We need to think about ways to evaluate the students' progress toward the outcomes we've specified. We're concerned with children's thinking processes and their ability to use content in the exploration of challenging problems."

Evaluative processes are continuous, pervading all learning and teaching. When we consider assessment carefully, we are also considering the reliability and validity of what we teach, and even the development of curriculum.

Interdisciplinary inquiry requires us to move beyond conventional forms of assessment and to use open-ended, complex challenges that enable children to demonstrate ways in which they construct their own meanings. Such approaches to assessment provide variety in modes of expression and can appraise both the processes and the products of the activity. Assessment procedures in thematic studies should be appropriate for a variety of tasks, accommodate children's individual strengths and needs, and promote evaluation across the fields of study.

In thematic studies, teachers use multidimensional forms of assessment in order to gather information about student progress toward learning outcomes. Learners are viewed as capable of actively constructing knowledge through several different modes of thought: imagic, symbolic, and affective. Assessment procedures must be able to examine the process of inquiry and these diverse modes of thinking.

Classroom teachers have a number of assessment procedures available to them. The literature on assessment describes a variety of methods designed to evaluate students' thinking and their ability to use knowledge: observation, checklists, interview/conference documentation, inventories, writing samples, performance tests with rating scales, video- and audio tapes, reading records, and responses through the performing arts. Planning for assessment in interdisciplinary theme studies is an integral part of planning for instruction. Objectives, learning activities, and assessment procedures are so closely interrelated that they cannot be designed independently.

Criteria for Significance

Earlier in this text, we presented criteria for the selection of themes. Figure 9.1 shows the criteria for assessment procedures. These criteria can be applied to all types of assessment, formal and informal.

The literature on assessment describes a wide variety of options. Teachers select those most relevant to their students' learning. In thematic studies, we have found the following options particularly useful: portfolios to document individual student learning, rubrics to provide criteria that make assessment meaningful, and learning records to permit teachers and students to keep track of learner progress.

USING PORTFOLIOS IN EVALUATION

Evaluation procedures include the collection of information over time, the analysis of data, and the search for meanings about learning. For years, architects, models, and photographers, among others, have used portfolios to chronicle their best work. The portfolio is equally applicable to the documentation and evaluation of student learn-

Figure 9.1
Criteria for assessment procedures

1. Is there consistency between the learning objectives and the means of assessment?
2. Do the means of assessment enable students to demonstrate their learning?
3. Are the means of assessment reliable? Are they consistent over time?
4. Can the means of assessment demonstrate student development in the mastery of content and process?
5. Can the means of assessment and their findings be clearly understood by all involved: teachers, students, parents, and administrators?

ing (Wiggins, 1992). When using portfolios, students can claim ownership in the evaluation process through self-evaluation and critical reflection about their work samples and the learning they represent. Teachers using student portfolios in their classes can monitor children's development, and can make changes in curriculum and instruction to meet individual student needs. Parents can look at their children's portfolios in order to follow their progress.

A portfolio is a purposeful collection of dated student work that highlights the individual efforts of students in one or more areas of classroom study. Students and teachers are active participants in the selection of the content of the portfolio and in the identification and application of criteria for judging the merit of the portfolio's contents. An added dimension of the student portfolio is that it can show evidence of students' reflection about their work.

A number of potential purposes for portfolio assessment include the following:

▼ To examine growth over time

▼ To involve students in self-evaluation

▼ To help students and teachers set goals

▼ To validate how students learn

▼ To help students connect process and product

▼ To provide student ownership, motivation, sense of accomplishment, and participation

▼ To look at the development of process skills and thinking

▼ To assess curriculum needs

▼ To improve communication

In interdisciplinary theme studies, the portfolio documents learning and provides an ongoing record of development in exploration and inquiry.

Selection of Materials

How will material be selected for the portfolio? Teachers need to help children choose samples of work that represent the knowledge, processes, and affective abilities fostered in the classroom. Students need guidance and time to learn how to select the items that represent their learning. For instance, a teacher might ask students to identify the items that represent their greatest challenges, best work, or most satisfying learning experiences. Materials selected for a portfolio used during an interdisciplinary theme study might indicate

1. Information that the student has gathered relevant to the subquestion;
2. Processes that the student used to explore the subquestion; and
3. Resources that the student identified in those investigations.

As the portfolio develops, the quality of the work is assessed according to criteria related to the prior experience of the students, their developmental levels, the planned learning outcomes, and the task itself. Such criteria may be applied through the use of rubrics.

▼ READER INVOLVEMENT

Look back at the activity cluster(s) that you have developed. Identify the activities that would result in materials for a portfolio. How might student portfolios contribute to the culminating activity that you designed?

USING RUBRICS IN EVALUATION

A rubric is a clearly established set of criteria that specifies gradations in achievement. The rubric is criterion-referenced rather than norm-referenced, which allows students to work toward mastery of developmentally-appropriate learning outcomes.

Rubrics may be general or specific to a particular task. A holistic rubric might outline general criteria that can be applied to many different areas of the curriculum. For example, the California Assessment Program (Stenmark, 1989) includes a detailed rubric that was designed for problem solving in mathematics. It uses these broad categories:

Rating	*Type of Response*
6	Exemplary response
5	Competent response
4	Minor errors, but generally satisfactory
3	Serious errors, but nearly satisfactory
2	Begins, but fails to complete, task/problem/question
1	Unable to begin effectively
0	No attempt

In addition to general rubrics that may be applied to a variety of tasks, rubrics may be designed to evaluate specific learning outcomes. For example, the Texas Education Agency (1993) developed the following rubric for the holistic scoring of student writing:

Score Point 4	*Score Point 3*
Correct purpose, mode, audience	Correct purpose, mode, audience
Effective elaboration	Moderately well elaborated
Consistent organization	Organized (but possible brief digressions)
Clear sense of order/completeness	Clear, effective language
Fluent	

Score Point 2

Correct purpose, mode, audience
Some elaboration
Some specific details
Gaps in organization
Limited language control

Score Point 1

Attempts to address audience
Brief/vague
Unelaborated
Wanders on/off topic
Lack of language control
Poor or no organization
Wrong purpose/mode

Score Point 0

Off topic
Blank paper
Foreign language
Illegible/incoherent
Copied prompt
Did not write enough to score (p. 20d)

For more focused assessment of specific writing objectives, a rubric such as the Selective Correction form (Texas Education Agency, 1993) might be used:

Selective Correction (Scoring for Specific Skills)

Example: Grading for Vivid Verbs

4 = Verbs exact, exciting

3 = Most verbs interesting

2 = Only a few verbs vivid

1 = Very few verbs interesting

0 = No vivid verbs (p. 20f)

The Texas Elementary Science Inservice Program (TESIP), developed by the University of Texas at Austin's Science Education Center and Texas Project 2061 (Barufaldi, Carnahan, & Rakow, 1991), matches specific rubrics to science tasks. One task on experimental design states its objective, materials, and problem as follows:

Objective: The student will design and complete an experiment, record observations, and draw conclusions.
Materials: Spring balance; wooden board (6 inches wide by 12 inches long); four textbooks; toy car or truck.
Problem: How does the angle of the board affect the force needed to pull the car up the board?

A rubric for each part of the task specifies several levels of performance. Note that the rubric for part 2 below is a five-point scale, while those for parts 1 and 3 have four points.

Part 1: Designing the Experiment

Describe the kind of tests you will do to find the answer.

Scoring

0	Fails to develop any type of plan
1	Design will not allow comparison of variable to standard
2	Design allows comparison of variables, but lacks sufficient number of tests to obtain meaningful data
3	Design allows comparison of variables and indicates sufficient number of tests to obtain meaningful data

Part 2: Collecting and Reporting Data

Record all of your observations so that someone else will understand what you have observed.

Scoring

0	Fails to collect any data
1	Describes observations in a disjointed manner
2	Makes a data table, but table lacks meaningful labels
3	Makes a meaningful data table, but fails to accurately record observations
4	Makes a meaningful table and records the data correctly

Part 3: Drawing Conclusions

What do you conclude is the answer to the problem "How does the angle of the board reflect the amount of force needed to pull the car up the ramp?" Be sure to support your conclusions with evidence.

Scoring

0	Fails to reach a conclusion
1	Draws a conclusion that is not supported by data
2	Draws a conclusion that is supported by the data, but fails to show any evidence for the conclusion
3	Draws a conclusion that is supported by the data and gives supporting evidence for the conclusion

These rubrics have been designed primarily for statewide assessment procedures. However, rubrics for general or specific learning outcomes can be developed for classroom use. Guidelines for designing rubrics include the following:

1. The behaviors described in the rubric should be the behaviors described in the learning objectives or in the description of the task.
2. There is no required number of points on the scale for a rubric; most useful rubrics include four to six points.

3. The descriptors for each point on the scale should be as clear and unambiguous as possible; complex tasks may be divided into separate parts with separate rubrics for each part.

4. Students may participate in the construction of rubrics by specifying the expected behaviors for each point on the scale. This helps students to gain a clear understanding of the nature and requirements of the task.

Even if students do not participate in the development of rubrics, they need to be actively involved in applying the criteria by which their products will be evaluated, so that as they construct knowledge through inquiry, they know the standards by which to judge their learning. Student participation in self-evaluation is extremely important. When students see connections among their work products, learning outcomes, and evaluation, they can recognize their strengths and build upon them. Their learning is more focused and can emphasize interdisciplinary connections and the use of habits of mind.

Teachers can work with students to assist them in self-evaluation. For example, when fourth graders were studying plants, they were able to apply a rubric designed to evaluate observational skills.

The children visited the botanical gardens to observe the tropical rain forest and desert areas. They examined each area, comparing and contrasting the vegetation for specific examples of ways that plants adapt to the different environments. The focus of this inquiry was the use of observation to find similarities and differences among plants in the two areas. After the children had recorded their findings, they applied the following rubric to assess their ability to make accurate and detailed observations:

Observing

5   *Makes six or more comparative observations related to the question under investigation; observational notes include accurate and detailed drawings*

4   *Makes five comparative observations related to the question under investigation; observational notes include accurate drawings with limited detail*

3   *Makes three or four observations related to the question under investigation; observational records are partially accurate, with limited detail*

2   *Makes three or four observations; observational records are inaccurate, with limited detail*

1   *Makes one or two observations; observational records are inaccurate and incomplete*

0   *Fails to make observations*

Another form of rubric can be developed in response to student work. This content analysis of student response allows teachers to analyze the ways in which individual students complete a task and perform a process. It also permits teachers to develop open-ended rubrics in which the highest level of performance is not initially defined. Rubrics of this type are often found in the research literature, largely because they permit evaluators to discover subtleties in student responses that adults might not anticipate, and because they may be applied to the work of children at different stages of development. Rubrics that evaluate the observation skills of 5-year-olds are not usually applicable to evaluating the observation skills of older students. For instance, if teachers want to evaluate student ability to make inferences and to formulate questions, they may provide an unknown stimulus and direct the students to interpret the object (e.g., artifact) or phenomenon (e.g., physical action or chemical reaction) and to list all the questions they have about it.

Using a fossil, a crinoid, Martinello and Kromer (1990) asked second grade students to respond to questions such as: (1) What do you see? (2) What do you think the object is? (3) What would you like to know about the object? Student responses to the first question were examined for the number and type of descriptors used. Responses to the second question were evaluated for the reasonableness of the inference and whether it was supported by evidence. This permitted the evaluation of inferences that might not be correct but were logical. Some student questions were intended to gather data; some tested hypotheses.

Because the categories were formed from the students' responses, students had significant input into the rubric's design. In all cases, there was no ceiling attached to any category, so students were not limited by a predetermined set of standards. By administering similar tasks with open-ended rubrics early and late in the studies, teachers could evaluate students' development of sophistication in using the thinking processes that are central to any curriculum strand. When developing this type of instrumentation for the evaluation of student learning, teachers were acting as inquirers, creating and testing their own professional methods.

▼ READER INVOLVEMENT

Choose one of the materials that you selected for the portfolio and design a rubric to evaluate its quality. Select a learning activity from your activity cluster and design a rubric that assesses the processes students develop through the activity.

LEARNING RECORDS

Chapter 6 presented ways of planning learning activities for interdisciplinary studies. Every learning activity cluster and learning activity plan specifies the central question under study and the main thinking processes that students will use as they conduct their inquiries. Well-chosen portfolio items will document the ways in which students explore and find answers to subquestions and central questions. The teachers with whom we have worked appreciate the portfolio's documentary value. Additionally, they have expressed the need for more summary record keeping, with the specific purpose of assessing each learner's abilities (1) to formulate answers to an activity cluster's central question and (2) to use the main thinking processes that the activities were designed to develop. Teachers have devised formats to accomplish this for individual students, small groups of students, and even an entire class. We call these *learning records.*

The learning records for the interdisciplinary theme studies that we have developed with teachers focus on central questions and thinking processes, as indicated in Figure 9.2. In some cases, teachers have chosen to include subquestions for each activity cluster as well. The degree of specificity depends upon teacher preference and student need; both use learning records to monitor learning and to establish new goals.

Figure 9.2
Learning record

Name	CQ1	TP: e.g., OBS	CQ2	TP: e.g., HYP	CQn	TPx

Abbreviations: CQ, central question; TP, thinking process; OBS, observing; HYP, hypothesizing.

Individual learning records simply use one form per student; group learning records list the names of all students in a small group or the entire class. In some classrooms, students keep their own personal records, which are periodically compared with those kept by the teacher. In others, students may examine and react to those kept by the teacher. In all cases, learning records are shared with parents.

Whether completed by teachers, by students, or by teachers and students in consultation, learning records permit holistic, subjective assessments. These provide varied evidence of student ability to formulate answers to questions or to use the thinking processes under examination. Teachers may base their assessments on their examination of student work products and their observation of student verbal and nonverbal behaviors. For students, the process is self-evaluative, and their notations give their impressions of their own learning.

How well students formulate answers to the central questions of an activity cluster may be noted by using a generalized rubric. Whether or not they can formulate reasoned answers may simply be noted by the presence or absence of a check mark. Dated observations indicate when they were able to do so. Comments, of course, are useful to clarify the nature of the observation and the evidence. Student ability to use the central thinking processes associated with a learning activity cluster is usually assessed by a specific rubric, but examples of evidence are always helpful in clarifying the depth and sophistication of the thinking demonstrated.

GRADING AND COMMUNICATING

Throughout this chapter, we have taken the position that evaluation is primarily for the learner's benefit. Therefore, all of the methods we recommend involve students in the evaluation process, through consultation with the teacher and with parents and through self-evaluation. Whatever the methods used to document, record, and assess learning, they should be used to guide each student toward maximum development in all instructional areas within reasonable and appropriate time frames. We do not believe this is accomplished by assigning evaluative letter grades or number grades with nebulous meanings and by communicating solely through report cards. In our view, nothing can or should replace individual conferences between teacher and student and among teacher, student, and parent. The evidence used in these conferences is contained in portfolios and learning records that, by their nature, permit sharing and consultation.

Teachers who view themselves as inquirers into their own practice will also use these documents as evidence of their own teaching effectiveness. Through careful analysis, they may uncover, in these documents and records, clues to their students' understandings or misconceptions, clear or fuzzy thinking, areas of interest or disinterest, inventive or mundane ideas, and even reasons for boredom or sources of challenge. Evaluation in interdisciplinary theme studies directs teaching and curriculum development as much as it assesses learning.

REFERENCES

Barufaldi, J. P., Carnahan, P. S., & Rakow, S. J. (1991). *Texas elementary science inservice program* (Education for Economic Security Act Title II, Project 00690401-04). Austin, TX: Texas Education Agency.

Engel, B. S. (1975). *A handbook on documentation.* Grand Forks, ND: University of North Dakota.

Martinello, M. L., & Kromer, M. E. (1990). Developing and assessing lower-SES Hispanic children's inferential thinking. *Journal of Elementary Science Education, 2,* 21–36.

Stenmark, J. K. (1989). *Assessment alternatives in mathematics: An overview of assessment techniques that promote learning.* Berkeley, CA: Regents, University of California.

Texas Education Agency. (1993). *Writing inservice guide for English language arts and TAAS.* Austin, TX: Author.

Wiggins, G. (1992). *Portfolios: Design ideas and criteria.* Geneses, NY: Center on Learning, Assessment, and School Structure.

Additional Reading

Herman, J. L., Aschbacher, P. R., & Winters, L. (1992). *A practical guide to alternative assessment.* Alexandria, VA: Association for Supervision and Curriculum Development.

Tierney, R. J., Carter, M. A., & Desai, L. E. (1991). *Portfolio assessment in the reading–writing classroom.* Norwood, MA: Christopher-Gordon Publishers.

Chapter Ten

Implementation of Interdisciplinary Curriculum

IMPLEMENTATION OF INTERDISCIPLINARY CURRICULUM IN THE SCHOOL

Curriculum development and implementation take place on a number of levels simultaneously: the classroom, the school, and the district. If interdisciplinary curriculum is to be successfully implemented, all three levels must be involved. Teachers must develop understanding of the principles of interdisciplinary curriculum and a commitment to them, and must be able to translate these principles into practice for their own unique group of students. Administrators at the school level must provide time and support for teachers as they experiment with new approaches, recognizing that significant change takes time and that their own commitment to the interdisciplinary approach will facilitate the commitment of teachers in their schools. Central office personnel must understand and support the dynamic nature of curriculum at the grass-roots level. The most important ingredients in successful curriculum implementation are mutual trust and true collaboration among all the people involved: students, teachers, administrators, and the community.

Many questions about interdisciplinary curriculum relate to implementation: Where do you begin? How do you schedule theme studies? How can theme studies be introduced in ways that do not disrupt the regular and necessary flow of activities in the school? How do teachers do everything they're supposed to do and theme studies, too, and maintain their sanity? These and related issues of implementation of interdisciplinary curriculum have many and varied responses. In this chapter, we present some suggestions for implementation, giving examples from our experiences with teachers and their schools. As we have done throughout this book, we invite readers to select the most suitable methods, and to invent their own.

BEGINNING THEME STUDIES: PATTERNS OF IMPLEMENTATION

There is no one prescription for successful implementation and administration of interdisciplinary curriculum. Our work with elementary and middle schools has shown that each school must develop its own ways of getting started with an interdisciplinary curriculum. The unique character of these approaches emerges from school culture, the character and needs of the student body, the experience and knowledge of the teachers, the expectations of the community, the broad goals of the school district, and many other factors.

We have found several patterns of implementation of interdisciplinary curriculum:

1. Individual teachers introduce theme studies in their own classrooms without involving other teachers and without altering established school schedules.
2. Grade-level teams initiate theme studies, with teachers collaboratively working out schedules for their grade level's population of students.
3. Particular sections of schools, such as the primary or intermediate grades or several middle-school grade-level teams, collaborate to offer students opportunities for theme studies.
4. Whole schools work toward this purpose.
5. Several schools collaborate so that interschool grade-level teacher teams work together.

Individual Teacher Initiatives

Many interdisciplinary theme studies are initiated by individual teachers. Teachers often communicate their interest in an event, an object, or an idea to their students, such as the teacher who was studying for her pilot's license and shared her experiences with her fifth graders. Sometimes students bring interests to school that have potential for short-term or more extensive theme studies. A group of second grade Girl Scouts brought to school their enthusiasm for a patch project, and ultimately involved their classmates in the extensive study of a historic route in their state. As we discussed earlier, teachers who think in thematic ways and who seek to engage their students in inquiry invite questions about these interests. They guide their students' inquiry toward the exploration of big ideas to develop interdisciplinary theme studies that ensure curriculum standards are at least met, if not exceeded.

Spiders intrigued a third grade teacher who had a passion for arachnids. She was enrolled in a graduate course in curriculum and supervision that required the design and development of an interdisciplinary unit. Searching for a focus, the teacher looked to her interests and the availability of resources for her students' explorations. Spiders surfaced immediately as a topic; adaptation for survival became the thematic concept. The teacher completed her own inquiry into the topic and theme, then designed a curriculum plan and implemented it over several years, with different children, and, eventually, with a student teacher. This theme study has become part of the teacher's regular curriculum. She schedules the children's theme studies during times that she can control, without altering regular grade-level and schoolwide activities. Her students typically share their theme study with parents and with other grade-level classes. And the teacher has presented her work at a national meeting of the National Science Teachers Association.

Grade-Level Team Planning

Many middle schools begin by restructuring one or more grade levels into interdisciplinary teams. Occasionally the interdisciplinary curriculum is introduced in a "school-within-a-school" setting.

Teams provide ways for students to know each other, for manageable block scheduling, and for teachers to have common planning periods. It is possible to begin with one team, one grade level, several volunteer teams across the grade levels, or to make a schoolwide commitment to interdisciplinary curriculum.

This approach enables teachers who come with expertise in specific subject areas such as math or history to participate in developing interdisciplinary curriculum. Grade-level teams in the elementary school can also work together to share ideas and resources to enrich their own theme studies.

Cross-Grade Interaction

Theme studies are particularly suited to nongraded or multigrade situations. They can encompass a broad scope and sequence of content and skills that cross traditional grade lines. They allow students to move through that scope and sequence at their own pace because theme studies provide many and diverse opportunities for individual and group work.

Oaklea Middle School has a media center at its hub from which classroom clusters called rivers radiate. Each river is a school-within-a-school for multiage groups of students in grades 5–8. Interdisciplinary teaching teams within each river develop theme studies.

All teams within each river have common planning periods and hold regular meetings after school. Each river sends curriculum and scheduling representatives to meetings of the four schools.

Students are assigned to a river first by parent choice and then according to recommendations from their elementary teachers. Attempts are made to balance each river with students who have different levels of achievement and differing needs. Students in each river stay with their homeroom teacher for 4 years.

Oaklea's teachers teach three to six subjects per day. All curriculum is proposed by teachers, individuals, and groups. The faculty seeks to implement the best research-based practices and, because of the organization for effective decision making and communication, is able to do so with ease and speed.

The school, recognized in Oregon and nationwide as a model school, recently obtained federal funds to enhance its work with "at-risk" students and to develop the interdisciplinary concept. Monitoring, assessment alternatives, and interdisciplinary curriculum are the focus of Oaklea's new efforts (Martinello & Cook, 1992).

Whole-School Commitment

Schoolwide implementation of team organization and interdisciplinary curriculum must be supported by all involved. Support from the central office is essential. Every new program should develop from a sound philosophy and from shared commitment to it among teachers and administrators. Also, staff development is crucial. Interdisciplinary curriculum often requires teachers to change their approach to teaching and learning. This change may be difficult and even painful. The principal plays a vital part in ensuring that time and support are available. After a year of staff development to familiarize the teachers at Anson Jones Middle School with the concepts of interdisciplinary teams and curriculum, the entire faculty voted to adopt this approach. Classrooms are grouped so teachers can work closely together, and movement in the halls is minimized. Bells during the day have been eliminated, and flexible scheduling allows teams to block their class time in different ways.

Curriculum integration is planned carefully by teachers at the daily team meetings. Interdisciplinary teams of teachers at each grade level interface on various levels to provide integrated learning experiences for their students. Every team develops at least one integrated theme unit each semester that incorporates some or all of the content areas (Martinello & Cook, 1992).

Interschool Collaboration

Several schools can work together to encourage teachers of one, several, or all grade levels to plan together for theme studies that cross school campuses. This can occur when several school principals join forces—and budgets—to facilitate interschool curriculum development. Grade-level teams, composed of teachers from several campus sites, are given time to meet for planning and to reflect on their work for evaluative purposes. In addition to administrative commitment and support, which includes provision of substitute teachers to release the classroom teacher for a half or whole day and materials for instruction, this approach usually requires that at least one teacher from each team assume responsibility to facilitate interaction and serve as liaison across the participating school grade-level teams.

A group of four schools, all serving lower socioeconomic minority students, came together because of the leadership of their principals. The intent of the four administrators was to implement site-based management that dealt with curriculum issues. The principals selected interdisciplinary curriculum design and development as their focus, then consulted university faculty for ways to begin. Through several planning sessions that involved the principals, school district personnel, and classroom teachers who had some experience with interdisciplinary theme studies, an in-service plan was developed and implemented with the entire staffs of the four schools. The four schools sought and were granted special permission to develop their program by expanding the time allotted for in-service work and teacher planning. As part of the program, teacher facilitators from each grade level were invited to enroll in a graduate course on interdisciplinary teaching and learning, with tuition, fees, and books paid from the schools' budgets. These teachers developed curriculum outlines in consultation with their teaching teams. Each grade-level team in each school works in its own way, with communication among the facilitators maintaining the flow of ideas. Some teams have done extensive work with theme studies. Others have been more moderate in their introduction of theme studies into their classrooms. Still others have elected to move more slowly, or have chosen not to participate. As this experiment in interschool collaboration continues, data is being collected to evaluate the project's impact on student learning and teacher professional development. Preliminary findings show expected variation among the teachers in their development of theme studies, but experience does not seem to be a significant factor. Novices and experienced teachers alike are showing evidence of implementing interdisciplinary studies that challenge students to exceed grade level standards. Their minority students appear to be meeting those challenges.

SCHOOLWIDE SCHEDULING

When entire schools are involved in theme studies, teachers and administrators are faced with the task of scheduling to meet several types of need:

1. Keeping groups of students together;
2. Attending to the role of the special-area teachers; and
3. Providing time for teachers to plan.

Teachers working on a grade-level team work with the same students. This permits them to plan an appropriate sequence within the theme study. For instance, in a theme study on conservation, a seventh grade team needed to schedule their students' study of statistical treatment of data in math class before the science teacher involved the students in analyzing data on industrial waste products and related health problems, and before the social studies teacher asked the students to map locations of the highest incidences of health hazards associated with industrial waste.

In both elementary and middle schools, it is important to work closely with special-area teachers in art, music, physical education, special education, English as a second language, and bilingual education. Each of these teachers can bring a unique dimension to theme studies. Art and music teachers are usually the first to be involved because their areas traditionally have been integrated into other curriculum areas. Special education teachers can include learning activities in the resource room that complement children's theme studies in their regular classroom. Careful scheduling for interdisciplinary theme studies allows resource-room experiences to enhance the educational purposes of inclusion and mainstreaming programs. Students who are assigned to bilingual classrooms can conduct interdisciplinary thematic explorations in a sheltered language context.

Time for teacher planning is mandatory for the successful implementation of theme studies. When teachers work in interdisciplinary ways, designing and developing inquiry-oriented experiences for students, they are also engaged in constructing and, perhaps, redefining their own practice. When teacher teams work together for this purpose, they are forming professional relationships and refining collaborative skills that can have lasting impact on the team's abilities to achieve excellence in educational programming and in teaching. Such teachers learn from one another and contribute significantly to the learning opportunities for all children on the grade level. This is a professional endeavor of tremendous importance to the individual teacher, the teaching team, the school, and the school community that deserves administrative support. Planning meetings are staff development sessions; a sequence of productive and collaborative planning sessions can become a powerful in-service program for self-directed and peer-guided continuing professional education. Adequate time for these meetings must be allocated on a regular basis and scheduled within the regular school day in ways that do not conflict with other uses of out-of-class time, such as parent conferences, record keeping, grading, or other teacher responsibilities.

COMMUNITY AND PARENTAL INVOLVEMENT

Parents and other members of the community are invaluable resources for students' explorations of many and diverse themes. One of the most significant ways to involve parents and community members in student inquiries is to invite them to serve as resource people. Of all the sources of information, the human consultant who lives or works in the community may well have information to share that is not available elsewhere.

During a four-school study of the "Seeds of Change" idea that the Smithsonian Institution developed to mark the Columbian quincentenary, an in-service workshop for all participating teachers was planned by teachers at one of the schools. The workshop focused on using community resources to encourage students of all ages to gather information by asking questions of guest consultants. The teacher planners looked to their local community for resource people.

For the study of the horse, they found a member of the local Charro Organization, a highly respected and award-winning horseman with remarkable skills in riding and using a lariat. The Charro delighted his audience of teachers with dazzling demonstrations on a champion horse. He shared in Spanish (with an interpreter for monolingual English-speaking teachers) a wealth of knowledge about horses and riding and the Mexican rodeo and vaquero traditions.

To show the significance of sugar as a seed of change, an African-American central office supervisor came in native dress to share how the history of her people was inextricably bound up with the sugar trade.

For those who were studying corn as another seed of change, two mothers demonstrated the creation of very different types of tamales. One, from Mexico, showed how to prepare a traditional tamale by spreading masa paste on corn shucks. The other, from Guatemala, used banana leaves and a masa mixture the consistency of pudding. Each explained their variations in the use of ingredients and cooking methods, demonstrating the versatility of corn as an American foodstuff.

The study of disease as a seed of change encouraged teachers to look to the local health science center for experts on contemporary epidemics. The teachers invited an AIDS researcher to speak to the group of teachers and parents who were involved in the workshop. Prior to his arrival, the workshop participants wrote out the questions they had about AIDS, then synthesized them and posted their queries around the room (just as they would do with their students). When the researcher arrived, he responded to many of the questions.

Parents may also contribute to the process of planning theme studies. When asked to consider themes for student study, they can suggest questions to explore and identify community resources for research. Children may be able to identify those parents who have the most to contribute to a given theme study, and to help in soliciting their participation.

Parents and community members who are willing and able to take an active role in school activities may be invited to in-service workshops, where they can work with grade-level teacher groups and parent groups to explore possibilities for children's theme studies. They may also be invited to work with teachers during their weekly planning sessions. By working collaboratively with teachers in this way, parents gain a sense of ownership of their children's studies. They also develop a better understanding of teacher expectations for children's learning and of the methods the teachers are using—methods that probably vary considerably from those the parents experienced when they attended elementary and middle school.

CELEBRATIONS AND SHARING

Culminating activities are planned to encourage students to share the results of their explorations. Individual classes may hold open-house events to demonstrate the findings of their theme study and to share their knowledge with others. Schoolwide celebrations of learning acquired through theme studies may be day-long events, involving presentations as well as exhibits, or they may be open-house activities of 2 to 3 hours during or after school. Another approach is to record learning and student presentations on videotape, which can be copied and shown in varied venues, including the home. A more ambitious and longer term effort might be a multimedia project, like the Santa Ana Kids' Project (see chapter 8). As students at McFadden Intermediate School in Santa Ana, California, explored the history, economy, culture, literature, architecture, and other characteristics of their community, they created a Hyper-Card program including music, still graphics, and QuickTime movies made during field trips to community sites. This dynamic program invites inquiry about Santa Ana and enables others to discover the substance and methods of the students' studies. This is a notable example of how the community may serve its learners and how the school may serve the community.

By celebrating and sharing children's learning in all communities, especially in the ghettos and barrios of our cities, we underscore our commitment to education as a means of achieving equality of opportunity for all.

CHANGE PROCESS AND TEACHER DEVELOPMENT

Why is change often so uncomfortable? Why do people appear to resist change? Why does it take so long for a new idea to be put into practice? Human reactions to change often seem paradoxical. On the one hand, life itself is constant change. In Western cultures, change is generally seen as desirable and often as synonymous with progress. Yet, at the same time, change is often perceived as confusing, upsetting, time-consuming, and even threatening.

This paradox cannot be avoided as we seek to implement interdisciplinary curriculum in the schools. Rather, we need to explore its implications and seek to understand the nature of successful change. In our own observations of individuals, groups, and schools as they begin to implement interdisciplinary curriculum, certain principles emerge that are supported by the literature on change and change processes.

1. *There must be motivation for the change.* Czajkowski and Patterson (1980) identify three causes of change: *mandate, attractive alternative,* and *discrepancy. Mandate,* the imposition of change from above, may be effective in cases where change is short-term and fairly routine, but it tends to create resistance, suspicion, and lack of real commitment among those expected to carry out the mandate. It is therefore unlikely to be effective in a complex and interactive change process such as the implementation of interdisciplinary curriculum.

Teachers frequently react positively to an *attractive alternative* such as a new textbook, appealing materials, or promising teaching strategies. However, if the attractive alternative is not fully understood, or if its early promise is not easily fulfilled, teachers tend to abandon it and return to previous dependable methods. When beginning to work with interdisciplinary theme studies, for example, teachers often tend to embrace the surface elements of the model without understanding its philosophical or pedagogical base. If they are not given the opportunity to internalize those principles, they may become discouraged or confused and reject the idea.

Discrepancy implies a perception of a gap between what is and what should be. Another way of describing this cause of change is a felt need. Research has shown that perceived needs are powerful motivators (e.g., Berman & McLaughlin, 1977; Emrick & Peterson, 1978; Rosenblum & Louis, 1979). Teachers know that they cannot fulfill all the needs of every child, yet they want to see all their students learn. This sense of discrepancy is a deep motivation that tends to be ongoing and long-lasting. It is also more internalized and personal than external motivators such as mandate and attractive alternative. Too often, teachers are put in a position where discrepancies are seen as failures and therefore should be downplayed or covered up. The inquiry-based character of interdisciplinary curriculum treats discrepancies as invitations for exploration and as ongoing opportunities for learning by teachers, students, administrators, and the community.

2. *Successful change involves shared meanings and beliefs.* While perceived needs are powerful motivators, long-term commitment to change requires shared meanings and beliefs. Fullan (1991) cites Marris (1975) as saying that all significant change involves loss, anxiety, and struggle, a point of view reiterated by Schön (1971), who indicates that real change involves uncertainty, discomfort, and confusion. In order to cope successfully with such feelings, people need to work collaboratively with others to develop a vision of where they are going and to support each other in their efforts to move toward that vision. Such collaboration can occur at various levels. At the school or district level, carefully planned staff development programs empower teachers and administrators to develop joint visions. At the grade or team level,

opportunities for ongoing, regular planning times allow teachers to meet together, share successes and work out problems, and discuss ways in which the curriculum is implemented day by day. In the classroom, students and teachers engage in an ongoing dialogue and shared inquiry as they explore significant themes together. Members of the larger community share in the process as supporters, resources, participants, and audience.

3.   *All participants must have ownership of the change.* Participation provides ownership, but only if such participation is meaningful and appropriate. In a school community, roles are defined in many ways, formally and informally. The culture and character of a school often depend in large part upon participants' perception of their roles. Problems frequently arise from contradictory perceptions of roles.

It is not enough to say that in an inquiry-based curriculum all interested parties have an opportunity to participate in inquiry. While teachers may be coinquirers with children, their roles and responsibilities are not identical. Parents and community members have an important part to play, but they play special roles that must be defined and clarified. Teachers take responsibility for curriculum development for their own students, but they must work within given guidelines. Administrators need to work closely with teachers to define the visions, purposes, and practices of the school, but they have particular responsibilities in setting up and maintaining such a situation. Shared ownership does not imply that everyone has identical responsibilities and roles. It rather indicates that one of the major and continuing tasks in the implementation of interdisciplinary curriculum is the constant definition and redefinition of roles and responsibilities to ensure that each individual can play an appropriate, significant, and rewarding part.

4.   *Change takes time.* This can be understood in two ways. First, change is a process that involves a great deal of interaction, negotiation, and energy. As Fullan (1991) indicates, change is a process, not an event. It cannot ever be completed, because each step in the process leads to new changes.

Teachers are already overburdened with what Huberman (1983) terms the "classroom press": the press for immediacy and concreteness, where they are called upon to make hundreds of decisions in a day, most of them involving the well-being of other individuals; the press for multidimensionality and simultaneity, where they are required to carry out a multitude of tasks at the same time; the press for adapting to ever-changing conditions or unpredictability, for in any complex human situation, the unexpected always happens; and the press for personal involvement with students, so that the teacher is involved emotionally as well as physically and intellectually (cited in Fullan, 1991). It is unrealistic to expect teachers to fit into their crowded days the effort involved in implementing an unfamiliar way of working with children. Time within the regular work day must be provided for planning, reflection, and assessment if there is to be successful implementation of interdisciplinary curriculum, especially when this approach is an innovation.

Change also takes time in another sense. It has been suggested that even moderately complex changes take 3 to 5 years from initiation to institutionalization (Fullan, 1991). Joyce and Weil (1992) found that while teachers could master a new teaching model by seeing it demonstrated 15–20 times and practicing it about a dozen times, most of them experienced great discomfort in putting the model into practice in the classroom, and needed extensive coaching over time before they could make the model a comfortable part of their own teaching. This long-term change means that results must be measured in small and frequent increments, rather than expecting dramatic results at the end of a limited period.

There is often pressure upon administrators and teachers to declare a program a success or a failure at the end of a brief period in order to justify further investment in the program. Accountability must be redefined in terms of the program itself. Standardized test results may not reveal the types of learning inherent in integrated theme studies. It is therefore incumbent upon teachers and administrators to search for and to design and develop appropriate evaluation procedures that will show accurately the learning that has occurred over short and longer time periods.

5. *Change is a developmental process.* People react to change in different ways and adjust to change at different rates. The reasons for this are multifaceted, related to personal variables such as age, career stage, personality, teaching and learning style, and contextual variables within and outside the school, such as school climate, community support, family situations, and external demands. We cannot explore all these factors here, but they must be taken into account.

One model that does have particular significance for the implementation of interdisciplinary curriculum is the Concerns-Based Adoption Model developed by Gene Hall and his colleagues (Hall & Rutherford, 1976; Hall & Loucks, 1978; Hall & Hord, 1987). This model proposes a hierarchy of "Stages of Concern" that people go through when faced with an innovation, such as the introduction of a new curriculum approach (Figure 10.1). Research suggests that when introduced to an innovation, people are concerned about *self,* first seeking information, and then wondering how the innovation will affect them. Once these questions are satisfied, concerns about the *task* emerge; the innovations seem unfamiliar, uncomfortable, and time-consuming, and then the effect upon others is an added concern. As the innovation is gradually mastered and becomes familiar, new concerns arise related to its *impact.* People become interested in collaborating with others to implement the innovation more effectively and, finally, at the *refocusing* stage, they begin to develop refinements and improvements to the original innovation. If these refinements and improvements constitute new innovations, then there may be a return to earlier stages of the model.

At any time in the process of implementing interdisciplinary curriculum, different teachers may be found at different stages of concern about it. In addition, even teachers who have reached a higher stage of concern may revert temporarily to a lower stage because of changes in the program, or because of personal factors such as fatigue, ill health, or family problems.

Figure 10.1
Stages of concern

Source: Excerpt from Hall, Gene E. & Rutherford, William (1976). "Concerns of Teachers About Implementing Team Teaching," *Educational Leadership, 34,* 3. Reprinted with permission of the Association for Supervision and Curriculum Development. Copyright 1976 by ASCD. All rights reserved.

	Typical Expressions of Concern About the Innovation	
	Stages of Concern	Expressions of Concern
I M P A C T	6. Refocusing	I have some ideas about something that would work even better.
	5. Collaboration	I am concerned about relating what I am doing with what other instructors are doing.
T A S K	4. Consequence	How is my use affecting kids?
	3. Management	I seem to be spending all my time getting material ready.
S E L F	2. Personal	How will using it affect me?
	1. Informational	I would like to know more about it.
	0. Awareness	I am not concerned about it (the innovation).

The approach we describe provides a flexibility that can accommodate a wide variety of stages of concern. For example, teachers who are struggling with "personal concerns" may be implementing the curriculum in a limited and "safe" way that allows them to involve students in integrated curriculum studies for only a part of the day, or even on only 2 or 3 days a week or for a limited number of weeks. At the same time, teachers at the "consequence" stage may be working with the students to design a study that builds upon individual interests, while teachers at the "refocusing" stage may be modifying the curriculum further, or working with teachers in another school to help them design their own interdisciplinary curriculum.

A similar model of change processes was described by Rogers (1962), in which he identified five stages: awareness, interest, evaluation, trial, and adoption. Parallels may also be found in Dewey's "scientific method" (1922), which includes five steps: becoming aware of the problem (or felt need), clarifying and refining the problem, evaluating proposed solutions, and experimental verification. All of these models, of course, occur over some extended period of time, and stages in the models may be revisited several times during the change process.

It should be remembered that developmental change processes affect students as well as teachers, and administrators and community personnel as well as those more immediately involved in the change process. Indeed, it is possible that at times students may have achieved a greater understanding and acceptance of interdisciplinary learning than the district administrators.

Continuing discussion and reflection about the curriculum by all involved will lead to deeper understanding and more sophisticated levels of implementation.

6. *Change is never simple or linear.* It is interactive, dynamic, and highly complex, and is affected by environmental factors. It is tempting to treat curricular change as if it were one process, with a beginning, a middle, and an end. However, curricular change cannot be isolated from the complex realities of schooling: state mandates, standardized testing, community expectations, current events, and so on. As Dewey, Flexner, Oberholzer, and the Bank Street educators emphasized, society and the curriculum are, and must be, closely interrelated. Teachers and other curriculum thinkers continue to struggle with the balance between immediate relevance and universality.

Outside influences may be perceived as threats to the successful implementation of new curriculum. How can standardized testing be reconciled with inquiry-based curriculum? How can children's immediate interests relate to the district guidelines? Yet such perceived obstacles may be seen as exciting challenges and as opportunities for rethinking ultimate aims and philosophies of education, and as such may lead to clarification and enrichment of the curriculum itself. For example, the Interdisciplinary Studies Degree program at the University of Texas at San Antonio was developed in response to a state mandate that abolished all elementary education degrees at the baccalaureate level in the State of Texas, and limited the number of hours in professional education to 18, including student teaching. This new teacher education program is designed to engage students in diversity of thought, incorporating integrated courses in arts and sciences such as "Science and Humanity," "Music and Related Arts," "World Civilization," and "Modes of Inquiry Across the Fields of Study" to prepare them for interdisciplinary teaching. The philosophy underlying this program has now become the basis for a university-wide core curriculum project that is revising undergraduate general education through collaborative planning by faculty and administrators from the university, the local community colleges, and the secondary schools.

Implementation is a complex and dynamic process that takes time, commitment, and patience. The implementation of inquiry-based curriculum is itself a process of inquiry.

REFERENCES

Berman, P., & McLaughlin, M. (1977). *Federal programs supporting educational change: Vol. 7. Factors affecting implementation and continuation.* Santa Monica, CA: Rand Corporation.

Czajkowski, T. J., & Patterson, J. L. (1980). Curriculum change and the school. In A. W. Foshay (Ed.), *Considered action for curriculum improvement.* Alexandria, VA: Association for Supervision and Curriculum Development.

Dewey, J. (1922). *Human nature and conduct.* New York: Holt, Rinehart and Winston.

Emrick, J., & Peterson, S. (1978). *A synthesis of findings across five recent studies in educational dissemination and change.* San Francisco: Far West Laboratory for Educational Research and Development.

Fullan, M., with Stiegelbauer, S. (1991). *The new meaning of educational change.* New York: Teachers College Press.

Hall, G. E., & Rutherford, W. L. (1976). Concerns of teachers about implementing team teaching. *Educational Leadership 34 (3),* 227–233.

Hall, G. E., & Loucks, S. F. (1978). Teacher concerns as a basis for facilitating personalizing staff development. *Teachers College Record 80 (1),* 36–53.

Hall, G. E., & Hord, S. M., (1987). *Change in schools: Facilitating the process.* Albany, NY: State University of New York Press.

Huberman, M. (1983). Recipes for busy kitchens. *Knowledge: Creation, Diffusion, Utilization, 4,* 478–510.

Joyce, B., & Weil, M., with Showers, B. (1992). *Models of teaching* (4th ed.). Boston: Allyn & Bacon.

Marris, P. (1975). *Loss and change.* New York: Anchor Press/Doubleday.

Martinello, M. L., & Cook, G. E. (1992). Interweaving the threads of learning: Interdisciplinary curriculum and teaching. NASSP *Curriculum Report* 21(3), 1–6.

Rogers, E. M. (1962). *Diffusion of innovations.* New York: Free Press.

Rosenblum, S., & Louis, K. (1979). *Stability and change: Innovation in an educational context.* Cambridge, MA: ABT Associates.

Schon, D. (1971). *Beyond the stable state.* New York: Norton.

Additional Reading

Alfonso, R. J., Firth, G. R., & Neville, R. F. (1981). *Instructional supervision: A behavior system* (2nd ed.). Boston: Allyn & Bacon.

Flexner, A. (1923). *A modern college and a modern school.* Garden City, NY: Doubleday.

Mayhew, K. C., & Edwards, A. C. (1936). *The Dewey school.* New York: Atherton.

Mitchell, L. S. (1950). *Our children and our schools.* New York: Simon & Schuster.

Oberholzer, E. (1937). *An integrated curriculum in practice.* New York: Teachers College Press.

References to School Curriculum Implementation

Anson Jones Middle School, Northside Independent School District, San Antonio, Texas

Brauchle Elementary School, Northside Independent School District, San Antonio, Texas

LINCS Schools, San Antonio Independent School District, San Antonio, Texas:

Ball Elementary School

Beacon Hill Elementary School

Herff Elementary School

Stewart Elementary School

Oaklea Middle School, Junction City, Oregon

Afterword

A pebble drops into a pond. The ripples spread, each ripple complete, comprehensive, circular. Ideas within ideas within ideas like ripples spread out to reach invisible shores.

An idea is sparked, questions form, and an inquiry begins. . . .

AS A CHILD

Gill: A windy day on the springy turf under wide spring skies; we walked, my father and I, on the hill known as Caesar's Camp, an old place, a natural fortress overlooking the hills and valleys of England's West Country. The short grass was dotted with little holes, home to some insects or small animals. "Look," my father joked, "that's where Caesar's men put their tent pegs!" Suddenly, for me, the hill was peopled with the ghosts of long-dead armies; I heard in my mind the soft stamp of marching sandals, the jingle of harnesses as the officers rode by, the clatter and clang of a military camp. The history books and the stories of long ago took on new significance as the old camp came alive for me, and my mind was full of new questions that I had not thought to ask before.

Marian: For as long as I could remember, people commented about my eyes. "They're so dark," they said, "such a deep brown." My mother would say, "You have Grandpa's eyes. You're the only one, you know." And during those special Sunday dinners at the dinner table in my paternal grandparents' New York apartment, Grandpa would whisper to me: "You have my eyes, Marianna. You are like me." I took pride in being special to Grandpa and during those long Sunday afternoon dinners, I often amused myself by surveying the eye colors of several generations of our extended Italian-American family. There were only two who had blue eyes. Grandma stood out as one. My godfather was the other. Everyone else had eyes of different degrees of brownness. My mother's eyes were light brown; so were my father's and my brother's. I was about 9 years old when the specialness that Grandpa and I shared became a source of inquiry: I wondered, "Why are we the only ones with dark brown eyes?" I began to explore that question by doing a more serious survey than I had done earlier, making a chart of the eye colors of my aunts and uncles and cousins, and connecting them in a sort of family tree. I discovered that there are many shades of brown, noting each on my chart, and found that, like me, many children did not carry the eye color of their parents—there were differences that could not be explained by parent–child heredity alone. I figured that it had something to do with grandparents. I asked the members of my family about this, and although I didn't get clear explanations, I got clues. One of my uncles by marriage referred me to the eye colors of his parents. But the best clue of all occurred at least a year after I had begun the inquiry, when it first came to my attention that my godfather had been adopted. He was a great ally in this search, because he had no sense of his inheritance. This shared interest paired us in an intriguing investigation of our origins. That was when the search got serious and I learned the meaning of the word *genetics*. We explored Mendelian tables together and made charts for our personal data. We worked with my question because it was quantifiable. We could assign a genetic code for eye color to each person on the family tree. We even tried predicting which of the younger generation might have children with different eye colors from the rest of the family, depending on the genetic characteristics of their spouses. And we inferred possible eye colors of generations past, people who had lived and died in Italy, like my grandfather's father who had died when Grandpa was a small boy—and for whom he had a passion to know about that lasted into his old age.

It may be that my fascination with my own genetics in childhood fanned my intrigue with things biological into my adulthood. And yet, that early scientific study that used probability and statistics to explore personally meaningful questions also caused me to investigate my cultural origins. I discovered the European places where my family had come from and much about the ways in which they lived. And the companion study of my godfather's origins caused me to learn about the drama of human life. When I look back on it now, I am amazed at how much I learned about myself and others and about the conduct of inquiry through that interdisciplinary study. To think that it all began with a little question about the eye color I shared with my Grandpa.

AS A TEACHER EDUCATION STUDENT

Gill: A little flint church in a tiny Kentish village; the teacher education students clustered in the doorway, wondering what was the point of this expedition to a Norman church. "What does this have to do with teaching?" we asked each other. The college lecturer began to ask us questions: "Why do you think this was built of flints? Why was it built here? Where did the flints come from? How has it lasted for 8 centuries?" We began to look more carefully at the location, at the chalk downs studded with the hard, sharp flints. We examined the construction. We compared this church with others we knew, and used our knowledge to make sense of this unfamiliar building. As we explored, new questions bubbled up: "Who built it? Why is it this shape? What determined the angles of the roof timbers, the shape of the narrow windows? Who worshiped here? Where did they live? What did they do? Who carved these whimsical characters under the choir seat?" Then, slowly, it occurred to us that this field trip had everything to do with teacher education, with the processes of learning, and of learning to learn. As we became learners, we were learning how to become teachers, to lead children to this exciting process of discovery of our world and ourselves.

AS A TEACHER

Marian: I was teaching third grade in an inner-city school. Most of my students were about 8 years of age; some had been retained and were 9 or 10. Few could read well, and some couldn't read at all. The reading materials that I had available were irrelevant to the experiences and interests of my students. I decided to disregard the readers altogether and work from the children's personal experiences, recording their stories for them, where necessary, to create our own books. This we did, drawing from the children's personal stories, until one day it occurred to me that all the stories took place in the immediate neighborhood. When I questioned my students about other places in our city, they seemed to have very limited knowledge of their larger environment. That's when I decided to engage them with a study of their city: its places, its people and their life styles and activities, its institutions, and its natural and built environment.

At first, the children didn't know enough about their city to begin asking questions. So we took a series of walking trips to gain a sense of the place and to spark inquiry. We followed these with some longer trips to places more distant from the school. And we reflected on the experiences through drawings and captions and dictated notes. We weren't long into this open exploration when the questions began to flow: just a few at first, then floods of them. The early questions focused on what the children had observed on the trips; they simply wanted to know more. As they learned more, the questions became more probing and specific. They wanted to find out more about the courthouse and the legal system; they wanted to find out more about the food markets and the food distribution system; they wanted to find out about the theaters and the entertainment enterprise; they wanted to find out about newspapers and the broadcast media. We organized ourselves so that different groups of children could explore different aspects of their city. Some parents came along to help us interact with different people and to experience different places. As the studies proceeded, I was amazed at how much I was learning with the children. The parents made similar comments about having lived their whole lives in our city without really knowing the place.

As teacher, I vigilantly guarded the regular class time for structured math and reading instruction. That caused me to notice something. The further we got into the study of our city, the easier a time the children seemed to have with the regular curriculum. The more the children wrote about their experiences in finding answers to their questions about their selected aspect of the city, the greater their facility in reading the standard reading materials. As they studied the economics of their topic and regularly computed distances and costs of the trips they took, the children discovered numbers to be useful tools. When they lost their fear of numbers, they were able to approach workbook assignments with confidence. They were, in fact, learning more than was required at their grade level. I was overjoyed. They were proud.

The city study, with all its pathways, went on for a full term and dwelled in every subject area of the curriculum. When it was done, the children compiled the bulk of their data into a rather extensive book, with illustrations, which they dedicated to the school library in a formal ceremony. The school librarian later told us that the book was well used by many children and adults. That book invites inquiry because it was born of a children's search to better know and to understand their environment. In the process, the students developed their tool skills and began to comprehend the concept of *city.*

Gill: A hot, sultry summer afternoon; the classroom was restless though quiet, the children heavy-headed and bored. "Miss, can't we go outside?" Outside? Of course! But where? The park was half a mile away, the playground hard and hot. I looked out of the big windows at the tiny enclosed courtyard, full of weeds and inaccessible to all but the janitor. The children's eyes followed mine. "We could go out through the window," suggested one enterprising youngster. Why not? A quick check with an understanding principal, and we were out, plucking grasses and collecting dusty pebbles. Back in the classroom, the children excitedly examined, classified, compared, and recorded our finds. They found books and pictures to help in our inquiries. Who would have thought that the tiny patch of city weeds could have yielded more than thirty types of grass, a dozen unknown flowers, and a wide variety of stones and rocks? For the rest of that year, the classroom was filled with the fruits of children's exploration and inquiry: grasses and grains, rocks and mountains, ecology and the environment.

AS A UNIVERSITY INSTRUCTOR

Marian: One summer, I was asked to teach an undergraduate course for academically gifted high school students, through which they might earn advanced academic credit. The course was to focus on primary-source research and use the resources of our community. To prepare some challenging assignments for the students, I worked with curators and educators in the local museum to create albums of primary-source references for selected families in the community. We created one for each student, making sure that sufficient resources were available in the community's libraries, archives, and artifact collections that were accessible to the students. On the first day of class, I described the task and distributed the albums, confident that the students would welcome this very different and highly individualized assignment. They accepted the assignment without many questions. I suggested that they begin their explorations in the university's special collections library, where materials for their use had been carefully selected and were awaiting their perusal.

The next day, a telephone call from the special collections librarian gave me a start. The students, she reported, had indeed gone to the library. They had looked at the materials she had pulled for their reference. But they were uncertain about what they would do with them. In fact, the librarian told me, they claimed that I had given them an *impossible* task.

During the class session immediately following that telephone call, I sat down with the students and told them that I had heard about their concern regarding the assignment. "What seems to be the problem?" I asked. There was a long silence. The students looked at each other. "I really want to know," I assured them. Then one youngster timidly raised her hand. I acknowledged her. "What you've given us," her voice quivered, "well—we can't look it up in the encyclopedia."

I wanted the students to be detectives. They had inadequate experience in doing self-directed research that required them to construct patterns of meaning from bits and pieces of evidence. I was asking the students to formulate questions by themselves about people, places, things, and events they knew little about, and, hardest of all, to find resources that contained clues to answers for their questions, none of which could provide direct and complete answers. I knew then what I had to do. The students had no model. I needed to offer them one.

I began my search for an artifact that would involve me in a study about a person or place or culture that I knew hardly at all. I wanted to demonstrate to the students that you don't need to have a great deal of knowledge about your subject before you begin your search, and that as your knowledge grows, so will the depth of your exploration. But you can start from scratch.

And then I found the house. It is maintained as a living history farmstead in a state historic park. Although the house and grounds have been reconstructed to represent life in the Texas hill country during the early 20th century, only some of the senior members of long-established families in the community had clear memories of the original resident couple in their youth, in the days when the house had been built. But the house stood as testimony to their presence, as did three additional material sources that, with the house, became my "signpost artifacts": a wedding portrait, the bride's wish list for her dowry, and a medicine bottle. So began my search for the story of a German-Texan woman named Emma, an inquiry whose questions traveled through more disciplines of study than I could have imagined at the start, an inquiry that immersed me in an ethnic group about whom I knew little and a rural culture that was foreign to me, and propelled me back into a time before my birth. From a personal perspective, that inquiry made strangers become like family: Emma now lives in my mind. From a professional viewpoint, that inquiry provided a model I could share with my students to help them see how one question leads to another and others; each query and uncovered clue ripples outward to form ever-larger concepts and to reveal ever more universal ideas about our living and our world.

Index